KITTY

KITTY

An Autobiography by Kitty Carlisle Hart

St. Martin's Press
New York

Every reasonable effort has been made to trace the ownership of photos included in this volume. Any errors which may have occurred are inadvertent and will be corrected in subsequent editions, provided notification is sent to the publisher.

Excerpt from *Heartbreak House* by George Bernard Shaw is reprinted courtesy of the Society of Authors on behalf of the Bernard Shaw estate. Excerpt from "I'm Just Wild About Harry" by Noble Sissle and Eubie Blake © 1921 Warner Brothers, Inc. (renewed). All Rights Reserved. Used by permission. Excerpt from Lotte Lenya letter reprinted with permission of the Kurt Weill Foundation of Music, New York. Excerpt from "Time does not bring relief; you all have lied" by Edna St. Vincent Millay. From *Collected Poems*, Harper & Row. Copyright 1917, 1945 by Edna St. Vincent Millay. Reprinted by permission. Quote by George Jean Nathan reprinted with permission from *Esquire*. Copyright © 1937 by George Jean Nathan. "Vom verwundeten Knaben," by Brahms (page 107) translation by Anne Grossman © 1965 by Juilliard School of Music. Excerpt by Rupert Brooke from *The Collected Poems of Rupert Brooke*, reprinted with the permission of Dodd, Mead & Co. Excerpt from "My Most Intimate Friends" from *Jubilee* by Cole Porter © 1935 Warner Brothers Inc. (Renewed). All rights reserved. Used by permission. Excerpt from "The Rain in Spain" by Alan Jay Lerner, Frederick Loewe © 1956 Chappell & Co., Inc. (Renewed). All rights reserved. Used by permission. Excerpt from "Searching for Her Glove" by Alan Jay Lerner, Frederick Loewe © 1960 Chappell & Co., Inc. All rights reserved. Used by permission. Excerpt from "Don't Let It Be Forgot" by Alan Jay Lerner, Frederick Loewe © 1960 Chappell & Co., Inc. All rights reserved. Used by permission.

Designed by Karolina Harris

Library of Congress Cataloging-in-Publication Data

Carlisle, Kitty.
    Kitty : an autobiography.

    1. Carlisle, Kitty. 2. Entertainers—
United States—Biography. I. Title.
PN2287.C27A3 1989b   792'.028'092 [B]   89–10077
ISBN 0–312–03373–7

First published in the United States by Doubleday.

FOR
CHRISTOPHER, CATHERINE, MARK,
and
JAMES

ACKNOWLEDGMENTS

I am blessed with good friends, and two of them have been extraordinarily generous with their time and their knowledge: Phyllis Cerf Wagner and Leonora Hornblow. They were both strict and kind in their comments, and each put forth a herculean labor of love. Although they have befriended me in the past, this time it was above and beyond the call of duty.

Through the years that I have been working on this book, there have been many people who have encouraged and helped me in different ways. Some have read the book, some have done research, some have provided photographs. I list them in alphabetical order: Mary Ellin Barrett; Laurie Baskin; Camilla de Chandon; Schuyler Chapin; Jeannette Suarez Ferretti; Clayton Fritchey; Ruth Goetz; Lisa Grossman; Kenneth Harris; Christopher Hart; Barbara Haspiel; Mary Hays; Jean Kerr; Gregory Kolovakos; Ivo Lederer; Kenneth McCormick; Anne Kaufman Schneider; Irving Schneider; Catherine Hart Stoeckle; Mark Stoeckle; Beth Taylor; Marietta Tree; William Walton.

I am grateful to Julia Pilar Miguel and Librada Gazquez who kept my household and my life running smoothly while I worked on this book.

I am particularly indebted to Sylvia Fine Kaye, who spent many hours going over the manuscript in detail, with a critical but affectionate eye.

I want to thank Carolyn Blakemore, whose sensitivity and understanding made the publication of this book as painless as possible. She started as my editor and ended as my friend.

AUTHOR'S NOTE

I had been trying to write this book for a long time when Anne Chotzinoff Grossman came into my life. I never could have finished it without her. For three and a half years her erudition and her skill have been a never-ending source of wonder. She is part of my world, and her understanding of it made the task at hand considerably easier. She has been patient, stern when necessary, but above all, ever encouraging. We laughed at the same things. It was her sense of fun which enabled me to go on with an exercise that turned out to take far longer than I anticipated. She gave me the daily push to continue.

She tells me she had as good a time working with me as I had with her.

Mother

Ah, lucky girls who grow up in the
shelter of a mother's love—a mother who knows
how to contrive opportunities without conceding
favors . . . The cleverest girl may miscalculate
where her own interests are concerned, may yield
too much at one moment and withdraw too far at
the next: it takes a mother's unerring vigilance
and foresight to land her daughters safely in
the arms of wealth and suitability.

Edith Wharton
The House of Mirth

My story rightfully begins with my mother. It was both my fortune and my burden to have been born to an extraordinary woman of enormous drive and ambition, not for herself but for me.

Mother had three passions in life: me, music, and bridge, in that order. One of my earliest memories is seeing her sitting in a rocking chair, dressed in a nightgown, her long black hair streaming down her back, her violin under her chin, a tin music stand in front of her, playing a Vivaldi concerto and rocking away as if the devil were after her.

Mother was born in Shreveport, Louisiana, where her father had settled. He came from Germany, but Mother said Alsace-Lorraine because she thought it was more exotic. (She would have preferred France, but since his name was Holtzman, Alsace was as near as she dared get.)

My grandfather arrived with the wave of immigrants who came to America to avoid the upheavals of Europe in the nineteenth century, only to find himself in the middle of the worst of our upheavals—the Civil War. He enlisted as a gunner on the *Merrimack,* and after the war he worked in a dry-goods store in Washington, where his claim to fame was that he had once sold a tie to Mr. Lincoln. His obituary in the *Times* of Shreveport, where he moved after the war, says he was also in Ford's Theatre the night Lincoln was shot—but alas, I have no program to prove it.

I remember my grandfather's beautiful white mustache. He was tall and good-looking, with a military bearing. He must have been a godsend to the young ladies of Shreveport, and he soon caught the fancy of Miss Stella Baer, pronounced Barr. In 1877 they were married on the Baer plantation, and they prospered. He opened his own dry-goods store, became a pillar of the community, and eventually Shreveport's first Jewish mayor.

They had two children, Aunt Sadie and my mother, Hortense (a name she hated). Sadie, the beauty of the family, had a sweet disposition, which threw my mother's character into sharp relief. It was said that my mother took after her grandmother, who whacked the slaves with her fan when they let the flies settle on her during her afternoon nap. Mother was the terror of the neighborhood, and parents would caution their children, "If you're not careful, you'll grow up like Hortense Holtzman!" She was constantly being punished, but it never did much good. She told me with great relish that once, after being naughty, she had been locked in a closet in the pantry where there happened to be a chocolate cake cooling on a shelf. Other children might have wept with remorse. *She* ate the cake. It's no wonder I grew up thinking Mother always had the last word.

Mother went to a small young ladies' seminary where, in keeping with the times, she had a classical education. She learned Greek and Latin, and she could parse a sentence in nothing flat. She played the violin remarkably well for an amateur, and at sixteen she was sent off to the Conservatory in Cincinnati.

When she returned she followed the crowd and started looking for a husband. Girls traveled a well-worn marriage circuit—Dallas, Galveston, New Orleans—passed from one eligible to another until true love or exhaustion tied the knot. Mother was already twenty-seven, and to make matters more urgent, her sister Sadie had long since married a millionaire and gone off to live in New York. Mother was on her second or third go-around when she met Joseph Conn, a struggling young doctor in New Orleans, and they were married soon thereafter.

My father was born in Hattiesburg, Mississippi, population 850. He had moved to New Orleans with two of his sisters and a brother. During the day he worked in a dry-goods store, and he went to Tulane Medical School at night.

My parents must have had a hard time in the beginning making ends meet. Doctors were the last to be paid, and Mother told me, with real feeling, of the humiliation of buying the groceries one bunch of carrots and a nickel's worth of spinach at a time. She never really got over it; it was probably the start of her lifelong tendency to economize on food.

They were an ill-assorted pair from the first. He liked camping, duck shooting, and his work. His specialty was gynecology, so he was often out at all hours of the night delivering babies. She didn't care at all for duck shooting, but she was out all hours of the night playing bridge. One of her partners once said to her, "I know how Kitty was conceived. You said, 'Doctor, hand me Culbertson's book on bridge and go ahead.' "

After I was born, my parents settled down on St. Charles Avenue. Though the address was good, the house was slightly rickety. The furniture seemed to be in the wrong rooms, and it all looked as if we were getting ready to move. There was white wicker in the dining room and heavy Victorian mahogany in my bedroom, while I longed for the dainty white enamel other children had.

Daddy's brother, Uncle Moïse, had a drugstore right down the block from our house, and a drugstore in the family is a lovely thing for a child. Aunt Hattie had married well; she drove a two-seater electric automobile, and she lived in a house with an elevator, the first one I ever saw. My Aunt Sophie lived on Prytania Street, in a gray frame house with a big fig tree in the backyard. She let me climb the tree to pick the figs. She put me in a bathing suit, because when I came down I'd be covered with ants and so sticky that I'd have to be hosed down. The picking was fun, but the reward was better, a big bowl of figs in thick unpasteurized cream—real lagniappe.

When I was six, Mother started teaching me the piano. While the other children on the block were outside playing, I had to practice the piano, two hours every day, with Mother rapping my knuckles and ignoring my tears. The worst part was the mice. I was always barefoot, and once in a while a mouse would run across my toes as I worked the pedals. Mother didn't see the mice. She was looking at the music, and she wore shoes. To teach me to sight-read, Mother would get out her violin and make me accompany her. I managed pretty well with the treble, but when I had to add the bass and all those chords and count at the same time, I ran into trouble. I was always losing my place, and her bow stabbing at the music across my shoulder terrified me; it was like a long, bony witch's finger.

Two friends of Mother's were talking about me one day. "That child has nothing," one said. "Don't be silly," said the other. "She has everything. She has her mother!"

Mother took me to concerts and operas, and I sat in a box waving a tiny pink feathered fan. Her friends would say disapprovingly, "Hortense, how can you keep that child up till all hours?" "That child" was enjoying it hugely. I can still see Rosa Ponselle in a bright red chiffon dress, and Caruso, short and fat, a red-faced penguin in his tails. *Faust* at the Opera House, with Mephistopheles disappearing through a trapdoor in a puff of green smoke, was a real dazzler. I'm eternally grateful that Mother gave me the habit of concertgoing.

When I was eight years old we finally moved to a better house, still on St. Charles Avenue but farther uptown, where the furniture sorted itself out. The new place boasted a music room and a brand-new baby grand piano. Daddy had more patients, and they were obviously paying on time.

It was Mother's love of music and her knowledge that made her vice president of the Philharmonic, certainly not her ability to contribute any money to the orchestra. But in her official capacity she entertained the soloists. Her parties were a toss-up: sometimes they worked, sometimes they didn't. At one dinner all the food tasted of kerosene (there had been an open can in the kitchen), and once, when a young Russian prodigy came for supper, shrimp was the main dish. The guest of honor could eat only kosher food. He practically starved, while the Philistines munched on.

Mother's violin and her impeccable manners at the bridge table were her entrée to the ladies who owned department stores and sugar plantations, and who went to Paris every year to do their shopping.

The ladies were generous in allowing Mother's seamstress to copy their children's French dresses for me. I remember two of those dresses with great affection. There was a rich brown velvet with a lace collar; and my favorite, a pale blue organdy with little puffed sleeves, pink and blue roses embroidered on the bodice, and a white organdy guimpe. I wore it at my debut when I was seven years old, at a recital at my piano teacher's studio.

The ladies were not so generous when they made fun of her attempts to keep up with their way of living.

Mother's bed had pink satin draperies, caught up at the head in a coronet like some she had seen in her friends' houses—except that Mother's was homemade and the coronet had a tendency to list, like a crown on a drunken king. She couldn't afford their table decorations, but she herself embroidered a fair copy of their tablecloths. Our own cook could do only simple things, so when Mother gave a dinner party, she got Aunt Sophie, who was a great cook, to come in and toil away unheralded in the kitchen.

But in spite of her pretensions, there was within her a saving grace. I saw a letter a few years ago that she had written to a friend: "I love to see others when they think I'm affected and think I don't know it. I've always been an affected puss—just love playing a part." When I was growing up, it would have made life a great deal easier if I had known she was on to herself.

Mother carried herself well, and with the help of high heels (I don't think she ever owned any low-heeled shoes) she looked taller than her five-foot-three. She had perfect white skin that never saw the sun, because she never did anything remotely athletic. She had lovely legs and tiny feet. (She never, but never, would say "feet." "Foot," yes, but heaven forbid "feet"!) Her nose was so-so, but she had the ravishing smile of a great actress, a wide, beautiful mouth, and gorgeous teeth—they were so strong that if she ever asked for a bite of my apple, she'd get a whole half of it into her mouth with one crunch, and she went to her grave with all of them firmly in place.

I went to a school called Isidor Newman, where the only thing I learned was to play a pretty good game of jacks. Then Mother sent me to Miss McGehee's. Her social ambition for me was beginning to show.

The photographs of the time show a serious-faced little girl who doesn't look as though she were going to be any fun at all. My talent at jacks didn't help. It was not the sport of choice at McGehee's. Worst of all, nobody noticed me, and I desperately wanted to be noticed. After all, I had already played the piano in public, and I knew I was noticed when I sat in the box at concerts; but the student body at Miss McGehee's school paid me no mind. No one would even eat lunch with me. The children always exchanged sandwiches; they had white-bread sandwiches with the crusts cut off, while mine were of french bread with the crust on (Mother thought it was good for my teeth) and holes through which the jelly dripped. No one wanted any part of them, or me.

For my ninth birthday I finally was given the white enamel desk I yearned for. It came with a complete set of Louisa May Alcott. There were almost no books in our house except my father's medical library. I never saw Mother read a book of any kind, though she could discuss every new one that came out— she read the reviews. I, on the other hand, devoured those medical books at night for hours under the blankets with the help of a flashlight.

The high point of our week was Sunday dinner, in the middle of the day. Mother must have splurged on Sundays. I have a memory of enormous meals, with big soup plates filled with river shrimp on a bed of cracked ice, roast chicken, and watermelon for dessert. After dinner the women took naps; there were many large ladies—Aunt Fannie, Aunt Nettie, Cousin Adele—all in Mother's kimonos, on every available sofa and bed. I don't know what the men did. Anyway, there were a lot more ladies than men. In the early evening, after the guests had left, we sat on the front porch in rocking chairs and watched the cars go by, and that was considered enough entertainment until it was time for me to go to the grocery store on the corner for our supper, a loaf of toasted french bread cut lengthwise and stuffed with fried oysters. We ate on the porch; Mother said it was so hot and steamy in New Orleans that even outside you just rocked and dripped.

Mother expected instant obedience at every command; the slightest hesitation on my part brought on the outbursts that were the worst features of my childhood. What could I have done to call forth such violence? Perhaps I was a convenient target for her feelings of deprivation in a marriage that afforded no companionship. Perhaps it was the never-ending social struggle; she must have suffered countless slights trying to make a place for me. Maybe there was something she wanted from me that I wasn't giving her. I was yearning for something she wasn't giving me—a physical sign of affection, a kiss, a pat on the head, a touch of some sort. In any event, the moments of physical closeness were so rare that when I was fifty years old, I was still trying to crawl into her lap.

It seems incredible that I cannot remember a word my father ever spoke to me. In my world, Mother loomed so large that she must have blotted him out. The things he did for me, however, remain vivid. He vaccinated me for smallpox, and it wasn't easy. I ran all over the backyard until he finally caught me. When I was sick he would bring me calf's foot jelly flavored with sherry, which I adored, and when I had what in those days was called growing pains, he would rub my legs and then bring me a thimbleful of Danziger Goldwasser, a liqueur that had little flecks of real gold dancing in it.

He took me on his rounds to see his patients, and on these visits he let me chew gum, a great secret between us, because Mother disapproved. His presence was kind and loving, but I never remember him saying my name or talking to my mother. Meals were like a silent film. We sat down, moved platters about, ate, in my recollection all in total silence.

My father died when I was ten years old. This kind man and dedicated doctor wore himself out caring for his patients in the influenza epidemic of 1918; two years later he was on one of his frequent house calls when he had a heart attack. He managed to stop the car and get out; he died on the sidewalk.

When they brought him home my mother was out at a concert. I was in bed in the dark, listening to ghost stories our young maid was telling me. She told them well, and they terrified me. Suddenly there was a commotion in the front hall, lights went on, and I heard loud voices. The maid ran downstairs. I got out of bed and looked over the stair rail in time to see a stretcher covered with a sheet being carried into the house. It was like a continuation of the stories I had just heard.

I don't know how long I stood there, shivering, bewildered, staring down at the stretcher. The house filled with people. Someone must have gone for my mother. She saw me at once, ran up the stairs, and took me into her bedroom. She sat in the rocking chair and held me on her lap, the only time I remember her doing that, rocking back and forth. "We're all alone now," she kept repeating. "We're all alone, it's just you and me."

I was sent away for a day to Aunt Hattie's, and when I came home my father was on a raised bier in the front room. Mother took me in to kiss him goodbye. His cheek was colder than anything I had ever felt in my life, but I wasn't frightened because it was Daddy and I loved him.

After my father died, my mother's friends expected her to sit on her front porch and rock and bring up her child and wait for another husband. She did none of those things. She sold the house, took my father's insurance money, tucked her violin under one arm, me under the other, and made off for New York.

New Orleans was behind her. She said it made you old to recollect the past. She never mentioned my father to me again, except to tell me that he had loved me. I had loved him, but I never missed him, at least not consciously. Now that I look at the photograph of his rather thoughtful face, I wish I had known him.

We went first to stay with Aunt Sadie on Riverside Drive. It seemed to me that after the flat New Orleans landscape, New York was all hills, particularly the big one from Riverside Drive to Broadway. The atmosphere at Aunt Sadie's apartment was grim. Her husband, who was in the clothing business, had just lost all his money. I must have been a nuisance to Aunt Sadie's children who were older than I, particularly to my cousin Hortense, who had to share her bed with me. After a few weeks we moved to the Gotham Hotel on Fifth Avenue.

Mother made an unexpected turn to the avant-garde, brought about by an old friend of hers from the south, Mabel Goldberg (whose granddaughter, Kitty Dukakis, wife of the Massachusetts governor, later became a friend of mine).

Thanks to Mabel's recommendation, Mother sent me to the progressive Dalton School. Academically it was a complete mystery to me. At home almost every moment of my time was apportioned, and I was never asked to use anything like my own judgment. At Dalton it was the reverse. Each pupil was supposed to advance at his or her own pace. What my pace was I never found out, because I went neither forward nor backward. I arrived there knowing very little, and I left in exactly the same condition.

What pushed my mother to Europe after that winter in New York? I think one reason was that she had heard enough about Paris from her New Orleans friends to want to see for herself. Another was the mood of the times. Americans were flinging themselves into the sea like lemmings to get to Paris. After the war, with dollars, one could live very cheaply, and by the end of the twenties the American colony had swelled to 100,000 souls. (There was even a joke current: a woman says to her husband, "If one of us dies, *I'm* going to Paris!")

I think the real reason was her ambition for me. She wanted me to make a suitable marriage, which in her terms meant well above my station. She was like the ladies in the Henry James stories who took their daughters to Europe to make brilliant marriages, except that unlike them, we had no money and no entrée. But somewhere in the back of Mother's mind was the idea of grooming me for a rich prince or, failing that, a not too-impoverished baron. She was very farsighted; I was only eleven years old.

ON the boat, the S.S. *Champlain,* Mother met a gentleman, kind and helpful, the first of many, who suggested that we stay at the Hotel Lotti, a small but very "good" hotel in the Rue Castiglione, where we had a tiny room under the eaves with one little window that looked out over the chimney pots of Paris, the first of many such rooms. Mother was already searching for the key to European society. To further her grand design, we had to be in the right place at the right time to meet the right people, but we had very little money, so we always stayed in the worst room in the best hotel.

Mother obviously hadn't learned the game yet, because we left Paris after a few days and set out for Germany. That August "nobody" went to Germany, and for very good reason. In 1922 there were sporadic riots, unemployment and political unrest; when we arrived in Hamburg there was shooting in the railroad station, with bullets flying. I was frightened, but that's when I learned I could count on Mother in a crisis. With complete composure she pulled me down behind a pile of trunks, and we crouched there until she decided it was safe to come out.

This trip was the beginning of a lifelong battle with our luggage, and single-handed combat at that. In those days wardrobe trunks were shipped ahead, and people traveled with heavy leather suitcases reinforced with wood. Also hat boxes. Our hat box was the most devilish piece of our luggage. It was made not of leather but of corrugated tin and looked like a sawed-off garbage can. It was painted a disgusting mustard brown, and the top fitted tightly over the bottom without a handle or pull to lift it. Inside there was an evil spirit that sucked all the air out of it and held the top fast shut, and when my knuckles were bleeding with the effort to pry it loose, it would shoot up with a *whoosh* and hit me on the chin.

I soon learned that Mother would have nothing to do with the luggage. She stalked ahead of me through the train like an empress in exile, while I followed like a juvenile Sancho Panza, hat over my eyes, with luggage in both hands, under my arms, on my back, all of it bumping and banging from side to side. When we arrived at our destination, Mother descended imperiously from the train as if an entourage of maids, couriers, and secretaries were following, leaving me to pull the suitcases off the racks and hand them through the window. I was always afraid the train would go on before I got them all out, leaving Mother on the platform and me going heaven knows where. I learned travel language quickly and could yell for porters in German, French, and Italian with the best of them.

At the hotel, the wardrobe trunk would be waiting. It contained everything else we owned (Mother obviously had decided the move to Europe was to be more than just a summer holiday). It was so full that no matter how carefully I had packed, when it was opened drawers jammed and hangers tangled, even though in the interests of economy Mother had ruthlessly jettisoned all but the essentials when we left New Orleans—there wasn't even room for my teddy bear. After I unpacked, it was my responsibility to press and spot-clean anything that needed it, and help Mother dress. Meanwhile I had to be dressed and ready to open the door for her to sweep out and into the dining room.

Mother engendered in me a lifelong enthusiasm for sightseeing. I was a wide-eyed tourist at eleven, and in this respect the child was mother to the woman. I'll still go anywhere and see anything. I kept a diary-and-memory book where I pasted everything I collected: postcards; coins; a replica of the Iron Maiden of Nuremberg; a bit of china from the factory at Meissen; an autographed photo of Anton Lang, who played Christ in the Passion Play at Oberammergau; and a fistful of opera ticket stubs. I still have the book.

Mother took me to the opera in every city—Hamburg, Dresden, Berlin. I remember *Die Meistersinger* in Munich best of all, because it started at four in the afternoon and didn't end till ten, with time out for supper. Mother thought nothing of having me sit through five hours of opera, and through three days on a very hard wooden bench at Oberammergau.

I don't remember the next venture ever being discussed between us, but in September Mother made up her mind to put me in school in Switzerland. We arrived in Lausanne ten days after the term had started; we made the rounds and Mother discovered all the schools were full. We had no family connections, no letters of introduction, and to the practiced eyes of headmistresses were as short of money as we were of credentials.

The first time I saw Mother's talent for casting spells over people was when she went into action to get me into a school. When she switched it on, her vitality was like a surge of electricity, and everyone was susceptible to her charms. She did a good job on the American vice-consul. He took us back to the exclusive École Mont Choisi, where we had already been turned down, left us alone while he spoke with the headmistress, and returned to announce that I was enrolled.

Next day Mother deposited me at the school. It must have been wonderful for her to be free to make a life for herself, knowing I was in good hands. Living alone with me in hotel rooms had been a terrible strain on both of us, but especially on her.

Mother took off for Egypt for the public opening of King Tut's tomb. She was learning to go where the action was. On the way she said she made a side trip to visit Sigmund Freud in Vienna. (When someone asked her why she did it, she replied, "It's the thing to do." She made him sound like a tourist attraction.)

Mother had a knack for letter writing. She wrote often, with enormous energy and humor, and her letters were filled with tales of her travels. But most wonderful of all, they were filled with affection. She was able to put on paper all the things she had never said to me. Her letters were my lifeline, and as long as they kept coming I felt safe.

Mont Choisi was a lovely old villa set on a hill overlooking Lac Léman, and I loved it from the start. Its main purpose was to teach French to English and American girls. The school was short on science and mathematics, but long on history, literature, sewing (I can still do fine hemstitching), sports, and French. The faster you learned French the quicker you got to the best teachers. I found I had quite a gift for languages, and with a little academic success (two prizes—a beautifully bound volume of Victor Hugo and one of French poetry) my brains woke up.

Mont Choisi gave me a lasting present as well as an education. There were too many Catherines in the school, and the headmistress asked me if I minded being called Kitty. I was delighted. Catherine (I had never had a nickname) had always seemed a bit ponderous, while Kitty sounded sprightly, gay, and lighthearted. Names *do* make a difference.

I also made an earthshaking discovery: how babies are made. The older girls were instructing the younger ones, and *les petites* were incredulous, crying out, "Oh no, my parents never did *that!*" I, on the other hand, thought about it and from that moment on never doubted that the Lord had invented a wonderful thing.

I had special piano lessons, but without Mother there to supervise me I just stopped practicing. I really hated practicing the piano. But even this major disobedience didn't stir Mother up, and the two years I spent in Switzerland were a time of truce between us.

Things were looking up for Mother; the opening of King Tut's tomb brought hordes of society people and a great deal of publicity to Cairo. It also brought her a romantic attachment.

Enter Major Spratt. He came face to face with Mother in the elevator at Shepheard's Hotel, took one look at her, and fell madly in love. He was a portly little man with a white mustache and a trim goatee. He was with the Red Cross, in charge of disbursing funds to the Balkans, and he introduced Mother to King George of Greece, Queen Marie of Rumania, and King Boris of Bulgaria, all of whom gave her signed photographs.

There was also a diamond necklace that has always been a mystery to me. There was nothing fanciful about Mother, but her tale of how the King of Bulgaria gave her the diamond necklace seemed to me to be full of holes. She was in Sofia some years later, and one day she went shopping. It had been raining, and a racing car came roaring down the road. As it passed her it ran through a mud puddle and the mud came splashing onto the sidewalk. The car pulled up, and out got a gentleman who said, "Oh, Madame, I hope I haven't muddied your dress." "Oh no," said Mother. And then, she told me (and here's where the biggest hole is), "There was a weekend in a monastery somewhere in the hills outside of Sofia, and this diamond necklace turned up and it was the King of Bulgaria." (I still have the necklace, and it's a stunner.)

While I was at school Mother traveled with Major Spratt, and during my holidays they took me along. Major Spratt really didn't know what to do with me—he'd never had children. He was polite and distant—even from Mother when I was with them, because she and I continued to share a room. He intruded very little into my life; I can't even remember his first name. He must have had money, because we had a large touring car and a courier. The car had the luggage strapped on the back. One day while we were driving through Italy I saw the hated hatbox come loose, jiggle up and down for a moment, and tumble off into the road. I watched without saying a word or moving a muscle. When we arrived at our destination and Mother discovered it was missing, she was furious. Usually when things went wrong, Mother would retrace the course of events to lay the blame at my door. This was one of the few times I really was responsible, but I never felt even the slightest twinge of guilt.

One rarely got the best of Mother. She and Major Spratt and another couple made a safari into the desert from Cairo, traveling by camel and spending the nights in tents. The Arabian guides carried rifles slung over their backs, and one evening while the guide was lifting Mother down from her camel (which she had come to loathe, saying it was the vilest form of transportation) his rifle came forward and banged her on the nose. She declared that she would never get on a camel again. It was explained to her that they were in the middle of the desert and the only way back was by camel. Mother said she didn't care; she'd stay in her tent until hell or the desert itself froze. She would die there if necessary, but camels were out. So they had to send to Cairo for a car on caterpillar treads to get her back.

Mother got out of the desert and she expected me to get myself from Switzerland to the Savoy Hotel in London on my spring vacation. I had to travel alone from Lausanne to Paris to Calais to Dover to London. That meant two trains, a ferry across the Channel, and another train, plus two sets of customs, before getting into a taxi in London to get to the hotel. Not bad for a thirteen-year-old, and when I walked into the lobby there was Mother waiting for me.

I remember our first trip to Venice, but not for the usual romantic reasons. We left Paris by train; by the time we arrived in Italy Mother had a serious case of tonsillitis. Her throat looked like raw meat and had swollen so that she couldn't utter a sound. When we got to the Hotel Danieli I had to do the talking. I told the desk clerk that my mother was ill, and please could we have our room right away. He wanted to know what train we had come on. When I said the Orient Express, he excused himself and disappeared, keeping Mother standing there. I was frantic with worry for her.

After what seemed a lifetime, the clerk came back and said forbiddingly, "I'm sorry, you can't stay here." Not "We don't have any rooms" or "We can't find your reservation," just a flat "You can't stay here." I was dumfounded. "Why not?" I asked. "There is the plague in Constantinople," he answered. "What has that got to do with us?" "The Orient Express comes from Constantinople. Isn't that where you came from?" "No!" I practically shouted. "We came from Paris! Here are our tickets to prove it!" "In that case," the clerk said, "you can have your room." I said I needed a doctor for Mother. He told me to take her up to the room, come back to the desk, and he'd get me a doctor.

I got Mother settled and rushed back to the desk clerk, who by now had lost his horns and big tail. He had a bellboy ready to escort me to the doctor, who apparently had no telephone, with instructions to bring him back to the hotel.

We scurried off through the back streets of Venice to the doctor's office. He seemed to have no patients waiting and returned with us right away. In spite of his poking around in Mother's mouth with the dirtiest fingernails I ever saw, she recovered. It was just one more lesson in learning how to cope with the unexpected.

After two years Mother tired of living out of suitcases. When I was fourteen she took a furnished apartment in Paris, on the Avenue Victor-Hugo, which became the pattern for all future flats: a good address, a decent drawing room, a piano with Mother's Spanish shawl and her photographs of the Balkan royals, a dark, dingy bedroom which we shared, and an awful bathroom.

Teachers also had to be found for Mother's violin and my piano. "Go to the top" was like the cry of the Valkyries for her. She managed to get to the world-famous violinist Jacques Thibaud, of the Cortot-Thibaud-Casals Trio, who in turn recommended Madame Chaigneau, of the Chaigneau Trio. Madame Chaigneau's only daughter, Irene, who became my friend, was the prettiest thing I'd ever seen, and a *Wunderkind* on the piano. She came by her musicianship naturally: her grandfather was the great nineteenth-century violinist Joseph Joachim. Irene was studying with Madame Leschetizky, so I too was sent to this legendary teacher. My lessons didn't last very long. Mother gave up trying to force me to practice on my own, so Madame Leschetizky was my last piano teacher.

Mother's lessons didn't last very long either, but Madame Chaigneau was the open sesame to the musical world of Paris. We had chamber music at home, where Mother played second fiddle. We met Bronislaw Hubermann, who helped Mother buy a good violin. Watching from the auditorium of the Salle Pleyel as he tried several instruments, I noticed he was quite walleyed. (Later I was told that he might have developed this condition from trying to count both sides of the house at once while he played.)

I went to a school in Neuilly, scholastically very tough, and I had four hours of homework every evening. Mother was suddenly undemanding: "Don't worry about bad marks in mathematics; you'll learn to add when you learn to play bridge." The school seemed to be quite secular until Easter, when I discovered that there was a tiny chapel, and girls who wished to could make a retreat. I had had no religious training in New Orleans—we never went to a synagogue—but I longed for a mystical experience. I spent quite a lot of time on my knees in the chapel practicing to be a nun.

I soon discovered I had no real vocation for the nunnery, so I followed two school friends into the American Cathedral for instruction in the Episcopal Church, with an eye to confirmation ceremonies. After two or three sessions I told Mother I didn't think I should go on with it. "I'm doing it because that's what my friends are doing, and that's not right." Mother just said, "Then forget it." She didn't try to persuade me to a course that might have protected me in a society that still entertained a great deal of prejudice.

That winter Mother left me with Madame Chaigneau and Irene while she went off to America to look after some business affairs. When she came back from New York she began to play the stock market. She did well, because we soon moved to a more elegant apartment, Avenue du Président-Wilson, with a series of three small drawing rooms opening one into another, whose windows looked out onto a tree-lined street. There was, however, the same dingy bedroom and awful bathroom.

I had a truly progressive education: I learned what I needed to know when I needed to know it. I stopped formal school at fifteen, but I was tutored at home. I had lessons in everything: languages, elocution, history of art, and comparative religion. No one cared about college or degrees for girls in those days in Europe, but Mother believed in culture—for me. When I complained I had nothing to do and no one to play with, Mother, who had her feet firmly planted under the bridge table, would say: "There's a museum on every corner in Paris; go to the Louvre or the Musée Grévin. Or go to a concert. Go to the Opéra-Comique. Your mind is your house. Furnish it!"

I had just started singing lessons, and it wasn't hard to persuade me to go to the Opéra-Comique. I would sit in the upper balcony with my score, following the singers.

The idea of singing lessons had come to Mother during our travels. She didn't sleep very well in the wagons-lits and sometimes would call to me in my upper berth to sing to her. There must have been something in my voice that made Mother think that perhaps singing lessons would be worthwhile, not in a professional sense but in place of the piano, as an "accomplishment."

Much as I had hated practicing the piano, I adored singing. Nothing was too much trouble. I practiced scales and arpeggios by the hour to improve my agility, and I started the lifelong search for a high pianissimo.

Even though we were better off, Mother still spent an awful lot of time jotting down figures on the backs of envelopes, and she gave me to understand that our money wouldn't ever stretch quite far enough—especially not for the clothes from the famous houses we needed to move upward into society—so her strategy was to buy at the sales. Mother was at her worst at these sessions but one season there was a respite. A friend of Mother's introduced her to an Italian lady who was just beginning to design sweaters. They had geometrical designs, very modern-looking, and I thought they were exceedingly smart. We never went in for impulse buying, but Mother bought me one. Mother hated going to the sales so much that she arranged for the Italian lady to take me. So for one whole winter my wardrobe was chosen by the great dress designer-to-be, the inventor of "shocking pink," Madame Elsa Schiaparelli.

We traveled a lot. The people Mother was after seemed to go everywhere together like flocks of birds, migrating to their own inner time clock. That meant St. Moritz in the winter, Paris in the spring, Venice in August, Villa d'Este in September.

Mother was learning the ropes so fast that sometimes we arrived ahead of the crowd. We got to the Hôtel du Cap at Antibes in 1927, long before they had built their cabañas and their famous restaurant by the sea.

The south of France had been frequented by the crowned heads of Europe for many years, but only during the winter months. Suddenly the world turned into sun worshippers, and it was a race to see who could get blackest quickest.

There seemed to be a lot of writers. The Michael Arlens were there; F. Scott Fitzgerald was there; I once saw George Bernard Shaw lying on the rocks sunbathing. He was very thin, and his silvery beard and white shorts were in startling contrast to his skin.

Grace Moore was also there. She came from Slabtown, Tennessee, and she was one of the most glamorous opera singers of her day, but unlike the European divas she had an easy, breezy American manner. She was clearly impressed by my eagerness to learn, for she listened to me sing and gave me much good advice on beginners' repertoire.

She was learning *Louise* with her coach, the conductor Moranzoni. When they were working she left the door of her suite ajar and I sat on a stool outside. I was aware that I was being singled out for something quite special. I was being allowed to listen to a famous opera star study an important role from scratch.

Miss Moore invited me to her first performance of *Louise* at the Opéra-Comique in Paris. *She* certainly didn't have to search for a high pianissimo. In "Depuis le jour" hers was faultless, yet what I remember most about the third act is her silver kid pumps. She had rather flat feet and a sideways walk that made her look like an Egyptian figure on a frieze, and the spotlight picked up her shiny shoes to the exclusion of all else. Those shoes were a lesson. I never wore silver kid pumps on the stage—ever.

Outside of my mother there were no witnesses to my growing up—except for the concierge at Villa d'Este. We started going to Villa d'Este when I was thirteen, and every September when we arrived at the hotel I would wait eagerly for the concierge to say, *"Signorina, com'e cresciuta!"* ("Young lady, how you've grown!") He was my only real source of continuity and he never disappointed me.

Villa d'Este was wonderful because most people stayed for the whole month, and the chance of real ties was easier than it was in Venice or Paris. Villa d'Este was a summer resort so there were organized activities for the young people. We sailed on the lake and swam. Mother stubbornly provided tennis and golf lessons despite the fact that I was totally uncoordinated at any sport involving the eye, the hand, and a ball. There was tea dancing, and Mother discovered I had one important social grace: I was a good dancer.

Mother had never paid too much attention to improving my looks, but she started me with an orthodontist almost before I had my second teeth. I had braces until I was about fourteen. I wore a gold wire retainer at night and instead of putting it away in the morning as I was supposed to, I would often leave it on the night table. Every hotel maid thought it was the wire that goes on top of champagne corks and would throw it out. It was very expensive, and I spent a lot of time frantically scrabbling around in hotel dustbins and incinerator rooms looking for my retainer and trying to keep from Mother that I had lost it—again.

One night before dinner she decided to do something more about my appearance and she put a little rouge on my cheeks. I looked in the mirror and saw a rather sallow, solemn face sparkle. Mother seemed as pleased with me as I was with her. I felt I had been touched by a fairy godmother.

However, there were still the explosions that caused Mother to push me out of the room and lock the door behind me. I would retreat to the service end of the corridor, sit on the back stairs, and wait; it was so humiliating to have chambermaids and waiters look at me inquiringly or pityingly. I tried hard not to cry. Sometimes the wait became too long for comfort, and nature's call would take me downstairs to the lobby. On the way back I would filch a few flowers from the public rooms to leave outside Mother's door. I'd put the bouquet on the floor and scratch gently at the door—it was too early to do anything as forceful as knocking. When the door stayed shut, I'd go back to the stairs. After what seemed to me to be the right time, I'd try again. If the flowers were still on the floor outside, it was too soon to knock. Instead, I would slip a note under the door, return to the stairs, and try to figure out what I had done to offend. I'd run the scene through in my mind: I could see my mother, the blood rising slowly as it always did in her rages, covering her bosom, her throat, then suffusing her whole face. Suppose the door never opened? Suppose she had died of a stroke? It was possible. Oh God! The frightening thought propelled me back to the room. This time I rattled the doorknob a little. At last the door would open, the atmosphere would be like summer lightning, the flashes growing fainter and gradually receding, until I would burst into tears and be forgiven.

I think Mother's nerves were tightened to such a pitch because Villa d'Este was a microcosm of the world that she was trying to fit me into, with all its accompanying frustrations and rebuffs. But I loved Villa d'Este, and I made many friends. It was there that I first met Wally and Wanda, the daughters of the conductor Arturo Toscanini, an undisputed genius in the music world and already a personality of monumental proportions. Wally and Wanda had come over from neighboring Stresa, where the family was staying for the summer. They took a real shine to me and I to them. Luckily Mother liked them both enormously, and whenever they asked me to go anywhere, Mother encouraged it. The girls took me to Stresa for lunch. It was my first glimpse of the Maestro. He was sitting at the piano when I was taken in to his study to meet him. I was aware of the electricity of his personality. He looked up at me with a piercing gaze from under his bushy eyebrows. I had heard stories of how tyrannical he was at the Metropolitan Opera, and I thought he was handsome and very scary.

Wanda, Wally, and I met on and off for years, and they took me to their father's concerts on two continents. Once in Venice they even changed Mother's mind in the middle of the Grand Canal. We were on our way to the railroad station, and they begged us to stay for another few days. Maestro was conducting at the Teatro La Fenice, and they wanted me especially to see the theater, one of the most beautiful in the world. To my amazement and delight, Mother had the gondola turn around, luggage and all, and go back to the hotel.

It was also at Villa d'Este that we met a family from Rome

named Suarez. They had three daughters, one of whom, Jeannette, was near my age. They were originally Egyptian and enormously rich. When Madame Suarez traveled, she had her own sheets, blankets, and pillows put on her bed in the wagon-lit and at the hotel. She even had her own lampshades. There were silver-framed family photographs set out all around the room. She was one of the most elegant and beautiful women in Europe, a strawberry blonde with white skin and large green almond-shaped eyes set wide apart in her face, like a Zuloaga portrait. Her entrance into the dining room every evening was awaited by the diners like the raising of a theater curtain.

Jeannette Suarez and I became close friends. In the fall she came to Paris with her family, and I was allowed to take her to lunch at the Ritz.

The Ritz for lunch was *the* place to be; one went to see the smartest ladies in the newest outfits of the season. Women today have conniption fits if they turn up at a party in the same model that someone else is wearing. I've never understood it. French ladies never minded being seen in the same Reboux hat or the same Patou outfit as three or four others. The most popular outfits were known as "Fords," and the women congratulated each other on having picked a winner.

Mother's rule, always order the least expensive dish but let the guest have whatever she wants, was hard to follow. Maybe food has always played an important part in my life because Mother's economies centered around it. At our cocktail parties the hors d'oeuvres were carefully counted. I wasn't allowed to taste one before the guests arrived, and generally there were none left when they departed. At the Ritz I would have to watch my friends gobble up lovely chicken dishes while I made do with tripe. Even though it was *à la mode de Caen,* it was still tripe.

Mother made many important decisions concerning my education that I accepted without question. The next summer at Villa d'Este, when I was sixteen, she managed to wangle an invitation for me from Madame Suarez to visit them in Italy.

Heaven knows how she did it. Perhaps Jeannette asked for me. All I knew was that I saw Mother walk over to Madame Suarez in the garden at Villa d'Este. They had tea together, and when Mother came back she told me I was going to spend the winter in Rome. Madame Suarez said I could have lessons with Jeannette, and since she was being presented to society, I could be presented too. That I wasn't quite old enough didn't matter from her point of view. The rules were not applicable to "American girls," always pronounced a little disparagingly. Mother wouldn't dream of turning down such an opportunity just because it was a year or so premature. As far as she was concerned, expediency was a necessity.

My wardrobe was terribly important. Mother pulled out all the stops. She found a copyist who made me a ball gown, a strange green shot-taffeta with a cockade of pink velvet ribbon over one shoulder (copy of a Lanvin); a tea-dancing outfit of beige crepe with silk fringes (copy of a Poiret); a beige dress trimmed in red and a red wool coat (copy of a Chanel); and a red hat (copy of a Reboux).

I thought the whole wardrobe the most elegant thing I'd ever seen. I had never had so many good clothes all at once. When Mother finally added the pièce de résistance, a brown caracul fur coat, it was like a real trousseau. That nobleman Mother was looking for didn't come cheap.

THE Suarezes lived in a villa near the Villa Borghese. It was richly if somewhat dramatically furnished. Madame Suarez's bedroom was hung with purple velvet and the bed, strewn with pillows, was on a raised platform covered with tiger skins. Her bathroom was the most impressive room of all: it was quite large, with a coffered ceiling more suitable to a ballroom, and the plumbing was hidden by carved wooden panels. In the middle of the room was a black marble sunken pool, and when Madame Suarez wasn't in it, it was filled with water lilies. The Romans certainly understood bathrooms.

I have always said I stayed with the Suarezes, but that's not quite true. I lived in a house nearby with a lady who took in paying guests. Madame Suarez took complete responsibility for me, but Mother paid for my lodging. There was a little upright piano in my room, and any spare time I had I spent practicing singing. I didn't have singing lessons in Rome, but I had brought with me my books of vocalises and the Italian eighteenth-century songbook that is the backbone of any singer's training.

Whatever Madame Suarez thought of the rest of my clothes I will never know, but she took one look at the ball gown and immediately took me to Ventura, the best dressmaker in Rome. She ordered a beautiful smoky, subtle blue tulle, which suddenly turned me into a rather attractive young girl. I was terribly worried about the cost, but since I heard nothing of a bill, it had to have been a present from Madame Suarez.

The Roman season was in full flower. "Princess Giovanelli is having a ball next week, and we must get you an invitation," Jeannette would say. But how? An extra American girl of no particular distinction was not easy to slip in. The first question asked about a newcomer always was, "Who is she?"—meaning who are her antecedents. In my case, the answer that echoed through the elegant halls of society was, "Nobody." I was very much aware of my social handicap, but in spite of it Jeannette did get me invited to a lot of parties.

Ever since Miss McGehee's school in New Orleans, Mother had been trying to open doors for me, pushing me through (giving my arm a pinch as she did it), and saying, "Be grrra-cious!" and then leaving me to make good. Up to then I hadn't been spectacularly successful. Rome was a turning point. I wrote to her after my first ball wearing the blue tulle dress, "You won't believe it, but I danced every dance!"

Jeannette and I had a fairly fixed routine. We had lessons in the morning at home, art was taught by visits to museums and concerts, and every day at noon we went for a walk with our governess-chaperone to the Villa Borghese. The governess thought we were walking for exercise, but we were walking to meet our beaux. We were never allowed to be alone with young men, so we met in groups, and since gossip about a girl was to be avoided at all costs, flirting had to be as subtle as possible.

My particular interest was the son of the Brazilian ambassador. We met at a *thé dansant* at the Palazzo Doria, where the ambassador, Baron de Teffé, lived. Jeannette and I walked up the grand staircase of that beautiful palace and at the top we paused. I looked into the ballroom, and there was Prince Charming. He came right over to where I was standing in the doorway and asked me to dance.

Maneco de Teffé was tall, dark, and handsome and not too bright. He was waiting to get into the university at Urbino, where boys who were not all that good scholastically were accepted. He had a sweet disposition, danced divinely, and had a beautiful silver-and-blue racing Alfa Romeo. He was a great driver and to me he was like a centaur, half man, half car. I was at an age when cars were a part of the attraction, and when he and his Alfa roared up the Pincio to meet us at the Villa Borghese, my heart quickened at the sound.

Maneco and I became more and more serious about each other, and we were indeed being gossiped about. Madame Suarez must have known we'd been seen holding hands at the movies—a serious breach—but she never said anything to me. Things came to a head one evening at a ball. Maneco and I had wandered away from the sharp eyes of the chaperones into a small sitting room to talk. The door was open, but we were alone, and although I knew that this was frowned upon, I had no idea that it would cause such a scandal. We were discussing our future when Madame Suarez loomed in the doorway. She was like a live volcano, apt to go off at any minute. "American manners!" she said with icy contempt. "In Rome, sitting alone at a ball with a young man is *not* allowed. Surely you must know *that* much by now. I shall write to your mother at once!"

I was disgraced. Mother's hopes of my advancement, the investment of the clothes, all was lost.

Madame Suarez's temper made Mother look like Little Nell, but her flare-ups seldom produced long-term results. I think I made more of the incident than she did, because I was so afraid of not being in her good graces. Apparently she forgot about the whole scene by the next morning, for I never heard another word (and my mother certainly didn't, because *I* would have heard about it).

Mother arrived at the end of June and we left Rome amicably, thanking Madame Suarez with sincere gratitude, and Jeannette and I swore eternal friendship (which lasts to this day).

I heard from the Toscanini girls that they were going to Brioni and they suggested we come along. I told Maneco of our summer plans. He said he wanted to be with me and he joined us. Brioni (Brijoni) is a lovely island in the Adriatic halfway between Venice and Trieste, and we all sailed together up and down the Dalmatian coast. There was only the hotel, a bathing pavilion, a private zoo, and a polo field. Lord Mountbatten came with his polo ponies from Malta, where he was stationed. When he went to the polo field in the hotel's ancient touring car, the only automobile allowed on the island, we all followed him on our bicycles as if he were a movie star.

After Brioni Maneco followed me to Villa d'Este and then to Paris. The Baron and Baroness de Teffé were not at all pleased by his proposal to marry an American girl whom they took to be the daughter of an adventuress. His father must have thought it was time for him to have a hand in the matter, and he fired the first torpedo aimed at sinking our romance. I translate from the French:

Madame,

I have learned with the greatest surprise . . . of a possible engagement between your daughter and my son Manuel. . . . my wife and I will never give our consent, nor our pecuniary assistance, to a union which does not have our approbation . . .

Manuel has more than once been madly in love with other young women—whom after a while he has completely forgotten—and I have always made it my duty to warn the parents in time. . . .

I remain yours faithfully

Oscar de Teffé

For the next couple of weeks there were telegrams from Madame de Teffé, explanations from Maneco, and further letters from his father.

The final salvo was a two-page letter from de Teffé:

". . . the responsibility for whatever may happen is yours—yours alone—and I would then be forced, to my great and keen regret, to have my son and your daughter followed by the police and to communicate the same to your Embassy. . . ."

Mother, much more sophisticated than I, knew his threats were empty ones, but she was delighted to see the end of a schoolgirl crush she didn't approve of anyway. She hardly welcomed as a future son-in-law a boy who had not even completed college and who wasn't bright enough to make his way in the world. He was hardly the pot of gold at the end of the rainbow.

Mother resorted to a Victorian stratagem to break up an infatuation—a sea voyage. We went back to New York for a short visit and then on to New Orleans. Almost by the time we arrived, I realized the whole episode with Maneco had been a winter romance. I saw him for the last time the following year in the south of France, and the "what might have been" was very emotional, but for both of us it was make-believe.

My social life seemed to have come a cropper in Rome, and I

fared no better in New Orleans. Mother thought she was going to show me off, a perfect product of European education, but every asset in Europe was a liability in America. Curtseying to old ladies was fine in Paris; for a seventeen-year-old girl in New Orleans it was ludicrous; while my conversation, larded as it was with dukes and countesses and castles, did nothing to endear me to my contemporaries.

I was only too happy to find that Mother sized up the situation. She took me right back to Paris.

As far as I was concerned, Paris in the twenties was made up of musicians and the frivolous post-World War I social set bent only on pleasure. I knew nothing of the other world of Paris—the expatriate artists and the literati, Hemingway, Sylvia Beach's Shakespeare & Co., Ezra Pound, Picasso, and Gertrude Stein, to name a few.

We were floating along on the outskirts of society, but it took a real swim to catapult me into the thick of it. That summer, at the Hôtel du Cap in Antibes, a beautiful girl about my age and I came to the diving board at the same time. We started in French: "After you!" "No, you were here first, it's your turn." "No, it's *your* turn," until it was resolved, and we met in the water. "What's your name?" I asked. "Jacqueline Stewart," she replied. "What's yours?" "Kitty Conn," I said, and we both laughed—two American girls, speaking perfect French.

Jacqueline was part of the *beau monde* of Paris. She had the best of both worlds—the Americans in Paris thanks to her American mother, and French society through her step-grandmother, the dowager Countess de Roussy de Sales. She was enormously popular and I was carried along in her wake. Jacqueline was going to Princess Mestchersky's fashionable finishing school that fall as a day student, and she thought it would be fun if I went too. Mother agreed. It was most unusual for a girl to return to boarding school after coming out, but Mother wanted to go to New York for the winter and it suited her to have me off her hands. I knew why. By then Major Spratt was among the missing and she had another beau, Edwin M. Otterbourg, a distinguished New York lawyer.

Princess Mestchersky was one of a large contingent of Russian nobles who fled to Paris after the revolution and were forced to earn a living. She had been lady-in-waiting to the Grand Duchess Hélène, the mother of Princess Marina (later the Duchess of Kent). The Grand Duchess used to come to teach us to make court curtseys and pour tea, which were presumably two of the things one learned at finishing school.

I was treated differently from the other girls because even though we were all under eighteen, I was the only boarder who had already been "out" in so-called society. I was allowed to go to parties at night and I was given my own key.

Among the younger girls at Princess Mestchersky's was thirteen-year-old Irina Yusupov, the daughter of the Prince Yusupov who had murdered Rasputin.

Yusupov came every Friday afternoon to take Irina to their house in Boulogne for the weekend. We all knew his lurid history, and we clustered at the top of the staircase to stare down at this fascinating man in the front hall. He was tall and dark and always wore an overcoat with an astrakhan collar; his hand, which was bejeweled with rings, held a lace handkerchief and rested on a silver-handled cane. His cheeks were lightly rouged and so were his lips, and he wore green eyeshadow.

Every Sunday night when Irina returned to school she had screaming nightmares. Hearing her screams and talking over all the terrible ways Yusupov and his friends tried to murder Rasputin: the poison cakes, the shootings, and throwing him into the freezing Neva River, where finally he drowned, we wondered what went on in that house in Boulogne.

Forty years later, during the intermission of *Pique-Dame* at the

old Metropolitan Opera House, I was sitting in the public rela-
tions office when the door slowly opened, and the first thing I
saw was the hand with the lace handkerchief, the jeweled fingers
on the silver-handled cane, and I knew instantly who was coming
through the door. Yusupov sat down beside me and I asked for
news of Irina. He told me she was a *vendeuse* for one of the big
French dressmakers. Then I asked him how he liked the opera.
He said it interested him very much, because *Pique-Dame* had
been written by Pushkin about his great-aunt, who had been an
inveterate gambler. She had lived in France; Yusupov and his
brother were sent to visit her when they were children, and every
night after dinner she would offer them a box of chocolates.
"She was very rich and very miserly," he said, "and the chocolates were . . . were . . ." he hesitated. I cannot think why,
but I pulled the word "moldy" out of his thoughts. "Yes, yes,"
he said, "they were moldy, and my brother always refused the
chocolates but I always took one." There was a long pause, as if
he were remembering the taste of moldy chocolate. Then he
added brightly, "And she left *me* all her money!"

ONE of the few times my mother misled me was when she told
me the "good" girls got the good husbands. It seemed to me
that if anybody had an edge, it was the bad girls. (We lived in a
world where people's sex life was freely discussed. I had read
French paperback novels at thirteen and Pierre Louÿs' *Aphrodite*
and *Chansons de Bilitis* at fourteen.) Everyone seemed to have a
lover or a mistress; the kept women were in a different class, and
they were graded for their chic, their jewels, and the length of
their liaisons. I wasn't a bad girl, but to tell the truth there were
no battalions trying to seduce me. However, when an attempt
was made, it was pretty elaborate.

Roland de l'Épée was as romantic as his name. He had the

reputation of being irresistible to women, and I was wary of being alone with him. One day he told me he was giving a cocktail party at his house in the country near St.-Cloud. When I arrived, it soon became plain that I was to be the only guest. We had a bit of a tussle, but Roland was a good sport and took me home *virgo intacta*.

He didn't give up, though; he invited me to his mother's château in the country. Brissac was a storybook castle: moat, turrets, one hundred rooms, no electricity, and one bathroom to a floor that must have been put in just after the château was built for Diane de Poitiers. When we arrived the servants were lined up on the steps of the terrace to greet us, and we were ushered into an enormous hall where I met Roland's mother and stepfather, the Duc and Duchesse de Brissac. Madame de Brissac was a sensitive and clever woman with psychic powers, as I was to learn later.

There was a large house party. We were thirty at dinner, and we were serenaded by musicians seated in the balcony. At the end of the evening we assembled in the great hall, where our lighted candles were set out on a large table, ready for the procession up to our rooms. It was a lovely sight, all those people carrying glowing tapers up the impressive staircase.

Forty candles wouldn't have been enough to illuminate my huge bedroom. I've always been afraid of the dark, and I was frightened out of my wits by the shadows and the unknown, convinced that Things with long octopus-like arms lurked under the bed waiting to grab my ankles.

Once in the four-poster I felt fairly safe; however, I was wrong. Within minutes the door quietly opened, and my heart stopped. What ghostly figure was coming to claim me? It was no ghost trying to get into my bed, but Roland himself, in bathrobe and pajamas. I remonstrated with him and convinced him that it was not to be.

The next morning, when we all gathered on the winding stairway for a chance at the bathroom, there was a lot of giggling over who was seen coming out of whose bedroom. Either it reached the duchesse's ears or she consulted her psychic powers, for the next time I came to Brissac I was put in a room adjoining her bedroom on the ground floor, and Roland turned his attention to someone more accessible.

That weekend the duchesse's gift for seeing into the future was brought home to me. Everyone had gone stag hunting except the duchesse and me, and we were going out to join the hunters with a picnic lunch in the dogcart. We met in the grand salon. "What a morning!" she said. "I was doing the farm accounts and all the time footsteps were going up and down the stairway in the tower." "What footsteps?" I asked. "The footsteps of all the people who used to live here," she answered, as if ghosts were a normal feature of castle life. Then she said, "We have a few minutes before we must go. Would you like me to read your cards?" "Oh yes, please!" I said.

Mother had never let me go to fortune-tellers. She said *she* could because she didn't *really* believe them, whereas I would believe everything they said. (She did, however, believe in reincarnation, and when she was pleased with me she would say I was an "old soul" who had been through many lives, and I had chosen to be her child for our mutual improvement.)

The duchesse and I went to the card table and she laid out the cards. I don't think she really read them; she seemed to me to use them to busy her hands and free her mind. "I see lights, music, and applause." Instantly I thought of the theater, and as I looked into her clairvoyant blue eyes, it didn't seem at all fanciful.

Then she said, "You have a beau in Paris; when you return tomorrow from this weekend he will be very ill and he may die." I did have a beau in Paris, Stuart Wiltsee, a young American whom I had met in the south of France that summer, and he had had a tooth pulled before I left for the weekend. But her words didn't frighten me. In my experience nobody got sick from having a tooth pulled, and as for dying, that was ridiculous. Nobody our age *ever* died. But this was before sulfa drugs, before penicillin. When I returned to Paris there was a message from his mother to come immediately: he was mortally ill. Poor Stuart had an infection which went to his brain, and an hour later he died virtually in my arms.

ALL young people move around in groups. Jacqueline and I went from balls to dinners to weekend parties, trailing the *jeunesse dorée* behind us.

Jacqueline's grandmother took us to all the balls, where I always obeyed Mother's injunction—never stay with the wallflowers in the corner of the ballroom; stand on the dance floor as if you were waiting for a partner. It was a terribly embarrassing thing to do, but it paid off.

The festivities were not limited to Paris—Jacqueline and I went often to England for weekend house parties and hunt balls. I was even invited to the Nottingham home of Charlie Birkin to go fox hunting with the Quorn, one of the most important hunts in England. When I told this to the Brissacs, they blanched. They had seen me ride, and they very encouragingly offered to meet me with an ambulance on my return at the Gare du Nord.

I was not to be deterred. Charlie showed me over the hunting terrain. At Brissac one hunted the stag down wide allées, and there was no jumping. Here in England I saw a series of five-foot fences, and though it may be my overheated imagination, I swear they had barbed wire on top. "Charlie," I said hastily, "I wouldn't *dream* of letting your father lend me one of his hunters. I'll just go out with the lunch!"

I met Charlie's father and mother and his sisters Violet (when she married Mr. Blue-Jones, she became Violet Blue-Jones) and Frieda Dudley Ward, the beloved of the Prince of Wales. The prince was off on a world tour, and she was taking care of his two Corgi dogs. To me it was exciting just being close enough to the Prince of Wales to pat his dogs and shake hands with his love. (I couldn't dream then that many years later I would sit next to the prince himself, then the Duke of Windsor, at a dinner party in New York. He was in a reminiscing mood, talking about his grandmama, Queen Victoria, who, he told me, taught him German songs when he was a child. He sang bits of them to me, and spoke to me in German. I have a limited knowledge of that language and a primitive vocabulary, but my accent is marvelous and with a few beautifully pronounced exclamations I fooled him into thinking I knew what he was talking about. Suddenly he said, *"Warum sind alle Führern Juden?"* I knew *Juden* were Jews, but to me *führer* meant only Hitler. Could he be asking why all Hitlers are Jews? Hardly. Then I thought, he's been talking about music, and *führer* also means leader, conductor. Maybe he wanted to know why all conductors were Jews. "Not all conductors are Jews, sir," I said in English. He seemed bewildered, and then he gave me a funny look. Luckily for me, at that moment it was time for him to turn to his other dinner partner. To this day I don't know what he was trying to say.)

THE curtain rises on my second chance at a brilliant marriage. I found him in an upstairs closet.

After every ball our group usually went to a nightclub, but this particular evening we went to a friend's house to play a game called Sardines. It was like hide-and-seek, except that the "it" had to hide, stay put, and as each seeker found him, he or she had to crowd into "its" hiding place. I was the first to find "it," and by the time the next person came in, Philippe Hottinguer and I were quite well acquainted.

Philippe was the younger son of an ancient banking family of great wealth. His mother was an American, married to the Baron Hottinguer, and Philippe himself was partial to Americans (he eventually married one).

The initial warning that Philippe was not to be my ultimate fate was sounded at my first dinner party at the Hottinguers' house in Paris. I was late, a major mistake. The taxi driver couldn't find the address, and Philippe's father, the baron, cared more about his chef than he did about his son's romance.

I made matters worse when Jacqueline and I and other friends were invited for a weekend at the Hottinguers' country house. After dinner the first night we assembled in the billiard room. The baron came in and said, *"Mes enfants,* do not sit on the edge of the billiard table with your coffee cups." The door had barely closed behind the baron when some evil genius impelled me to sit on the billiard table with my full cup, with the foreseeable result. I was not endearing myself to the family.

Nevertheless, Philippe and I saw a great deal of each other. One day he asked me to come to see his own small shooting box, Chambrulé. It was being winterized, he implied, so we could use it as a year-round weekend cottage. I was positive he was going to pop the question. Philippe, who had brought me there for quite another reason, was very much annoyed to find the place full of plumbers. He was furious when one suddenly came in to the library where we were sitting. "Monsieur, we're laying the hot-water pipes," the plumber said. "Do you want to come with us to show us where they should go?" "No, no," Philippe said, "put them wherever you think best." They laid the pipes where Philippe's father, not knowing about the modernizations, had temporarily stored his best wine and champagne. It ruined the lot, to say nothing of my chances.

The Hottinguers didn't think I was the proper wife for Philippe anyway. Philippe was sweet and gentle, but he had a strong family feeling, and he didn't love me enough to fight for me and I didn't love him enough to put him up to it.

For two years Mother had been making a little money in the stock market. I no longer saw her writing figures on the backs of envelopes. We moved into a little house off the fashionable Avenue Foch, the Villa Saïd, where Anatole France had lived. We even had a Rolls-Royce and chauffeur, hired for special occasions from the taxi rank in front of the Ritz. The car was so old I'm sure it had gone to the battle of the Marne with all the other taxi cabs, and it was painted, or had turned, a sickly green. Mother didn't care. It was a Rolls-Royce, and that made up for all its decrepitude.

We seldom gave dinner parties but when we did we hired a butler, whom we also pretended was ours. Because he wasn't, there were catastrophic contretemps. The first formal dinner I ever gave was very important to me, and I was allowed to choose the food and wine. Mother went off to play bridge, leaving me alone with my guests. We were twelve young people, including Jacqueline and Philippe. The main course was squab, and the butler couldn't find a platter big enough to hold twelve squabs. The dish went around with six aboard. In Europe, unlike in America, the guest of honor is served first instead of the hostess. My friends silently correlated the number of squabs to the number of guests, and each in turn politely said "No, thank you." I was so embarrassed that total paralysis set in and I couldn't utter a word. Why Jacqueline didn't say something I'll never know, but the six squabs went back to join the other six in the kitchen.

Mother loved the whole business of the stock market—the conferences with friends, and consultations with her broker. But the daily phone call to get the latest stock market figures fell to me because her French, except at the bridge table, wasn't all that good. I never remembered the quotations from one day to the next but repeated them parrot-like to Mother.

One day in October 1929 I put through the usual call. I was standing at the telephone in Mother's room; she was sitting on the bed. Halfway through, as I relayed to her what was being said on the other end, she gasped and turned pale. At that moment in New York people were jumping out of windows, but Mother just fell backward on the bed, her arm flung over her eyes as if to ward off a blow. I was too frightened to move. After a long pause, she sat bolt upright and said with finality, "We've lost all our money."

By the time it took to pack our clothes and pick up the Spanish shawl and the royal Balkan photos, we were back to one room under the eaves in a good hotel, this time the Plaza Athénée, in a room so small that we had to sidle around the wardrobe trunk to get to the door.

But as always Mother had a plan. "It's obvious you're not going to make a brilliant marriage." I was only nineteen, but I'd had two cracks at it, Rome and Paris. "You wear clothes fairly well, you could become a model." Even though I didn't know very much about modeling as a profession, I was aware that it was a bit of a dead end. I shook my head. "Well," she went on, "you're not the prettiest girl I ever saw, you're not the best singer I ever heard, and you're certainly not the best actress I ever hope to see, but if we put them all together, *we'll* find the husband *we're* looking for on the stage."

I was thunderstuck. I had long since forgotten the Duchesse de Brissac's prediction.

"I'll back you with what's left of the money, and you can go to the Royal Academy of Dramatic Art in London." It sounded a lot more exciting than trying to marry Philippe.

Mother decided on the Royal Academy, affectionately known as RADA, because she thought that renowned school would give me the best classical training, though I suspect she would rather have returned to New York and her beau, Ed.

In the months before I went to London, Mother threw herself into my career with as much passion as she had put into finding an entrée into society. She worked on getting introductions to top people. It was a very mixed bunch; she hadn't quite made up her mind what branch of the theater I was to dignify.

Acting lessons were first on her agenda. She found a remarkable teacher, Charles Dullin, who directed an avant-garde theater and acting school, "Le Théâtre vingt-huit," a forerunner of today's improvisational theater.

Next the opera world. I auditioned for a monumental opera singer, Emma Eames. She was monumental in every way. She lived in an apartment filled with the spindliest, most fragile gilt furniture I had ever seen, and as she moved majestically through the french doors to greet us, I wondered how on earth this enormous creature was going to sit down without the chair splintering under her. She was dressed as though about to give a performance in Carnegie Hall, except for an incongruous fur tippet hard put to cover her tremendous shoulders.

Eames didn't stand on ceremony and immediately demanded of my mother, "Well, madame, what is it you want?" "I would like you to tell me if my daughter's voice has operatic possibilities," said Mother. "Did you bring something to sing?" Madame Eames asked, barely acknowledging my existence. "I brought some Handel," I said timidly. It was a mistake to have brought the Handel, and I only did it because my singing teacher had told me to. It was far too difficult, and frightened as I was, to the point of dry mouth and cloven tongue, the aria was insuperable. (I've often wondered why singing teachers give students songs beyond their technical abilities, and why they insist on their singing them at auditions.) As I quavered through the Handel, I became more and more desperate, and finally on the last note my voice got completely away from me, and I let out a lamb-to-the-slaughter bleat that startled even me.

Madame Eames gave a prodigious sigh. It sounded like the wind coming up in a grove of oaks. I can see her tippet heaving now. "Opera, no," she pronounced; "operetta—perhaps." She made it sound as though it was slightly better than going on the streets. We took our leave.

Following Eames's advice, next stop was the composer Reynaldo Hahn, whose successful operetta *Mozart* was playing with Yvonne Printemps and Sacha Guitry in the starring roles. Hahn was a small gray man who lived five flights up in a tiny studio. We had a few sessions before he sent me on to a singing teacher with this note: "I recommend Miss Kitty Conn; she has a pretty voice, somewhat weak on the top."

We were going steadily downhill. Mother's next port of call was a famous *diseuse* of the Café Concert, Yvette Guilbert. A *diseuse* has been defined as someone who sings but hasn't any voice. Guilbert was tall, red-haired, and still beautiful, but to my young eyes an aging lady. She lived in a cluttered bohemian atmosphere surrounded by huge pouffes, oriental rugs, and potted palms. The walls were covered with posters from her every engagement, many of them by her friend Toulouse-Lautrec. A strong smell of incense filled the air. I never got around to singing for her, because as soon as she saw me she announced immediately that she didn't take pupils. She did, however, vouchsafe that experience was the best teacher; I should try to find an audience—any audience—and sing to it. We took our leave of her too.

Now for the audience. Mother found one, but it was most peculiar. In a suburb of Paris called Ménilmontant, there was a workingmen's club that held concerts periodically. The audience consisted solely of the workingmen, who would turn up for practically anything provided they didn't have to pay. The hall had a wooden platform and wooden benches. The men in their work clothes—rough navy blue butchers' shirts, corduroy trousers, and long-visored caps which they never took off—sat hunched, with no expression on their faces, not knowing what they were going to get. What they got was my Handel, which was in French, followed by "Can't Help Lovin' Dat Man," from *Showboat,* in English. What the men made of that combination I cannot imagine, nor indeed what possessed me to choose it. Perhaps I was thinking of Yvette Guilbert and singing in a nightclub, but this would not account for the Handel. Neither composition, however, proved congenial to the audience. The men went on sitting, looking as wooden as their benches. Fortunately my contribution was limited, and my place on the platform was soon taken by another victim, a nervous young man with a violin. Mother and I went out through the body of the hall. As I looked back I had an impression of this poor fellow sawing away at his violin and of the still motionless men in the audience. It struck me they looked the same from the back as they did from the front.

UNTIL now the permanent cast of characters in my life had been limited to one: my mother. Now another was added. Her relationship with Ed Otterbourg was to last for thirty years, until she died.

Ed was a bachelor; he was tall and looked well-fed. He wore a pince-nez and had beautiful gray hair, which he never lost. In a movie he would have been cast as the governor of an important state.

Ed was president of the New York County Lawyers Association. He came from a long line of lawyers and judges. His grandfather, Judge Otterbourg, had been the United States envoy to the court of Maximilian and Carlotta in Mexico. But more to the point, Ed was the nephew of Henry Wolfson, the Sol Hurok of his day, who had been the manager of such artists as Mischa Elman and Madame Schumann-Heink. Ed grew up in the world of music and the theater. He had a box at Carnegie Hall for the Boston Symphony, Monday night seats at the opera (which I have inherited), and a subscription to the Theatre Guild. Ed's interests were intellectual: books, music; he was a collector of fine prints and etchings—a thoroughly civilized man.

I didn't meet him on his first trip to Paris, but he was responsible for the only time I ever found Mother in an indiscretion: I had returned from a weekend visit and discovered one of his collars in my bureau drawer.

Ed had fallen in love with Mother, and she was in love with him, I think, but I never saw the slightest sign of physical affection between them, not even the obligatory kiss on the cheek when they met. From across the room she would say, "Hello, Ed," and that was it.

In the beginning I wanted very much for Mother to marry Ed. It would have made life easier for me. This way he had no official title. What was I to call him? My mother's boyfriend? My lawyer? Uncle Ed? (Which is what he became to my children.) Throughout the years he would ask me, "Why won't your mother marry me?" I would then ask her. "Every woman should be married once," she'd say, "and once is enough." Or: "I don't want to keep house anymore." Sometimes she was flippant: "If I did marry him, he wouldn't send flowers and call me twice a day." Finally she told me the truth: "I want to be able to go to my own apartment and close the door." And when she was in a three-day blow, that's exactly what she did. In the end I understood her reluctance; she had things just the way she wanted.

Ed fancied himself an impresario like his uncle and was eager to accept responsibility for me and my career. This suited Mother perfectly, and it became a lasting source of interest between them. When he returned to Paris, he said he wanted to talk to me alone. He needed to know from *me* whether I really wanted to go on the stage. Did I know what I was in for, or was I doing it only to please my mother? He warned me it would mean hard work, possible heartbreak, and I would need to develop the hide of a rhinoceros. "I understand all that," I said. "I want to do it." "Very well then, if you'll follow my advice and do exactly

as I say, I'll make you a star." I felt like Faust selling his soul to
the devil.

Ed returned to New York and his law practice, but he gave
Mother a detailed blueprint for future reference. She and I were
left to plan my trip to London and the Royal Academy.

Although Mother's main objective was the theater, she
couldn't bear the thought that I wasn't studying something else
at the same time. Why learn one thing when you can learn two?
"You're interested in politics; you can take a couple of courses at
the London School of Economics and enlarge your horizons."
So I audited some courses with Harold Lasky.

As RADA didn't offer singing lessons, Mother had to find me a
singing teacher; also a suitable chaperone. She herself was going
to stay in Paris for a couple of months and would join me later.

Mother's predilection for going to the top produced Madame
Karchowska, one of Lotte Lehmann's singing teachers; and the
mother of a fellow pupil, Trudy Ophuls, agreed to chaperone
me. Trudy, who had a lovely soprano, was born with that elusive
high pianissimo. We stayed at the Ambassador Hotel in Bloomsbury. It was a modest hotel. The food was predictable—some
sort of boiled fish and a boiled potato for lunch, and an uniden-
tifiable piece of meat and a boiled vegetable for dinner. Dessert
was invariably tired cooked pears. The first night we came in to
dinner, the dreary atmosphere was enlivened by a gramophone
playing the sextet from *Lucia*. Three months later, although I
still liked it, I was longing for a change of pace.

The magic carpet to the future was RADA. It had a stage; and
the very first moment I set foot on that stage, I knew I'd found
my element. The boards under my feet gave me wings. I floated,
I flew, taking strength from those boards as if I'd always lived in
the theater. Up to then everything had depended on something
or someone else. Now, for the first time in my life, I felt as if my
future was in my own hands. It was the most exhilarating feeling
I had ever had.

Madame Karchowska arranged for her students to get some experience singing in public at small musicales. The first was at Kensington Palace, for Princess Beatrice, the daughter of Queen Victoria. We were excited about going to a palace to sing for a lady of such antecedents—but the princess was very old, and at the first chirp she went peacefully to sleep.

At the end of three months I was in my first play at RADA, *Trelawny of the Wells*. I played the lead, Rose, but only in the first act. There were too many of us and we had to divide up the part. Mother came from Paris to see me. She was pinning all her hopes on my career. This was the acid test.

After the act was over I waited for the verdict. Mother came backstage and looked me straight in the eye. "My dear," she said, "we've made a ghastly mistake!"

Ordinarily this kind of criticism would have laid me flat. Not this time. I *wanted* the theater. I knew I had to keep on trying. Anyway, there was no alternative; for once Mother couldn't seem to think of anything else. But after three more months our money ran out. If I wanted to stay at RADA I had to get a job.

Mother cut our Paris ties and took up residence with me in Bloomsbury. Poor Mother; it wasn't the Ritz, it was shabby gentility and a shilling in the gas meter. Nevertheless, ever resourceful, she joined Crockford's Bridge Club where her days were happily occupied.

My teachers at RADA had friends in the theater. They arranged an audition for a Hawaiian musical, *Luana of the Jungle*. I was given a song about a maiden who was a human sacrifice and had to jump into a volcano. As I finished, on a good loud high B flat, the producer called out, "Can you take the last note pianissimo?" How could I do it? I hadn't found it yet! But I felt success or failure hinged on my trying. I took a deep breath and leapt into the unknown as that maiden might have leapt into her volcano, and I produced the same bleat I had produced for Madame Eames. (Years later I studied with the great Madame

Schoen-René, the teacher of Risë Stevens, whose lessons preceded mine. One day I asked Schoen-René to give me the same beautiful high pianissimo Risë had. Schoen-René looked at me as if I was mad. "Dose high pianissimos," she announced, "come only from Gott!" It was one of the few honest answers I ever had from a singing teacher.)

My next audition was for a tiny part in *The Great Waltz*. After I sang a simple song (with no high pianissimos), they said they'd hire me. Mother was delighted, even though it wasn't much more than a chorus part. In her day English chorus girls, known as Gaiety Girls, all married dukes—and revitalized the British aristocracy.

It was a rude shock to discover that I had to comply with all sorts of formalities to work in England. The first was obtaining a labor permit. I was in England on a student visa, and to change my status, especially in 1931 when everyone was on the dole, proved impossible. Obviously an English girl could say "The carriage is waiting, madam," which was all that my part called for. (The rule still applies on both sides of the Atlantic. When Rex Harrison was cast in *My Fair Lady*, Actors Equity refused him permission. We had to go to the prestigious firm of Dewey, Ballantine; Thomas E. Dewey himself negotiated with the union, and the rest is history.)

Mother tried very hard to beat the system, but we didn't know anybody who could get me a labor permit. Ed was in America, not available for day-to-day advice. Mother knocked on many doors, and all were shut. She made an abrupt decision—this time to return to New York and Ed.

My brush with *The Great Waltz* was the first signpost on the way to Moss Hart: he subsequently adapted it for the Center Theater in New York. I hadn't even heard his name then, but the lines of our lives were beginning to converge.

BACK to America in 1932, and a dive into the unknown. I had been living abroad for ten years except for that one short trip to New Orleans, and I remember being horrified when a customs official stamped "expatriate" on my passport.

Broke though Mother and I were, Ed said we still had to have a good address, so we went to the Ambassador Hotel on Park Avenue. We had a tiny apartment with a minute kitchen which was useless, because neither Mother nor I could cook. In Europe, where the dollar was high and living was inexpensive, we'd always had a cook, but in New York for the first few weeks I went around the corner to Child's for our breakfast, which I then brought home: coffee in a paper cup and soggy toast on a paper plate. I had to learn to use the stove. Mother must have longed for Southern food all those years in Paris, because every day I made grits and bacon for our lunch. Luckily, dinner was no problem. We had dinner with Ed every night. He loved good food (and it showed a little bit in his embonpoint).

First things first: I had to get a singing teacher. Mother and Ed produced Estelle Liebling, a bridge-playing friend of theirs who later became the teacher of many stars, including Beverly Sills. The voice is the only instrument that you can't see, can't touch, fix, or tune. Singing is an act of faith; it takes place for the most part in your head, and if the teacher can reach your mind with the right words and improve the instrument, that teacher becomes all-important. Miss Liebling taught me without compensation, except for my gratitude, both for her generosity and for her faith in me.

Singers have to keep in shape, so Ed made me walk around the reservoir in Central Park four times a week. One day as I looked south at the New York skyline I vowed that someday everybody in every one of those buildings would know my name.

But I needed a stage name, and I wanted something elegant. The telephone book proved useful for research, and after a few false starts with names that were *too* elegant (Vere de Vere was discarded early on), I came up with Kitty Carlisle. It was euphonious and I liked it.

Mother went to a numerologist to check it out. "My daughter is thinking of taking Kitty Carlisle as a stage name," she said. "What will it do for her?" The fortune-teller wrote down rows of figures and studied them, and then she said, "That name is a big money-maker." "Thank you," said Mother, "how much do I owe you?" "Don't you want to know if she'll be happy?" asked the fortune-teller. "No," Mother said, "that's fine, thank you." I became Kitty Carlisle, and overnight Mother became Mrs. Carlisle. It was one of the many stories she told on herself.

Ed picked up my cultural education where Mother left off. He took me to museums and galleries, and to the dealer where he bought his lithographs and etchings. He filled in the lacunae of my French education with the nineteenth-century English writers he loved: Charles Dickens, Anthony Trollope, George Eliot. There was music as well—concerts and opera—and theater.

Getting an agent was important, but for a beginner it was (and still is) difficult. Agents don't want to take you on until they can see what you can do; but how do you get the job to show an agent what you can do if you don't have an agent to get you the jobs? Ed must have been very persuasive to get Bill Liebling to represent me. He was no relation to Estelle, but Liebling was my lucky name.

Now it was up to me to get a job. This was exciting and urgent. I was being entrusted with a very grown-up mission, and it gave me a feeling of importance I'd never known before.

Ed lent me eight hundred dollars. (Why eight hundred dollars? And how did he know it would last me until I got a job?) He said it was for taxis to go to auditions if it was raining, and for good shoes, clean white gloves, and hairdressers. True to his word, he was guiding my career.

I started the audition circuit. I sang for shows that never saw the light of day, much less Broadway, and for composers who had no shows to offer and only wanted to hear what their own songs sounded like.

After many months of no offers, Bill escorted me to a now-defunct Broadway movie house, the 3,800-seat Capitol Theatre, to audition for the lead in a condensed version of *Rio Rita.*

In those days movie houses were huge and ornate. Live acts played along with the movie, and every so often an operetta or a play would be presented. A lot of stars toured in such productions. Mrs. Patrick Campbell and Ethel Barrymore went out with playlets by Sir James M. Barrie; George Arliss played in *The Green Goddess,* and Ginger Rogers did a shortened version of *Girl Crazy.* The movie started in the late morning; then the stage show, which took an hour and twenty minutes; then the movie, and so on. There were four shows a day during the week and five on weekends.

For the audition I had to sing the title song, "Rio Rita." I rushed out and bought the sheet music, but there wasn't enough time to learn it by heart. The next morning I arrived at the theater clutching the music and wearing what I thought was suitable for the early hour: a little Chanel-type wool suit and a simple beret to match. (*Everything* had to match then.) It was the depths of the Depression; nobody had a job, and the theater was filled with experienced Broadway prima donnas, all wearing their most glamorous clothes—black satin dresses slit up to mid-thigh, aigrettes and diamanté clips on their hats, and pearl necklaces to their knees. They sang without music, while I sat in a welter of misery in my wool suit and cap, the music in my hands getting damper and damper. When my name was called I walked quickly to the stage and sang from the printed page.

I stepped down off the stage and went home and waited. How many times have I auditioned and then waited, only to hear all those euphemisms adding up to "thanks but no thanks!" In spite of the competition I was optimistic, and whenever I was away from the hotel for any length of time I telephoned home to see if there was any word. One day I called from a phone booth, and

Mother was as excited as I had ever heard her. "You got the job, you got the job!" she cried. "You start rehearsing right away!"

Rio Rita was to open in three weeks at eleven in the morning. The pay was $200 a week, a fortune in the Depression. We would play a week at the Capitol, then go on the subway circuit—so called because you could get to Loew's 86th Street, Loew's Brooklyn, Loew's Valencia, and Loew's Paradise by subway—and then tour the country in the big movie houses for one-week stands.

At the first rehearsal I saw a group of show girls in a corner talking to one another, and I went over to make friends. As I approached I heard one say, "Why on earth do you suppose they hired *her* to play the lead?" I was wondering the same thing myself. Goodness knows, I was green.

But Louis K. Sidney, who had hired me, knew something about me that I didn't know: I had stamina. Lord, did I have stamina! I played eight months—1,000 performances—in *Rio Rita*. In the last scene I wore a white velvet wedding dress with a six-foot train and a veil, and I carried an armful of calla lilies. I swore, after playing in that outfit four and five times a day, that I would never wear a bridal gown again, not even if I got married.

After the week at the Capitol we started on the subway circuit, but I never went by subway. Ed had a Ford town car, and following his philosophy of "how-to-handle-a-star," I was driven to work in his car and came home the same way.

Then came the sleeper jumps. The routine was to get on the train Sunday night after the last show, travel all night, and arrive the next morning in time to rehearse and open at 11 A.M. I took my career seriously. I always tried to get a proper night's sleep in order to open refreshed and in good voice, with an eye to the critics.

One morning in the dead of winter we arrived in Buffalo after I'd had a bad night on the train. The company had decided to have a party, which meant noise, card games, and liquor. I arrived at the hotel a bit earlier than usual, in time for a nap. I got into my nightgown and fell asleep.

The telephone woke me up. A voice yelled in my ear: "Where the hell are you? You're on!" I jumped out of bed and threw on a fur coat that Ed had given me. It had belonged to his mother, who must have been very tall, and it fell to my ankles. I stuffed my bare feet into galoshes, the rubber kind with metal fasteners that came up to mid-calf. I rushed out the door, hailed a taxi, and arrived at the theater, where my dresser was waiting to get me into my costume. As the last hook was fastened my cue came, and I bounded on the stage and ran down to the footlights for my first number.

Having missed rehearsal, there were two things I didn't know about Shea's Buffalo Theatre. The first was that the stage was raked, so that in running to the footlights I gathered unexpected momentum; the second was that the orchestra pit, which rose dramatically to stage level at the start of the stage show, had fouled that morning. On it the band was playing a good four feet below me and rising slowly. From my running start over the slanting stage, I shot right into the orchestra pit. Miraculously nobody was hurt and I was able to continue with the performance, but it was, hands down, the most dramatic entrance of my life.

Mother traveled with me because she and Ed felt I should be chaperoned. It must have been terribly lonely for her, as I provided little or no companionship. However, she always found the local bridge club, and with her credentials from Crockford's in London, she had no trouble getting a visitor's membership.

Mother came to see the show from time to time. She was always trying to improve me, but she never praised me without first pointing out what I had done wrong: "The 'E' vowel on the F sharp was pinched . . . but it was a lovely performance." Too late; all I could hear was the criticism. In Detroit she called up the leading critic, Mr. McDermott, to ask him what he meant by his poor notice. It wasn't that she was complaining, she told him, it was to help me better my performance.

My days were spent in the theater, and when I wasn't on stage, I was eating or trying to nap. I am eternally grateful to Maurice Baring, for it was during the *Rio Rita* tour that I read his biography of Sarah Bernhardt and learned that she could fall asleep on the hearthrug in a roomful of people, sleep for ten minutes, and wake totally refreshed. I thought, I can't act like Bernhardt, but maybe I can sleep like Bernhardt, so I bought a cot which traveled with me. I could sleep in the theater and never miss a rehearsal or a performance. There was always the call: "Half hour!" to wake me in time to do a few vocalises, powder my nose, and go on again. I learned to nap anywhere and I still can.

I really needed those naps. After six months I was so tired I asked my understudy to do the six o'clock show for me, when the only people in the theater were a few traveling salesmen with their sample cases, there to get out of the cold. I paid her five dollars a show, and she was delighted.

When we got to Omaha, I sent Louis K. Sidney a telegram saying that my voice was giving out and I didn't think I could continue on the road. At our next stop the answer was waiting for me: "Stick with it, kid. From what I hear, by the time you get back to New York you'll be able to fill Yankee Stadium."

I stuck with it. By the time we returned to New York, I had saved some money. I paid Ed back and now I was ready, I hoped, for Broadway and what I had dreamed of all those months on the road: Stardom!

I had become the family breadwinner. I enjoyed making a living, but the only time I ever handled my own money was on the road with *Rio Rita*. It came in cash every week in a little brown envelope, and I pinned it to the inside of my girdle. That money was real. All subsequent salaries went to Ed, who took care of my finances. He gave me an allowance of fifty dollars a week.

Mother still hadn't made up her mind whether I was operatic material or not. *Rio Rita* was certainly valuable theatrical experience, but she hankered for a more classical career for me, and I tried hard to live up to her expectations. My wonderful teacher, Estelle Liebling, said I had a "dugazon" soprano. I never heard that expression before or since, and no one I asked ever had either, so I suspect Miss Liebling invented it to describe what she diplomatically called a "short" soprano. I never did have a good high C except in the "Miserere" in *A Night at the Opera.* The best part of my voice lay in the middle and lower register.

But Mother was looking for another opinion about my voice; through Miss Liebling, she got an audition for me with Rosa Ponselle, the greatest soprano of my time.

Miss Ponselle received me sitting at the piano with Romano Romani, her coach-accompanist. She looked surprised to see me, as if it had escaped her mind that I had an appointment. I was in and out in twenty minutes. It was Emma Eames all over again.

(As for Ponselle, though I heard her sing many times after that unfortunate audition, I never met her again until her seventy-fifth birthday, when I was asked to go to Baltimore to sing "Happy Birthday" to her. For me it was a great honor, but the best part was standing next to her and hearing that still-glorious voice join in and blithely sing happy birthday to herself!)

I waited four months for another job, and the time seemed endless. When you're very young time passes very slowly. As you get older, it whizzes by. Mother said, "Once you're past fifty, every fifteen minutes it's breakfast!"

Ed decided that it was time for me to have another agent. Agents had different spheres of influence; Liebling's was vaudeville, and Ed was already aiming for Broadway and Hollywood. One of the biggest agencies in town which had offices on both coasts was A. and S. Lyons. Ed figured that if he became their lawyer, he could control their handling of me; but I was not to meet them except on ceremonial occasions. I think Ed had delusions of my grandeur.

Arthur Lyons got an audition for me with Dwight Deere Wyman, a most distinguished theatrical producer, for a production of Johann Strauss's opera *Die Fledermaus,* which was to be called *Champagne, Sec.* I gave a good audition and landed the part of Prince Orlovsky. While not the lead, it was a showy role. It was written for a female and is usually played by one. There are many such in opera, and they're known as pants parts. The rest of the cast were Peggy Wood, George Meader (from the Metropolitan Opera), and Helen Ford, who had been the star of Rodgers and Hart's *Dearest Enemy.* Wyman had planned a week's tryout at the Westport Country Playhouse, and if it worked, he would then take it to Broadway.

Rehearsals were held in New York. I arrived at the theater to find everyone letter-perfect but me. In musical comedy you learn your part in rehearsal. Not so in opera. The conductor, with a reputation in symphony and opera, was authoritarian and choleric. In spite of those duets with my mother, I had never become a very good sight reader, and after three days of rehearsal he said, in front of everyone, "If you don't know your part by tomorrow, you will be fired." I sat up all night at the piano, blessing Mother for the lessons, the rapped knuckles, and even the mice. The next day I may not have been letter-perfect, but I saved my job.

We had three directors: Monty Woolley (later to play Sheridan Whiteside in the Kaufman-Hart *The Man Who Came to Dinner*), Lawrence Langner, and Lina Abarbanell. I couldn't tell who directed what.

Every company has a patsy, and this time I was it. I was made to feel that if anything gummed up the works at rehearsal, it was always my fault. In spite of the three directors, no one seemed to have any time for me. I was left to work things out pretty much by myself. The most important were the Russian accent and the boy's walk. The accent was easy; I went back in my memory to Princess Mestchersky's school. Between her, the deposed Russians and the Yusupovs, there had been a variety of Russian accents. For the walk, I remembered my lessons in improvisation from RADA. I would follow a man on the street, swinging my arms, trying to imitate his masculine stride. I must have been quite a sight walking down Park Avenue behind an attractive young man, altering my gait every few steps, shaking my head and saying out loud, "No, no, that's not right."

At the audition no one had asked to see my legs. On the day of the costume parade, just before we were to leave for Westport, when I came out on the little stage at Eaves Costume Company in black tights, I heard Mr. Wyman sigh with relief.

(Thank goodness in the aging process the legs are the last to go. Fifty-five years later, at the opening of Lincoln Center's Outdoor Festival, I said to the audience, "This is a wonderful occasion. There is something here for everyone: children, tourists, and senior citizens like me." Then Mayor Ed Koch, who followed me, said, "Senior citizen or not, Kitty's got the greatest pair of legs I've ever seen!")

The night of the dress rehearsal I walked up the hill to the Playhouse with the press agent. "How do you get to be a star?" I asked her, and she laughed, not only because it was a silly question, but because there was no answer.

I got into my costume and stood in the wings. Prince Orlovsky doesn't come on till the second act, and I had time to develop a full-blown case of stage fright. The stage manager, Eddie Mendelssohn of sainted memory, was my one buttress against total collapse. He patted me on the back. "Don't worry, kid," he kept saying through the first act, "you're going to be all right."

But I wasn't all right yet. Mother and Ed brought Arthur Lyons to Westport for the dress rehearsal. Obviously this was a ceremonial occasion. Directors hate actors' families and agents sitting out front during rehearsals, and stage mothers are anathema. Mother would have been appalled to have been thought of as a stage mother, but she did have strong opinions. That they were there this time was a lifesaver. When they came backstage, Arthur Lyons said, "Why are you being such a shrinking violet? It's *your* palace, it's *your* party. Take the stage!" I had never heard that phrase, but I had a flash of insight and I knew precisely what he meant.

Opening night, without changing a move or a single bit of business, I took the stage. After "Chacun à son Goût," I heard a sudden noise, like rain on the tin roof of the Playhouse. Oh God, I thought, nobody heard my big song. But it wasn't rain at all, it was applause!

After the performance, walking down the hill, the press agent said, "Remember what you asked me last night? Well, *that's* how you get to be a star!"

The next night I was told that Hollywood scouts would be in the audience. This time it *was* raining, and as I arrived at the theater, I slipped on the cobblestones outside the stage door and sprained my ankle. The house doctor told me I could go on, but I must not dance the big waltz in the second act.

I wasn't going to let a sprained ankle interfere with my chance at the movies. It was the time of the lavish movie musicals, and young singers were being shipped out to Hollywood by the carload. I gritted my teeth and performed with total abandon, ankle or no ankle.

I must have done well; a screen test was arranged for me as soon as we returned to New York.

Dwight Wyman decided that *Champagne, Sec* was worth a New York run. On opening night, as I arrived at the Morosco Theatre, I looked up at the marquee. There, with Peggy Wood, George Meader, and Helen Ford, was Kitty Carlisle. I sat on the fireplug in front of the theater, gazed at my name in lights, and wept for joy.

I hoped for good reviews on my singing and acting, and I did indeed get brilliant notices—one whole inch in the Herald Tribune from Percy Hammond—on my legs.

At the Morosco the pianist in the orchestra pit was a slight young Viennese named Frederick Loewe. Every evening he came up to my dressing room on the third floor, stood behind my chair, and watched me make up. We talked of the future and he would say, with great certainty in his Viennese accent, "Someday I am going to wrrrite the best musical on Brroadway." I would think, how many pianists in how many Broadway theaters are saying the same thing this very moment? (Lap dissolve, as they say in the movies: opening night of *My Fair Lady,* some twenty years later, as Moss and I stood in our usual spot against the back wall of the orchestra, Fritz came over to me and said, "I wrrrote the best musical on Brroadway!")

When I got my first *Champagne, Sec* paycheck, Ed decided I should have a checking account, so he took me to the Bank of New York and introduced me to the vice president, Ed Streeter, the author of *Dere Mable* and later *Father of the Bride.* I like the idea of belonging to a bank where the vice president was a literary man. After I'd had my checkbook for a few months, a correspondence started between Streeter and Ed. From Streeter: "Dear Ed: Would you instruct your valued client Kitty Carlisle, who seems to be on the brink of a fine career, in the principles of banking? She is overdrawn." Next letter: "Dear Ed: Your valued client Kitty Carlisle seems unable to grasp or follow the principles of banking, which I'm sure by now you have explained to her. She is overdrawn." (I hope, dear Mr. Streeter, wherever you are, that you know that I *have* learned, and that our fiscal practices at the Arts Council are in perfect accord with good banking principles.)

I stayed with *Champagne, Sec* for four months, and then Ed and Arthur Lyons negotiated a Hollywood contract. I had to get out of *Champagne, Sec.* I went to see Dwight Wyman and asked him to let me go. He was a great gentleman and he said, "You may go, but I advise you not to; you should stay in the theater and learn your business." I tended to agree with him, but Ed felt I had better grab this opportunity while I could.

I never had to make the choice, because *Champagne, Sec* closed before I left for Hollywood. I was spared the feeling of having deserted Dwight Wyman, who had given me such a fine opportunity.

ON the first trip to Hollywood Mother and I were bidden by the studio to get off the train in Pasadena, where we were met by the obligatory reporter and photographer and I made the usual statements: "I'm thrilled to be here; I'm looking forward to being in pictures." The truth was I was scared to death.

Ed laid out the rules of conduct in Hollywood. He thought Hollywood was a den of iniquity, and I would surely go right into the gutter without ironclad safeguards. I was never to go out with anyone without a formal introduction and never without my mother. He was very straitlaced; but indeed, Hollywood was to everyone, including me, a strange and exotic land where the stakes were so high and the pitfalls so deep that I fell in with his plan without any argument.

Leaving nothing to chance or memory, Ed wrote a guidebook for me called "A Mental Baedeker to Stardom for Miss Kitty Carlisle," a thirty-three-page manual illustrated with *New Yorker* cartoons.

I offer a few examples; as the Contents page shows, its range is quite broad.

Grooming—Do not go to the studio in slacks, but take trouble always to arrive there fully dressed as a lady should be in every respect . . . make this part of your professional equipment. It is very important.

Singing Songs in the Movies—In rehearsing a song for the camera, the best way to do it is by standing in front of a long mirror. If you find yourself making faces at yourself, you will be able to stop it. . . . No matter what anyone tells you, never sacrifice making a song comprehensible in order to hit a high note . . . you might make pretty sounds, but no one knows whether you are selling fish or whether you are brokenhearted, because the words are not understandable.

Love—of course you know too much to try to be coy or kittenish or to suddenly throw your arms about a hero and break his ribs. You certainly should be careful about this because there are not many good tenors in the movies.

Eating—In portraying scenes of eating, I hope you will restrain your eagerness and speed and show an indifference to food which will require real acting on your part. I understand that in pictures they have real food to eat, and I suggest that you always have something on your plate you do not particularly care for. . . . I think this is all I dare say on the subject.

Jealousy—Any time you have to register jealousy, try to assume the same look that you have in real life when I take a black olive from your plate. That is perfect.

Conclusion—At all times, remember that in a very short period you have accomplished a great personal success . . . be confident in your own ability and ultimate destiny. . . . So far as I am concerned, I have no doubts whatsoever of what is going to happen, and if this mental guidebook, which turned out to be a potpourri of many things, is of any assistance at all, it will have served its purpose.

When I first read it, I was impressed with the effort Ed had put into it, but I wondered if Ed really knew what he was talking about. He'd never been to Hollywood; what did he know about movie techniques? I regret to say I didn't follow it as I should have. Rereading it now, I wish I'd paid closer attention: I might have been more successful.

Paramount gave me feature billing and I was paid $1,500 a week. Ed fought hard to prevent their signing me up to a seven-year contract. He felt that a picture-by-picture deal would get me better pictures. Most of all, he thought it would be better for my cultural development if I could go back to New York after each film. Los Angeles in 1934 was hardly the Athens of the Western world. He even made me choose a newspaper that would offset the Los Angeles *Examiner,* in which every headline seemed to be a variation of "Black Dahlia Murders" or "Tot Hacked."

Out of intellectual snobbism I chose the Manchester *Guardian.* It came rolled up in a brown paper wrapper, and I kept the issues that I hadn't read unopened in a pile by my bed. When the pile formed a wall that I had to leap over to get out of bed, Mother called Ed, who said it was time to come back to New York.

Each time I went to Hollywood I tried to keep some perspective about its importance in the general scheme of things. As I got on the train, I would start a solemn litany that began: "Hollywood is not heaven and Louis B. Mayer is not God." Everything would be fine until we came to the Rockies, and as the train plunged down the other side of the Continental Divide toward California, the wheels would answer, with continuing crescendo: "Hollywood's heaven, and Louis B. Mayer is God; Hollywood's heaven, and Louis B. Mayer is God!"

Hollywood gave me the feeling of here today and gone tomorrow. There was no sense of belonging anywhere. Everyone was on the wing, either going up or going down. The first thing they told me at Paramount was to be nice to everybody when you're on the way up; they're the same people you're going to see on the way down.

Most people who went out to Hollywood lived at first in places like the Garden of Allah, which had little villas around a swimming pool, and then moved into their own houses. Not us. We set up housekeeping at the Beverly Wilshire, a big hotel just like the ones we'd always lived in. We could have been anywhere in any city. Mother made no concessions to California, and her attitude didn't help my feeling of being an outsider. She didn't participate in anything the climate had to offer—tennis, golf, and swimming were not in her repertoire, and she hated the sun. She liked city life; she missed New York, the theater, the opera, and Fifth Avenue. She was scornful of Hollywood customs, and continued to wear her little black dresses, her little black hats with the nose veils, and the white gloves.

Mother had some introductions from her New York bridge club, and spent her time playing bridge. For me, the big excitement on Saturday nights was to sit behind her chair with my knitting and watch her. I didn't rebel because I was supposed to be concentrating on my career; also, by following Ed's rules I didn't know anyone.

We hired a car and chauffeur for Mother, and I got a bicycle for short distances around Beverly Hills. I would no more ride a bicycle in Beverly Hills today than I would ride one down Fifth Avenue, but there was no traffic then. There were only three streets of any importance: Sunset, Hollywood, and Wilshire boulevards. There was no smog, and at Christmas there were fields of poinsettias blooming on Sunset Boulevard.

It was vital that I continue my singing lessons. We found a teacher, Morris Halpern, and I had a lesson every day.

If anything was going to undermine what little confidence I had as a movie actress, the first call for publicity photographs did it. While I was still in New York, Ed had tried to train me for the camera. He had set up a spotlight in his living room and taken pictures of me smiling, looking sad, quizzical, singing, right profile, left profile, full face. But the distance between Ed's living room and the stills studio at Paramount was enormous. After the first session, they told me to come in the next day and see how Carole Lombard did it. Did what? I asked. Lighted up when the shutter clicked, communicated her emotions. "Thank you," I said, hoping to learn the trick in one easy lesson.

The next day I came to watch Carole Lombard light up when the shutter clicked and communicate her emotions. I could see that she did it—but how? I said to the photographers, "That was very interesting. When can I learn some more?" "Come back tomorrow," they said, "and watch Marlene Dietrich." I came back, saw more magic performed, and left still baffled.

Makeup and hairdressing finished me off. Makeup said I had a dish-face—no cheekbones, no modeling. Hairdressing said my hair was too dark, no highlights. When I timidly inquired about Hedy Lamarr's very black hair, I was told condescendingly, "Hers is different; it's like a horse's tail." Why that was good I had no idea.

The real movie star in those days loved the way she looked and never tired of her own image. I would go into the makeup department at 6 A.M. and there would be four of the screen's matchless beauties, gazing at themselves in the mirror with absolute rapture, every eyelash, every pore, giving them unrivaled pleasure. I would look at myself and think, "Good Lord, who is *that*?" They shaved my hairline, they altered my mouth line, my eyebrows disappeared, and I accepted it all. I dieted to achieve the narrow body that movie stars had, which I could never have because as a singer my rib cage was already expanding.

Hollywood was a hardworking town, and there were no unions then. There were times when I didn't leave the set until 3 A.M. I would go home, drop into bed, and I'd have to start learning lines for the next day before I could go to sleep.

But I had a bit of luck in Hollywood: I made four movies and had a hit song in each. My first film was *Murder at the Vanities,* with Carl Brisson and Duke Ellington, and the song was "Cocktails for Two." It was directed by Mitchell Leisen, whose specialty was big musicals and big musical numbers. Cameras high on booms zoomed down on giant powder boxes which slowly opened and revealed beautiful girls lying in graceful positions, tastefully undraped.

I had a South Sea Island number with more beautiful girls lying on their backs, waving hundreds of aquamarine feathered fans. I was to rise out of the fans like a water nymph. When I tried on the costume I was too embarrassed to come out of the fitting room. It was just a body stocking, three strategically placed velvet fig leaves, and a hula skirt made of a few strands of green silk. I called my mother: "They've got me dressed up in practically nothing!" I cried into the telephone. "I'll be right over," she said.

She looked at the costume and said: "We'll talk to Manny Cohen." Manny Cohen was the head of Paramount, and he was so short that it was said when he got really mad he walked up and down under his desk. After a good deal of palaver it was agreed that I would wear the fig leaves in the movie, but there would be no still photographs for publicity purposes. We should have known they wouldn't keep the bargain.

Murder at the Vanities is a good movie, but it's never shown on television because one of the songs was called "Marijuana." It was sung with a backdrop of huge cactus plants, the blossoms of which were girls. Although marijuana was legal until the repeal of Prohibition, I had never heard of it. I knew that jazz musicians smoked "tea," but if I'd been asked I would have said marijuana was some kind of Mexican musical instrument.

The next picture was *She Loves Me Not,* with Bing Crosby and Miriam Hopkins. Miriam Hopkins had the reputation of being a termagant. To me she was the most generous of colleagues, offering to rehearse before each scene, run lines, and in every way help a beginner.

Bing Crosby's star was rising, and it was quite a coup to be singing with him. But any flirtatious notions I might have had were quickly dispelled when it turned out that he was considerably shorter than I was. Bing had to stand on a box in all our love scenes. It was death to romance.

Bing and I didn't have much in common. He was a natural movie actor, whereas I, who came from the stage, had to struggle for film technique. The only remotely personal conversation that I remember was when he showed me a modest diamond necklace he'd bought for his wife, Dixie Lee, and asked me if I thought she would like it.

His singing constantly astonished and delighted me. Into the recording studio he would come, chewing gum, eating chocolate and drinking milk, all things considered taboo before performing. Then out of his throat would come that heavenly golden sound. One day I asked him which would be the hit song in our movie. "If I could predict that," he said, "I'd be a millionaire music publisher, and I wouldn't be putting on this toupée. I'd be out on the golf course every day and never go to work again."

There was a hit song, "Love in Bloom," and Bing and I sang it together. It was the last song I ever sang that wasn't pretaped. We filmed it directly on the set with the orchestra, at nine in the morning, and I was so nervous that every time I watch the movie I can see the muscle twitching in my cheek. I thought eventually it might be my theme song; but soon after it was published Jack Benny picked it up, and when I sang it people laughed, because all they could remember was Jack Benny scratching it out on his violin.

I was coming up in the world and I wasn't enjoying it. What a waste. I went to see the rushes of every day's shooting, and every day I was disappointed by my looks and my performance. I had no perspective on what I was looking at, and I was bogged down with detail: the shape of my mouth, the shading on my cheeks, and the endless conversations about my hair with Mother, because of course she came to see the rushes with me. Everybody seemed preoccupied with the way I looked; even Jeanette MacDonald, whom I never met, sent me notes via the makeup department about the shape of my mouth—she said they were giving me too much of a bow.

At least and at last my social life was improving. Mother had discovered some stable, established Hollywood families, and I was finally allowed to go out on my own to dinner—I was now in my twenties. I dined with the Lewis Milestones. (He won an Oscar for his direction of *All Quiet on the Western Front.*) On one occasion they invited me and Charlie Chaplin to dinner, just us. Chaplin was fascinating, jumping up from the table to illustrate his stories with the deftness and precision of a genius pantomimist, which he was. When he got around to the business of politics, I found myself nodding in agreement like a wound-up toy. But reviewing the evening at home, I realized that I had been spellbound by his delivery and not by his radical theories.

I also dined with the de Milles, both Cecil B. and Mrs. William. Mrs. William de Mille was the daughter of Henry George, the single-taxer, and the mother of Agnes and Margaret, who became my friends. I joined Agnes's ballet class because Mother made me. Years later Agnes said that we had both suffered. She hated teaching but needed the money, and I hated being the only one with three left feet in a roomful of dancers.

After *She Loves Me Not,* we returned to New York by airplane. Our trip took sixteen hours. There was no food aboard, and we stopped for refueling and box lunches. About 7 A.M. the captain came into the cabin and said, "Who wants to stop for breakfast and who wants to go on to New York?" "On to New York!" everyone yelled. We wanted to get to New York as soon as possible because the cabin wasn't pressurized and we all had dreadful earaches.

NEW York was freedom. Mother had Ed, and I had friends. From the two movies I'd made I already had some small claim to fame, so there were guest appearances on radio shows. One day a real plum fell in my lap: I was booked on the Rudy Vallee show to sing "The Man I Love." It was an all-Gershwin hour, and Gershwin himself was to play his Concerto in F, with Rudy conducting.

I'd never met Gershwin, and I had no idea if my interpretation would please him. Composers can get very angry if they don't like one's interpretation.

I arrived for the rehearsal with a dry mouth and a pounding heart, symptoms of stage fright which have plagued me all my life.

I was introduced to Gershwin. "Would you like to run over the number?" he asked. "Yes, please," I said rather shakily. He sat down at the piano and we began. I was in a whirl of mixed emotions: fright, elation and, above all, a sense of standing to one side and saying, "Look at me! Am I not doing well!" I've never gotten over that, and it's been the extra pinch of salt that has added savor to many glorious occasions.

George didn't stop me once. When I'd finished, I asked, "Is it all right?" He flashed his brilliant smile and said, "Fine." My heart turned over; he was very attractive. I was also grateful, because radio was always a bugaboo. That ugly hanging mike was like a demon making horrid faces at me; and to change my interpretation of a song just before a broadcast would have completely unnerved me.

Rudy Vallee couldn't read music very well, and when it came to the concerto, I saw that every change of tempo was on a different colored paper—blue for 2/4, pink for 4/4, green for 3/8, and so on. The score unfolded like a multicolored fan. I cannot imagine why this made it easier for him; he must have had to memorize each color to correspond to the correct tempo!

After the broadcast, George asked me to go to a large party Elsa Maxwell was giving at the Savoy-Plaza. I had read about Elsa's parties and could practically recite the guest lists. When we walked in it was as advertised. They were all there: Gertrude Lawrence, Noël Coward, Beatrice Lillie. I also knew that people entertained at Elsa's parties, but when George said, "Let's do 'The Man I Love,' " I discovered something that has never changed over the years. When I sing at parties where I either know the people or admire them greatly, I never do my best.

My performance didn't seem to discourage George, for he kept asking me out. He was a very good dancer, and we went quite often to El Morocco.

George was at the center of everything that was happening—and he was the one that made it happen. He was enormously interested in jazz, and Harlem was the mecca. We'd go to nightclubs like Small's Paradise and the Cotton Club, where George was received as an honored guest. Sometimes we went in full evening dress. I remember one night when Gertrude Lawrence wore an ermine coat, and Bea Lillie had on a black beaded dress with ropes of large fake pearls. It was just like the song "The Lady Is a Tramp": we went "to Harlem in ermine and pearls."

One evening he took me to a prizefight, and he fought the whole bout in an ecstasy of transference. Every time one fighter landed a punch on the other, George landed one on my ribs with his elbow. I came out black and blue. I've never been to another prizefight.

George was a perennial student, and he was always trying to improve his craft. He studied harmony and composition with

Joseph Schillinger in New York, and he would strew the floor in Mother's apartment with bits of paper, explaining to me what he'd learned that day. Even though I didn't understand the complicated twelve-tone scale, I knew that he was reviewing for himself what he'd been over with Schillinger.

George talked about himself all the time. I don't remember his ever saying a word about me. His egocentricity didn't bother me at all. I had been brought up by egocentrics, and I was by nature and by choice a listener. It was just as well, for George was not the only talker in his coterie of friends. His crony Oscar Levant—pianist, wit, TV personality, sometime movie actor— was wonderfully funny and almost frighteningly articulate.

Oscar and I palled around, and once at a rehearsal for a Gershwin concert I asked him if George had spent a lot of time practicing hard for the performance. Oscar grinned at me: "George doesn't *have* to practice; he plays all the time." His playing at other people's parties was legendary. Cole Porter even wrote a couplet about it in *Jubilee:*

> 'Twill be new in ev'ry way:
> Gershwin's promised not to play!

George would say, "Come on up to the apartment while I do some work on *Porgy and Bess.*" I was tremendously pleased when he asked me to sing the soprano line of "Summertime" while he worked on the orchestration, but I soon realized he used that ploy the way other men said "Come up and see my etchings."

George was a marvelous companion, but he wasn't a serious beau. He never made me feel as though I were a very important part of his life, so after a few months, when I had to return to Hollywood for my next picture, I left him in New York without too much of a pang. His letters to me were flip, affectionate, and a little sophomoric except when he wrote about his work. They were hardly of a tone to inspire serious feelings:

Hello K.C.

. . . Are you off for the coast from Detroit? Let know, please. Let know please, plans. (It's the Gertrude Stien [sic] in me) Please let know plans, please. . . .

. . . I've been doing some work on the orchestration of my big opus. It's a big task, scoring 3 hours of anybody's music. Millions of notes. Some of my pages look like a home for gnats. It will take me at least 6 months to finish the scoring.

I hope this letter finds you and your nice mother in the pink—or as pink as you can be in February.

Take good care of yourself and think often of—and write often to—

yours,
George.

I had made a hit in *She Loves Me Not* and the studio rewarded me with a starring role again opposite Bing Crosby. As one of the newspapers of the day put it: ". . . Heretofore, Crosby has carefully avoided working with the same actress twice, but his . . . vocalizing with Kitty Carlisle in *She Loves Me Not* brought so much commendation that he sought to work with her again in . . . *Here Is My Heart.*"

Here Is My Heart was supposed to be a coup for Crosby and me. It was a remake of *The Grand Duchess and the Waiter,* which had originally starred Florence Vidor and Adolphe Menjou. It was my second role as Russian nobility—first a prince in *Champagne, Sec,* and now a Grand Duchess. The hit song was "June in January," a song I loved then, and I still sing it.

I had pinned my hopes on *Here Is My Heart* to establish me as a permanent star. It not only didn't turn the trick, it turned Paramount off, even though I coached the part with Akim Tamiroff and practiced singing as diligently as I could. With *Here Is My Heart* I thought I was on my way, and I was—on my way out.

There had been many shake-ups at the top level, and the people who had brought me out to Hollywood and who believed in me were no longer in charge. Paramount didn't seem to have any more movies for me.

Oscar Levant came to my rescue. He spent quite a lot of time in California, and we had become good friends through our mutual affection for George. Oscar thought I'd be right for the part of the opera singer in *A Night at the Opera* with the Marx Brothers, and he literally opened the door by taking me to dinner at the beach house of M-G-M producer Irving Thalberg.

Arthur Lyons negotiated a deal for Paramount to loan me out to Metro. It was exciting to be given the chance to sing opera straight, although many people remember Allan Jones and me singing "Alone" more than they remember our scenes from *Il Trovatore* and *I Pagliacci*.

Through the options in my contract I was now getting $3,500 a week. I was finally allowed to buy myself a little car and learn to drive. There was one proviso: at my first accident, goodbye car. It was a secondhand two-seat Pierce-Arrow, and I loved it passionately. I wasn't allowed a convertible, which I longed for; Mother and Ed insisted on a hard top for my safety. They were right: first crack out of the box I banged into the gates at M-G-M; I unhinged them and they collapsed together on top of me. I wasn't hurt, neither was the car, and Mother never found out.

The next time I had a mishap was after we finished filming *A Night at the Opera*. I was driving along Wilshire Boulevard and I must have been woolgathering—I ran smack into the car ahead of me. I hardly dented its fender, but the driver got out and we exchanged the usual formalities. Of all the cars to hit in Los Angeles, I had to pick Groucho Marx's! That night there was a preview of *A Night at the Opera*. I was hoping to keep Mother away from Groucho, and to my great relief we didn't run into him. After the film was over, we got into our car and were just pulling away from the curb when Groucho suddenly appeared, stuck his head in the window, and demanded, "What do you mean by hitting my car?" Our car drove off before I could answer. Mother looked at me suspiciously. "What did he mean by that?"

"Oh, he says that to all the girls," I said hastily; "that's his latest routine!" "Really?" Mother said. "I don't think it's up to his usual standard!"

I had no idea that *A Night at the Opera* was going to become a classic. It's been my passport to my children's friends. When they meet me they look at me as if I were a national monument. They behave as if they are shaking hands with the Brooklyn Bridge.

A Night at the Opera has endured because the Marx brothers were smart enough to get good writers like George S. Kaufman and Morrie Ryskind. They ensured its success by trying it out like a show, in theaters up and down the West Coast, so that by the time they came to the actual filming there was no question of *cinéma vérité,* or making it up as they went along. Everything was rehearsed and timed and, contrary to popular assumption that she didn't know what was going on, that great character actress Margaret Dumont knew exactly what she was doing, and what those rascals the Marx Brothers were doing to her.

Allan Jones and I prerecorded the songs and the opera sequences. Everybody seemed very pleased with the results. My first day of shooting was in a replica of the Metropolitan Opera House, with an audience of full-dress extras. The opera was *Pagliacci,* and I was on stage in costume, ready to sing the *Ballatella* to my own playback. High on the boom sat the director, Sam Wood, and at "Take One," I started mouthing the first phrase: *"Stridono lassù."* Something in the sound of the playback bothered me, and after a few notes I stopped. Sam Wood yelled down to me, "What's the matter?" "I don't know," I replied. "All right, Take Two," Sam said. Again I started, *"Stridono lassù,"* and again I stopped. Sam, somewhat irritated, said, "Now what?" "Mr. Wood, that playback doesn't sound like my voice!" Sam brought the boom and camera down to my level and said soothingly, "Don't worry, dear, just do it and I'll explain later."

I wasn't absolutely positive, but I had a feeling that I was being tricked into mouthing to someone else's recording. I had never heard of such a thing, and I was so bewildered that I walked off the set and called my agent, Arthur Lyons. He told me to sit tight while he went to see Thalberg.

When he came back, he said Thalberg hadn't trusted Allan and me to sing the arias, so he had sent to New York and recorded two Metropolitan Opera singers. He intended to film the operatic sequences two ways: first with Allan and me mouthing to *their* playback, and then to our own, and he would then decide which version he wanted. "But I only took this part so I could sing opera," I wept. "I know," Arthur said. "This is what you must do. Sit in your dressing room in costume and makeup, and wait." "Wait for what?" I asked. "Wait for me," he answered.

For three days I waited. The movie waited too, and it cost M-G-M a lot of money. On the fourth day Arthur came to my dressing room. "Thalberg wants to see you," he said. Thalberg received me sitting behind his desk and tried to talk me into his deceitful plan. I cried all over his office; I cried in his wastebasket; I cried on his desk, and I cried all over the top of his head. In the end he gave in. He used the recordings Allan and I had made, and when I see the movie now, I have the satisfaction of knowing that the high C in the *Miserere* is mine! Arthur Lyons, who became a friend of the family after his unselfish championing of my cause with Thalberg, was barred from M-G-M for a year for his pains.

Working with the Marx Brothers was unlike anything I had been led to expect. They never played tricks on me, they were unfailingly courteous, and Groucho paid me the compliment of asking my opinion about the jokes. He was the worrier of the three. He would read me a line deadpan and ask, "Is that funny?" When I'd shake my head he'd go away, only to come back with another deadpan reading. He did it over and over, till he finally came up with a good one and I burst out laughing.

Harpo, who was always mute in their act, was the most articulate offstage, and he was the beloved of the New York literary crowd; he had his own place at the legendary Algonquin Round

Table with George Kaufman, Dorothy Parker, Alexander Wooll-cott. Harpo was always hungry on the set. From 11:30 on, he'd lie on the nearest piece of furniture and yell "Lunchee!" every five minutes until lunch was called.

Chico had to be pried out of his dressing room. He would stay there—with a lady, or a card game—until the cameras were rolling. But once on the set he was brilliant, as when he and Groucho discuss the clauses in the contract scene, ending with, "You can't fool me, there ain't no Sanity Claus!"

Allan Jones was also busy with ladies, in and out of his dress-ing room.

George Kaufman not only wrote the dialogue, he directed it. I was very much interested in him, because I was always interested in the playwright and the director. He paid no attention to me whatsoever, except for being scrupulously polite. One day the call was 12 noon for a short retake, just Harpo and me. I figured it would take half an hour to reshoot the scene; then it would be 12:30, and George might ask me to lunch.

I arrived on the set and saw not one but two directors' chairs behind the camera, one for George and one for the prettiest woman I'd ever seen. When the scene was over, it was 12:30. George didn't introduce the lady and he didn't ask me to lunch. He just said goodbye to Harpo and me, turned, and escorted the beauty down the corridor, presumably to take *her* to lunch. It was not until I picked up the paper a few months later that I discov-ered that George's companion was the movie star Mary Astor of diary fame.

A Night at the Opera's significance in my career, even though it's still being shown all over the world, was as nothing compared to its bearing on my personal life. It was on the set of *A Night at the Opera* that I met Moss Hart for the first time.

George Kaufman came to me and said there were two friends of his from New York who wanted to meet me. They were look-ing for a leading lady for their new musical, *Jubilee*. Their names were Moss Hart and Cole Porter.

I became so excited at the prospect of meeting two of my heroes that I began running toward them. A movie set is one big booby trap, with electrical boxes, plugs, and coils of wire all over the floor. I tripped over one of them and fell flat at Moss's feet. Every time I saw him after that I kept falling down. (The most spectacular fall was down a whole flight of stairs at "21." When he married me, he said he finally set me firmly on my feet.)

After I had picked myself up and said how-do-you-do, Moss and Cole asked me to come up to their hotel suite to listen to the book and score of *Jubilee.* I was dying to get to know Moss Hart. I had heard so much about him; he was the kind of man people often quoted, and anecdotes about him were in constant circulation. He had already written *Once in a Lifetime* and *Merrily We Roll Along* with George S. Kaufman, *Face the Music,* and the best revue ever produced, *As Thousands Cheer,* with Irving Berlin. (*You Can't Take It with You, The Man Who Came to Dinner, Lady in the Dark,* and *Light Up the Sky* were yet to come.) He was one of the theater's most eligible bachelors, and when I met him that day I thought he was the best-looking, most arresting man I'd ever seen.

That evening I went to the hotel to hear Moss read the book and Cole play "Just One of Those Things," "Begin the Beguine," and "Why Shouldn't I?" Then I sang "Why Shouldn't I?" for them. They made polite noises about my singing, but that was all. They didn't offer me the part, and I lost more than a Broadway show. If they had engaged me, I might have had ten more years with Moss.

No offers came after *A Night at the Opera.* Paramount had no plans for me. In Hollywood the ups are fast, but the downs are faster, and I became more and more depressed. Failure doesn't always bring people together. Angry, disappointed, trapped in a hotel suite, Mother and I were having painful daily rows. We were boiling up in a cauldron of resentment.

Mother and Ed both wanted me to go back to musical comedy in New York, and they talked about it a lot on the long-distance telephone. Arthur Lyons wanted me to stay in Hollywood. "You won't get back into pictures by going to New York," he said (and it turned out he was right). Halpern, my singing teacher, wanted me to stay, forget about the movies, and study opera. Mother disagreed with both Arthur and Halpern. She said that whatever I had become was due to her and Ed, and I must listen to no one else.

It had become "them" and me, and far from being grateful for all they had done for me, I resented them, and Halpern too, for tearing at my loyalties in this tug-of-war.

THERE was a brief interlude. One evening Margaret de Mille invited me to a dance recital at the Hollywood Bowl. In the box was Bob Jackson, Secretary of the Democratic National Committee, who was in California to plan Roosevelt's 1936 campaign. Another guest was the young third secretary at the Brazilian Embassy in Washington. Brazilians seemed to find the way to my heart: first Maneco de Teffé, and now a real ladykiller, Decio de Moura. Decio was touring California with his boss, Ambassador Oswaldo Aranha. He had been with the embassy in London, and his English was perfect, as were his clothes and his manners. He had black patent-leather hair, wore a monocle, and now that I think of it, except for the monocle he was the same type as Rudolph Valentino, the only movie star I ever had a crush on. We went to a nightclub after the concert. I had danced with many good dancers, but no one could hold a candle to Decio. We fitted together like two halves of the same body.

He called the next day and asked if we could have dinner that night at the Ambassador Hotel. Mother said we could have dinner, but at the Beverly Wilshire Hotel, where *we* lived, not at the Ambassador, where *he* lived.

Decio was presented to Mother. He charmed women of all ages, and she was no exception. Then he and I went downstairs to the hotel dining room, and I flirted as much as I dared. He was a little older than I and a lot more experienced and not one bit impressed by the budding young movie star. He called me Little Monkey, and he teased me gently. No one had ever teased me before, and I had never been so attracted to anyone in my life.

At the end of dinner he asked me if I would go back to his hotel with him. I knew perfectly well what his intentions were, but I couldn't quite bring myself to say No. So I waffled. "Oh, I couldn't do that. My mother said we have to stay in the Beverly Wilshire." Without a word he put his hand on the table, opened his fingers, and there in his palm lay a Beverly Wilshire room key. "I have reserved a suite here," he said. "Will you come to see it?" It was irresistible.

Alas, Decio and Ambassador Aranha were going back to Washington within a day or two. I was in a terrible dilemma. Should I stay and keep trying for a movie career? Or should I go back East, where Decio would be the extra added attraction? The day before Decio left I was standing in our kitchen when Mother came in, brandishing my diary. She had found it, read it, and had zoomed in on the page where in a fit of childish passion I had said I hated her. She was already in the full fortissimo of one of her extra-special rages.

I stood silent, letting the storm break over me. When there was no defense from me, Mother's anger blew her right out of the kitchen.

I never should have underestimated Mother's ability to master any situation. She came back into the kitchen, and there were no histrionics from her. "I think you should get away by yourself for a while. Why don't you go to Arrowhead Lake for the weekend."

She must have realized at that point we were much better off away from each other.

So the day Decio left for Washington, I went to Arrowhead. He bombarded me with telegrams from every stop along the way.

Scene One: Young man lost, not knowing what to do. Love, Dee.

Scene Second. Young man wandering around lonely and miserable, discovering does care more and more. Dee.

Scene 3. Worse and worse, please do something about it. *Je ne rêve que d'elle, d'elle, d'elle; m'obsède, J'en suis fou.* [I dream only of her, of her, of her; I'm obsessed, I'm mad about her.] Love, Dee.

Although much better after call young man feeling very bad never thought so dangerous playing around with monkeys will try convince young lady come to Washington better do or I will keep on asking just discover am mad about love—Dee.

When I returned to Hollywood there was a letter from George Gershwin:

Dear Kitty-the-Great—
. . . I thought I was the forgotten composer. What strange effect has Hollywood upon New Orleans favorite chile that she gets writer's cramp as soon as she sets foot in movieland? Is it that you just can't stand the sound of pen scratching paper? Anyway I forgive you because I'm not such a hot letter writer myself. . . .
Bob Sherwood was in to lunch the other day and told me you are simply grand in the new Marx picture which he saw in a preview. I can't wait to see it. . . .
A little later I may come out to do a picture and I'll take the house next to yours . . . then we can play games, throw stones, break each other's windows and have lots of fun.

Next to Decio's telegrams, George's prose was hardly calculated to inspire passion; nevertheless, under the signature was scribbled a tiny line of music, the first nine notes of "Bess, You Is My Woman."

The final decision to stay or go was taken out of my hands when Paramount decided they didn't want me anymore and paid me off. As Fred Allen once said, "California is wonderful if you're an orange," and I was getting less sunkist by the minute.

The first part of our trip home was horrible. I felt that my Hollywood career could be summed up in two words: I was a Meteoric Bust. I stayed in my upper berth and cried all the way to the continental divide. Then the wheels of the train began to sing "I'll take Manhattan, the Bronx and Staten Island too!" and I began to perk up.

I bought an apartment at the Ritz Tower for Mother and me, and gave her the money I had saved from the movies. (When she died, the money was intact—she had kept it all for me.)

Decio was wildly romantic and I loved being with him, but he could only come to New York once in a while whereas George lived there, and he took me out a lot.

I knew I was far from the only girl in George's life. He had a little waltz that he would compose on the spot for whatever young lady took his fancy at a party. He would lead her to the piano bench and then and there he'd be inspired to write this very waltz just for her. The lyric had a blank space in it to fill in the name of the lady. I used to think of it as his mating call. It seems odd that I, who have a tendency to hang on to everything —letters, photos, old clothes—could never find that piece of sheet music. I remember the cover—it had large triangles of black and green in a geometric pattern. Maybe George whisked it away, and it reposes on some other girl's piano.

I didn't see George all the time. When Decio came to town we'd go dancing. We even won a waltz contest at the Rainbow Room, and I told him if he didn't make ambassador and if I lost my voice, we could always earn a living as a ballroom dance team.

During the Jewish holidays George asked me to a seder at his house. I had never been to a seder, and I was pleased and curious.

There were about eight of us, but the only ones I remember were Robert Sherwood and Oscar Levant and, of course, George. Neither Sherwood nor I knew what to do or what to expect. We needn't have worried; the whole ceremony, both prayers and songs, was done by Oscar, with George chiming in, in a kind of mad jazz rhythm.

Porgy and Bess had just opened, and George took me to see it. I felt proud to be sitting in the box with the composer. I never thought of myself as a prophet, but I disagreed violently with Lawrence Gilman's poor review. I thought it broke new ground between musical comedy and opera, and I was delighted when it became a towering landmark in American music.

Mother and George got along very well. He sent her beautiful flowers and made quite an effort to ingratiate himself. She was very fond of him, and I'm sure she hoped for him as a son-in-law. What mother wouldn't! He was rich, famous, and a marvelous catch.

George did ask me to marry him. It was a great compliment and I was tempted. But when he went to Hollywood, leaving me, as he said, to think it over, I told Mother I didn't want to marry him. I loved his talent, but I didn't really love him. I've always admired her for her answer. She didn't hesitate for a minute. She simply said, "Then forget it!" And no questions asked.

I agonized over my answer to George's proposal, not because of indecision on my part, but because I didn't want to hurt his feelings. I finally sent him a telegram saying I wasn't ready to marry; I was too involved in my own career, and if I married him I would have to give it up because he needed and deserved a full-time wife. I said I hoped we would remain friends forever.

He consoled himself rather too quickly with the Hollywood ladies after I said no. I felt he had asked me because he thought it was time for him to get married and I would make a suitable wife. I fit in with his social friends, I was musical, and I respected his talent.

It was six months after George went to Hollywood that the brain tumor which finally killed him began to cause terrible symptoms. One Sunday morning I received a phone call from California. His friend Emil Mosbacher said George was in the hospital and asked me if I could get in touch with a famous brain surgeon, Dr. Dandy, who was somewhere in Maryland. After many telephone calls I learned that Dr. Dandy was fishing in Chesapeake Bay and couldn't be reached. That evening I was scheduled to do a broadcast with Ed Wynn on his Fire Chief variety show. I went to the studio only mildly worried.

I was sitting in my dressing room when Harry von Zell, the announcer, came down the hall and stopped at each door, murmuring something I couldn't hear. I heard only shocked voices saying, "Oh, my God!" "Oh, no!" He came to Helen Hayes, whose dressing room was next to mine. And then I heard what he was saying: "George Gershwin is dead."

I don't know what is so sacrosanct about "the show must go on," but I had been schooled in that tradition, and on I went.

In New York nobody seemed to care that my Hollywood career was over. I was hired to sing on quite a few variety radio shows including Ben Bernie's and Jack Benny's, and eventually I landed the lead in the biggest musical of the 1936–37 season, the role of the innkeeper in *White Horse Inn,* with music by Ralph Benatzky, which had played all over the world. I had seen it in London when I was at RADA, never dreaming I would ever star in it. In New York it played the Center Theater in Rockefeller Center, a 3,200-seat house that had been rebuilt to accommodate an entire Tyrolean village, with yodelers, donkey carts, goats, geese, and villagers strolling along ramps built along the side walls of the theater. People talked more about the scenery than the actors. Six rows of seats had been removed so that the Emperor of Austria could arrive by boat, and the pièce de résistance was a rainstorm at the end of the first act that required 1200 gallons of water for every show. The theater is gone now (an awful lot of theaters that I played in are gone), and its dressing rooms have become offices. It's a pity; they were beautiful dressing rooms.

After we'd been playing for a few weeks I went to the author, Dr. Hans Müller, and said, "That line in the first act never gets a laugh. May I cut it?" He looked at me and said, *"White Horse Inn* has played 2,000 performances in Tokyo, 1,500 in Berlin and 2,000 in London," and I was sure he was going to tell me the line always got a laugh. Instead he said plaintively, "That line *never* got a laugh, but someday, maybe?" I didn't have the heart to cut it, and like Dr. Müller, throughout the run I kept thinking, "Maybe?"

White Horse Inn didn't play on Sundays, so I could go to Washington to see Decio and stay till Monday afternoon. Bob Jackson, who had been at the Hollywood Bowl where I'd met Decio, had introduced me to his daughter, Sarah, Mrs. Forbes Morgan. She lived in Washington and she was my excuse whenever I went to visit Decio. I thought I was fooling my mother pretty well until one day she called out to me, as I was at the door with my suitcase, "When Decio isn't around, phone me—I just want to know you arrived safely."

It was through Sarah that Washington political life opened to me. Her dinner parties were filled with politicians and senior diplomats. I found I *loved* politics! I went to lunch at the Senate, where many of our legislators were so isolationist that they thought Sofia was only a girl's name. And one day Sarah's father told me he had arranged for me to sing "The Star-Spangled Banner" at the National Democratic Convention in Philadelphia. This was a great honor, and forever after I felt that in 1936 I had elected FDR single-handed.

The first time I ever went to the White House was with Sarah. We were invited by Mrs. Roosevelt for a ladies' luncheon, and I was startled to see the guests pick up their plates without any attempt at subterfuge and turn them over to see where they came from. People didn't steal the silverware quite as unashamedly as they looked at the undersides of the china, but Mrs. Roosevelt told us they put a lot of spoons in their pockets. (Things haven't changed. Nancy Reagan told me they still lose an awful lot of spoons.)

The one I really wanted to meet was President Roosevelt. I got my wish at the annual dinner he gave for the Cabinet at the Mayflower Hotel. I was part of a group of performers invited to dine with them and then entertain in the ballroom, which was set up like a nightclub. I sang my best audition song, "Giannina Mia," and a waltz medley from *The Chocolate Soldier,* always good for a big finish. There was a magician who treated us to feats of legerdemain. For his grand finale he went around the tables and removed suspenders, belts, and wallets from the Cabinet and even purloined the President's watch. I doubt that any such close contact would be allowed today.

After the show the performers were all invited back to the White House for sandwiches and drinks. The President made the cocktails, and Mrs. Roosevelt bustled about serving us. Mrs. James Roosevelt, the President's mother, dressed all in black, sat in an armchair off to one side and dominated the proceedings without saying a word. The President drew his wheelchair up to the fireplace, and we sat around, some on the fender, some on the floor, and he regaled us with stories. The best one was about Calvin Coolidge's secret fondness for practical jokes. Roosevelt had been told the story by the Secret Service. They said that every afternoon while Coolidge was having his nap, all the alarms went off in the White House and no one could figure out why, until one day a Secret Service man stationed himself behind a screen in the hall outside the President's bedroom. To his astonishment he saw Coolidge quietly open the door, peek around to see if he was observed, go to the alarm, pull it, and tiptoe back to his room! Under the heading of unasked questions (Moss said I always wanted to know what happened to the characters in a play after the curtain went down): Did they ever tell Coolidge they were on to him, or did they let him go on playing his little game?

Forbes Morgan, Sarah's husband, died suddenly, and Sarah asked me to come to Washington for the funeral. Forbes had been the Secretary of the Democratic Party after Sarah's father, and he was also a cousin of Mrs. Roosevelt, so the President was coming to the funeral, as well as the Supreme Court and the diplomatic corps.

It was a very hot day. While the family and I waited in the sacristy for the Roosevelts to arrive, I wandered out onto a little back porch to get some air. I had to find a place to rest my poor feet. There was no chair on the porch, so I sat down on the steps and dangled my feet over the edge. Because my mother, who wore a size four shoe, said that big feet were "common," I always tried to stuff my feet into shoes a full size too small, and I had sore feet all my early life. Pretty soon next to me was dangling another pair of feet, in high laced shoes. I followed the feet up and up and up, and there sat a very tall gentleman with a shock of white hair who looked like an Old Testament prophet. "Hello," I said, and added, "my feet hurt." "Mine too," he said, and that was our bond and the start of my friendship with Bernard Baruch. He wasn't Old Testament, but he was something of a prophet, also an elder statesman, friend and adviser to presidents, and financial wizard. And he seemed very old indeed.

Baruch took Sarah and me back to New York in his private railroad car—the first one I'd ever been in. After that he often asked me to lunch at his Fifth Avenue house. In those days Fifth Avenue was still quite grand, and I loved going there. Through Baruch I learned the difference between money and big money. His house had a ballroom; his food was different—his lima beans were so small and tender they were practically unborn. His private secretary had an ermine coat and a diamond necklace, and his valet died leaving a million dollars.

Bernie's feet always hurt, and once in a while after lunch he'd ask me to help him soak them. We would go up to a fifth-floor bathroom—I never knew why—which had a big old-fashioned tub with claw feet; Bernie sat on a high wooden stool with his feet in the water, and I poured in Epsom salts from a five-pound box.

Mother wasn't too happy about this friendship. She said, "If you think you're going to marry that old fellow and he's going to die and leave you all his money, you've got another think coming." She needn't have worried. I didn't want to marry him, nor did he want to marry me, and he lived another thirty years.

But I did ask once for some financial advice: "I've saved a little money, and I wondered if you could tell me something that I could invest in." He looked at me severely. "I've already given you the best advice in the world," he said. "What was it?" I cried. "Work hard," he told me solemnly.

Bernie invited me to go to Scotland to shoot grouse. It was the summer of 1938; he must have known it would be the last time before the coming war. *White Horse Inn* had just closed after eight months. Decio had been recalled to the Foreign Office in Rio for a couple of months, and I wanted a holiday. I was twenty-six years old and Mother thought it would be all right if I went to Europe alone, so I took the *Queen Mary*, quite exhilarated by my daring. Once I got to England my mother obviously lost track of me for a while, because I got a telegram: "WHERE ARE YOU?" I cabled back: "SHOOTING BARUCH IN SCOTLAND."

Bernie had rented a vast hunting lodge. Everything was done by Fortnum & Mason, down to chewing gum (!) on the night table; and we were piped in to dinner with bagpipes every night. I had asked what I should bring in the way of clothes, and Baruch had said, "Well, get some divided skirts; we ride ponies out to the moors for lunch." Ponies were all right, I thought, but when

I got there, the Scottish ponies had behinds like Percherons. Some ponies.

There were elaborate lunches on the moors every day, with wine in silver coolers. I didn't shoot, but I'd sit in the butts and keep my head down, which is all you're supposed to do when you're sitting in a butt if you're not shooting.

Bernie was writing his autobiography, and one evening he asked me to come to his room after dinner so he could read some of it to me. When I arrived he was in bed; he said he had a cold. He started reading aloud and it was quite boring. All of a sudden he leaped out of bed in his long winter underwear and made a grab for me. He chased me around the room, and all I could think of was, I must get this old gent back under the covers —he'll catch pneumonia! He finally did go back to bed, and that was the only advance he ever made in my direction.

One evening as we were being piped into dinner Bernie was called to the telephone. He asked me to come with him; because of his deafness he was afraid he might have trouble hearing. When he finished the call, his face was so troubled that I hesitated to speak. He walked silently to the great windows of the drawing room and stood for a long time staring out at the moors. Then he turned to me. "That was Lord Ismay, Churchill's military adviser," he said. "The British have no defenses, nothing but wooden staves to fight with. I must return to Washington immediately to talk to the President."

Bernie went back to America, and I went to Paris to see my old friends. I asked them all to come to my hotel for drinks one afternoon. I particularly wanted to see Philippe Hottinguer; we had remained friends. The air was electric with talk of the "phony war" and the Maginot Line, and I overheard Philippe say to a couple of chums, "I was mobilized today." They nodded: "So were we." It was my second warning in as many weeks. I was pouring champagne; I put the bottle right down in the middle of the floor and went straight to the telephone to book passage home.

ARTHUR Lyons made one more stab at my movie career: a screen test at Warner Brothers. He had recently married, and though I hadn't met his wife yet he asked me to come to Hollywood to stay with them. It was a good time for me to go. Decio was still in Rio.

I went to California on the Superchief. In the dining car a man introduced himself as the director of the Goodman Theatre in Chicago. He said he was sitting with Sinclair Lewis, who wanted to meet me.

Lewis, the first American writer to win a Nobel Prize, was a tremendous star at the time. He had lately turned to writing plays; he had with him the script of his work in progress, *Angela Is Twenty-Two,* and he asked me if I would look at it. I read it on the train, and I didn't think it was terribly good—he had a total lack of technical knowledge about the theater—but I was intrigued and in a way touched by his intense interest in it. He was like a stagestruck boy, and the reason he was attracted to me, I thought, was that I was an actress. We discussed *Angela* a great deal, and by the time we got to Pasadena he was trying to persuade me to do it.

Staying at Arthur's house was not all that comfortable. His bride turned out to be very pretty, very young; she seemed hardly more than a child, and I think she was frightened and bored by Arthur and his high-flown shenanigans to create a movie empire. Anyway, she stayed mostly in bed, and so far as I could tell all she ever did was eat popcorn and drink brandy. Arthur was at his office all day, and since the studio was taking its time scheduling my screen test, I had nothing to do. The movies are like the army: it's hurry up and wait.

Sinclair Lewis—he was usually called "Red"—didn't seem to have many friends, and he had a lot of free time, so I spent most of every day with him. We drove to out-of-the-way places for lunch, and afternoons we sat around in his bungalow at the Beverly Hills Hotel. What a talker he was; he never stopped the whole time I was with him. He was also working on a book, *Bethel Merriday,* and he showed me pages and pages of names he had jotted down for possible use. He had a wonderful knack for names, and I asked him how it felt to have created a generic name for a certain kind of person, Babbitt. He grinned: "I like it!" It was the shortest sentence I ever heard from him.

Red was tall and so thin that his clothes hung on him like a scarecrow. He never dressed casually à la California, but always as if he were going to a business appointment with his banker. Perhaps this was compensation for a distressing and painfully obvious problem—he had skin cancer.

Outside of his work, I knew very little about him—I didn't even know about his drinking problem, although he did drink an awful lot of iced coffee. We had no friends in common, not even the man who had introduced us, whom I didn't know very well, and who never showed up again. It was as though our meeting on the train had somehow encapsulated us in another dimension.

I have an enormous curiosity about people, but for some reason I never asked Red about his life. I was too concerned about my own career; the screen test was as slow in coming as molasses in winter, and I was beginning to wonder what I was doing in California in the first place. Also, I think Red talked so much I never got a word in edgewise. I came away from all that time knowing as little about him as when I met him on the train. I never questioned the loneliness of his Hollywood life or why he was dependent on me for companionship.

I thought that companionship was all it was, until he astonished me by telling me he loved me. I didn't take him seriously, because I had told him about Decio. Then he really frightened the wits out of me when he said he was going to tell his wife, Dorothy Thompson, that he wanted to marry me. Dorothy

Grandfather Holtzman

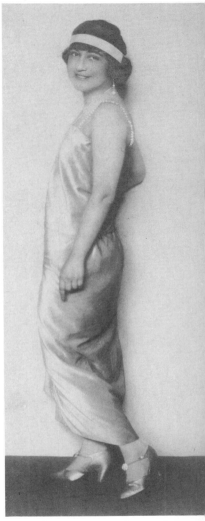

My mother, Hortense Holtzman Conn

My father, Joseph Conn

First formal photograph

Kitty in the brown velvet dress

Kitty at Mont Choisi

Mother and Major Spratt at the Alhambra in fancy dress

Kitty, age seventeen, in the green taffeta ball gown

Madame Suarez's bathtub, filled with water lilies

Château de Brissac

With Maneco de Teffé in Brioni

Arriving in Hollywood

Murder at the Vanities

"June in January," from Here Is My Heart,
with Bing Crosby, (Copyright © by Paramount Pictures.
Courtesy of MCA Publishing Rights,
a Division of MCA, Inc.)

With Bing Crosby in
She Loves Me Not

A Night at the Opera. *Margaret Dumont, Kitty, Allan Jones, Chico, Groucho, and Harpo Marx (© 1972 Freelance, Lansdale, Pa. 19446)*

George Gershwin

For Kitty — In appreciation of a grand girl — much admiration. George

"Summertime"

Decio de Moura (left)

Three Waltzes, *with Michael Bartlett*

Sinclair Lewis (Harold Stein photo)

Singing "The Star-Spangled Ban-
ner" during a World War II
bond rally

Popsy in his commodore's cap

Moss Hart and George Kaufman (Van Damm)

Being married by the Justice of the Peace (Wide World Photos)

The trees Moss planted   *Kitty and Moss at the farm*

*Moss and Darryl on the
Zanucks' croquet lawn in
Palm Springs*

*Chris in Kitty's arms, on stage at the
Bucks County Playhouse
(J. H. Melford photo)*

The Rape of Lucretia, *with Marguerite Piazza (left) and Brenda Lewis (Van Damm)*

Kitty in Carmen, *Salt Lake City*

The staircase at 1185 Park Avenue

Chris and Cathy

Thompson was a formidable creature—foreign correspondent, columnist, lecturer, and world figure. She had just arrived in California to make a speech, and Red said he was going to go to her lecture and give her this piece of news. I said if he told her any such thing I'd never speak to him again. All the time we were together he'd never asked me if *I* would like to marry *him,* or even if I loved him. It was Gershwin all over again: I loved his talent, but I didn't love him. I liked him, and I was pleased that he cared to spend so much time with me, but the idea of sharing my life with him had never crossed my mind, and I was scared to think what an announcement of this kind could do to Miss Thompson. (Red obviously didn't say anything to her about marrying me, because I never heard from her.)

The screen test finally came through, but unfortunately it was for *Anthony Adverse,* and Olivia de Havilland was better suited for it than I. Even Arthur's magic couldn't produce a movie; and I went back to New York to meet Decio, who had just returned from Rio.

Red's letters started the day I left, sometimes two a day. Considering that his lovemaking had stopped with a hug at hello and goodbye, and a kiss or two, I was dismayed at the depth of his feelings:

". . . I still don't quite believe you're not going to be here for dinner tomorrow, or a country drive. . . .

". . . Darling, I write words . . . I can't write my heart."

The letter is typed, but there is a blob of ink on the page. Next to it is a handwritten note: "I'd say this was a tear, but, darling, my tears are *not* of ink."

". . . Oh my dear, each hour speeding farther from me."

". . . My Kitty, small cat cream-covered, I do care a lot—perhaps you guessed that. I wish, for you, I were a Celebrity, not a small doubtful man in a hotel room, trying to get himself to work."

And then there were several poems, and once, when I forgot to return a phone call, there was a scene from *Romeo and Juliet:*

ACT I—SCENE XCIX

(A street in Verona, 7:30 P.M.,
May 18. Enter Romeo and Mercutio.)

MER. Thou pigeon's craw, thou cast-off lady's glove,
Why dost thou stare and sigh? Why art thou sad?

ROM. Juliet, singing in far Mantua,
Before the prince and his bedizened court,
Proud in the splendors of the Capitol,
So far forgot me that she did not phone.

She said she'd call me late this afternoon—
The silver moon had promised to turn gold,
The medlar tree had promised me its fruit—
They failed me. Why should I not be distraught?

MER. What? Oh, I chide thee! Dost thou blame her, then,
That singing, standing like a little queen
Before the cheering thousands, she forgot?

ROM. *Blame* her? I do not *know* that puling word!
Whatever she may do is fair and bright,
Whatever she may fail to do is right.

Yet—if her voice one second I had heard,
How radiantly I would dream tonight.

Yet, good Mercutio, sighing I confess
Love in its hunger is so limitless
That had she called—a minute's priceless dower!—
I would have begged her to talk on an hour
And had she talked an hour, I would have pled
With her to talk the skylark into bed.

Love is insatiable, Mercutio.
That is its grief—and glory. Let us go.

(Exeunt)

In the end his affection for me dwindled because I could
return so little of it. I never even managed to send the photographs he requested. But I treasure the time we spent together,

the autographed books, *Babbitt, Arrowsmith, Main Street,* and the photograph signed "To Kitty with Love."

In the theater, as in politics, either everybody wants you or nobody wants you. This time everyone wanted me. I played Reno Sweeney in *Anything Goes;* Maggie in *The Man Who Came to Dinner* for the first time, and *Tonight or Never,* all in summer stock. Mother was delighted that I was getting experience in so many varied roles, and Decio was a devoted camp follower. He visited me wherever the theaters were, and we had a wonderful time wandering around Hyannis, Amherst, Dennis, Cohasset.

One of my productions was Noël Coward's *Design for Living.* It is an intricate play, which needs a great deal of rehearsal, but for summer stock we had only one week. On opening night we were still rehearsing in the ladies' lounge at 8 P.M. in pin curls and bathrobes. At 8:30 the audience began stamping its feet in the auditorium overhead, and the director finally sent us to our dressing rooms to get ready. We had never seen one another in costume and makeup, which is a world away from the way in which we'd left one another—particularly in the case of Herbert Berghof, who was as bald as an egg, and who had never worn his hairpiece to rehearsals.

The curtain finally went up. I was discovered on stage, facing the audience, a breakfast tray on a coffee table in front of me, reading the newspaper. There was a knock on the door. I put down the newspaper, went to the door and opened it. There stood a man, beautifully dressed, wing collar, black coat and striped pants, four-in-hand, with a homburg perched on a full head of hair. I was sure I had never seen this person before in my life, and I didn't even recognize the character he was playing. I met this puzzlement by shutting the door firmly in his face and going back to the breakfast tray to try to figure out who it could be. Suddenly the light dawned. "Oh, my God, it's Berghof!" I ran back to the door, let him in, and the play began.

My career took a big leap forward when I was asked if I would come to Philadelphia, look at an operetta, *Three Waltzes,* and jump into the lead in four days. The Shuberts, who were the producers, had dismissed the current leading lady, Margaret Bannerman, so summarily that I never met her. The show was to open in New York in ten days. At the same time, I was chosen to be the star singer in a weekly Coca-Cola radio show.

There were twelve songs in *Three Waltzes* for me to learn, and the plot was rather complicated. I played three generations: a woman in the first act, her daughter in the second, and her granddaughter in the third act.

To complicate matters further, I had to commute from New York because of the Coca-Cola rehearsals.

When *Three Waltzes* opened in New York, there was a basket of flowers in my dressing room with a note: "Good luck for tonight and best wishes. Margaret Bannerman." She was such a good sport and this was such a generous gesture that I never forgot it. (I told Moss this story long after, and he never forgot it either. When he was casting the national company of *My Fair Lady* and saw that Bannerman was up for the part of Mrs. Higgins, he told the casting director to hire her on the spot—no audition necessary.)

I did well in *Three Waltzes.* George Jean Nathan, who was *Esquire*'s theater critic at the time, gave me the best notice I ever had. It was my first rave from a major critic, and I'm going to quote it all:

> A word about Kitty Carlisle, whose singing presence in *Three Waltzes,* along with the Strauss music and its derivations, made me oblivious of the spoken words. Here, I think, is the most likely female voice, the best singing actress and, certainly and by long odds, the comeliest woman on our present musical show stage. She never made any such impression upon me in her previous manifestations. Something has happened either to her or to me. Maybe she has improved, or maybe I have. I am impolite enough, I fear, to suspect that it is she. But, whether it is the great improvement that has come over her or whether I in the past have been a

defective critic, the fact remains that she now takes the palm from her musical-stage sisters.

I managed well enough doing both *Three Waltzes* and singing on the radio, because the Coca-Cola show was on Sunday nights when the theater was dark. However, New Year's Eve fell on a Sunday that year, and *Three Waltzes* did a special Sunday performance. The Shuberts solved the conflict neatly: I played my part in the first act; my understudy played me as my daughter in the second act while I was off doing the Coca-Cola show; and I returned to play the part of my granddaughter in the third act, all courtesy of a motorcycle escort provided by the Shuberts. The audience got 66⅔ percent of me, and 100 percent confusion.

In spite of my lovely notice, *Three Waltzes* wasn't much of a hit. It limped along, but when it closed the Shuberts wanted to take it on tour.

I didn't want to go. Decio was about to be recalled again to Rio, and we hadn't had much time together. Ethel Colt, whom I had met when she played the ingenue in *Anything Goes,* told me she would take me to her mother, Ethel Barrymore, for advice. "My dear," said Miss Barrymore, "*stars* tour; only show girls don't." So off I went, and was rewarded for my good behavior: *Three Waltzes* mercifully closed after three weeks, and I was able to get back to New York before Decio left.

I took over another show, *Walk with Music.* It remains in my mind for two reasons: a lovely score by Johnny Mercer and Hoagy Carmichael; and choreography by Anton Dolin, who tried to teach me a dance routine with Jack Whiting, the leading man. After laboring mightily, Dolin finally threw up his hands and said, "You're the only singer I ever met who can walk out of time to the music." I was quite offended; after all, I was a *very* good ballroom dancer.

Then after this burst of activity everything came to a standstill.

There were no offers for shows. What was left were big-name bands and vaudeville.

Big-name bands played the movie houses, and of course they had their own vocalists, but sometimes they accompanied headliners like me. I played a week with Harry James in Rochester, New York, and it was a week to remember. We opened on New Year's Eve. I had heard bloodcurdling stories about the New Year's Eve audience's rowdiness the year before, when Anita Louise was there. The curtain went up on a tableau: Anita, an ethereal blond starlet dressed in white tulle, was seated at a harp, a soft spotlight playing around her head like a halo. She was preparing to make celestial music on her harp, which she played quite well. But the tableau had struck an unexpected chord in the audience, and they started off with catcalls, followed by rolls of toilet paper thrown on the stage like streamers, which I am told was standard equipment for New Year's Eve audiences in that theater. They had to lower the curtain and Anita Louise never got to play a single glissando on her harp.

Harry James's audience was hardly my operetta audience. They were used to pop singers, and I had to deflect any feelings they might have that I and my songs were highfalutin'. I decided to talk before I sang. I turned on every ounce of charm I could summon; I tried to win them over with "we're all in this together." I think I confused them so much that in the end, though it may not have been my finest performance, I got away without streamers.

There was still plenty of vaudeville around in the thirties, even though you could feel it foundering under your feet. Loew's State was the big one to aim for; it was New York and it was Broadway; and there was always the chance that a famous manager or director might see you and sign you up for a real Broadway show. I never felt I did my best at Loew's State—there was too much riding on it, and Mother and Ed threw me off balance by trying to change the routine of my act at every performance.

But I learned a lot playing with the great comedians; it taught me the importance of verbal economy in getting a laugh, and it sharpened my timing. I played with some of the best of them: George Jessel, Jack Haley, Joe E. Lewis, Willy Shore, Henny Youngman. I had all the prerequisites for a good straight woman: I was dignified, wore beautiful clothes, and laughed up the jokes.

The comedians liked working with me. That was not true of all the animal acts, and I gave a wide berth to the ones I knew particularly disliked me.

Sharkey the Seal was at the head of the list. I admired him, make no mistake. As a performer he was altogether delightful; he could play three different tunes on his little trumpets, and he clapped his flippers together on cue. But backstage his true character came out. He was bad-tempered, he tried to splash water from his tank all over my evening dresses; and when I was going on stage as he was coming off, he deliberately barked at me and tried to step on my feet.

On the other hand, the little fox terriers who built houses in no time flat were courteous, and they went about their business with speed and dexterity, looking neither to the right nor left as they scampered up and down their little ladders carrying their buckets in their teeth, to the tune of the William Tell overture. I never tired of watching their act.

Nightclubs were also a possibility. I had never worked in a nightclub, but I got an arranger and we put an act together. Ed took me to Nick Prounis, of the Versailles Restaurant.

Nick was doubtful, but Ed told him if he'd give me a chance he could pay me anything he wanted, so long as he kept the amount a secret. Nick agreed.

Once I got the hang of it, nightclubs were fun for me. Holding a nightclub audience requires total concentration. Every good song tells a story, and it has to be so clear in your mind that the listeners become caught up in *your* vision. In a nightclub everything conspired to spoil my concentration: the drunks; the busboy who worked the lights—it was always a busboy, and if he was inattentive or hostile, soon I was floundering in bright light on the torch songs, and pin spots on the "up" songs. Then there was the waiter who dropped the tray on my pianissimo (which I had finally found), and the management who agreed to stop all service during my performance and had no intention of doing it.

Working at night brought its own problems. My last show didn't finish till 12:30 A.M.; if I invited a date to come back to my hotel for a bite of supper, it was nearly three in the morning before he left. "What will the bellboys think?" I asked my mother. She said crisply, "My dear, you can't live your life for the bellboys!"

After the Versailles I went on to the Persian Room at the Plaza, this time at a proper salary.

The Persian Room was very elegant. Hildegarde, the great nightclub performer, and the power behind her throne, Anna Sosenko, helped me prepare my act with routining and lighting. I wanted to make a big splash, and I planned my dress with the utmost care; It was red chiffon with red bugle beads and had a fairly short skirt. It was ravishing and very, very expensive.

I made my entrance into a packed house. I began my first song, "Love Is Sweeping the Country," by George Gershwin. After the opening phrase my mind went blank. I stopped. I broke out in a cold sweat, but smiling gamely I turned, nodded to the orchestra leader, who had brought the band to a ragged stop, and indicated I was ready to begin again. He struck up the introduction and I sang out "Love Is Sweeping the Country"— and at the same spot again I stopped. I turned to the orchestra leader, gritting my teeth, still smiling, and once more I indicated that I was ready, but this time I thought he knew that "Love Is Sweeping the Country" was a lost cause and we'd better forget it and go on to the next number. But no, he played "Love Is Sweeping the Country" still another time. By now I was so deaf with humiliation and fright that I didn't hear what he was playing, and I piped up with my second song. The orchestra was still playing "Love Is Sweeping the Country" but I was singing "The Man I Love."

We got together somehow and finished the act. It was one of the worst nights of my life, and I certainly never wore that dress again. Why more actors don't drop dead on opening night I'll never know.

Eventually I made good at the Persian Room, and I was engaged by the Chez Paree, the gaudiest and best nightclub in Chicago. It had gambling, big-name bands, and a line of show girls. It was run by Mike Fritzel and Joey Jacobson. Like almost everyone else in their line of work, they had a rigid code for girls. Judgment was made instantly, based on some mysterious mobster criterion. You were either a good girl or a bad girl. I was a good girl.

Nightclub dressing rooms provided a bare minimum, and the Chez was no exception. My room had a counter, two straight chairs, and hooks on the wall for the costumes. It was so small and airless that if anyone asked me to come out into the club for a drink, I accepted gratefully. I'd no sooner be seated at the table than a waiter would come and whisper, "Miss Carlisle, you're wanted in the office." There Mike and Joey would ask sternly, "Do you know the people you're sitting with?" If the answer was no, they'd say, "You'd better go back to your dressing room."

Mother was terribly worried about my singing in a club that had gambling. She decided to come to Chicago to protect me. But Mike and Joey were such a couple of nannies that Mother felt perfectly safe leaving me in their hands, and she went back to New York and Ed.

At my first rehearsal at the Chez Paree, I was immediately drawn to a girl with a lively, intelligent face. Her name was Sylvia Fine. She was married to the young comedian in the show, Danny Kaye. She wrote the material for him, and she was also his accompanist. They had already played one New York engagement, at the Martinique. But compared to the Martinique, the

Chez Paree was the big time, and both Sylvia and Danny were very nervous.

They needn't have been. Danny was an instantaneous hit. So were Sylvia's songs. She was—and is—a marvelous musician and a brilliant lyricist. Danny's reputation traveled like the wind from Hollywood to Broadway and back. Everybody in show business stopped between trains in Chicago to see him.

We did three shows a night, from 8:30 to 3 A.M. Sylvia had no dressing room of her own, so I invited her to share mine. Night after night for the next six weeks we sat between shows with our feet up on the counter and discussed only two subjects: should I marry Decio? and would Moss Hart *really* write a part for Danny? Moss had seen him in New York, was exceedingly impressed, and had promised to write a part for him in his new musical *Lady in the Dark.* Sylvia and I gave each other endless advice on both subjects with the greatest authority, though I'd only met Moss once and Sylvia didn't know Decio at all.

I enjoyed the challenge of singing in nightclubs, but on one occasion I brushed a little too close to the underpinnings of the business. On my first day at the Brook Club in Miami I was greeted by the owner, a handsome old gentleman with the manners of a Southern colonel. He wore a string tie and a black fedora, and his haberdashery was impeccable. He asked how long my act was. "Forty to forty-five minutes," I said, and added cheerily, "I can do a little longer." "Oh no, little lady," he said, "that won't be necessary. Three songs will do." At the sight of my crestfallen face, he added, "and an encore."

I couldn't figure it out. Why were they paying my entire salary for only three songs? After rehearsal the press agent showed me around the club. Then I saw the gambling room and, innocent though I was, I understood. The owner wanted to get the people to the gaming tables as fast as possible, and three songs was all the time he would allow for the show.

The press agent also told me that the slits in the ceiling were for guns, to protect the club and the patrons against thieves. It all sounded like an Edward G. Robinson movie until I went to get my things in the employees' cloakroom. I bumped up against something in an overcoat hanging on a hook. I have no idea what possessed me to put my hand in the pocket, but I pulled out a gun. If it had been a rattlesnake I couldn't have dropped it faster. The implications of the melodrama became frighteningly real when, the week after I had played there, the Mounds Club in Cleveland was held up and all the customers were robbed. If they'd had the same protection as the Brook Club, it wouldn't have happened.

Nightclubs can be lonely—I felt a little out of sync, working when everyone else was playing, sleeping when everyone else was working. The day I met Carleton Smith, all that changed. He introduced me to the most interesting people in all the towns I played in.

Carleton was a man of mystery, and I always suspected that he was a spy. He had been a music critic for *Esquire* magazine, and music was his life. He was a constant name-dropper. At first I thought he was making it up, but it turned out that he really *had* been staying with Sibelius in Finland, or sitting in the opera box in Berlin with Hitler and Winifred Wagner, and bringing messages back to Roosevelt at the White House. I once took him to the airport in Los Angeles during the war, when airplanes were only for VIP's. They were paging him as we arrived; he flashed a White House pass at the gate and boarded a plane that was obviously being held for him.

Carleton was persona grata with most of the great musicians of the day, and when we were in California he took me to meet Lotte Lehmann, one of my heroines ever since my student days in London, where I had heard her often at Covent Garden. I never forgot her Marschallin in *Der Rosenkavalier*, especially her final gesture of resignation at the end of the first act. She had retired from opera and was living in Santa Barbara, giving master classes. She invited Carleton and me to tea.

He told me to bring some music so I pulled out the only German song in my repertoire, Brahms' "Lullaby."

Lehmann lived in a comfortable, spacious house, with lots of windows and a pretty garden. She looked most motherly, and she received Carleton affectionately.

After tea, Carleton suggested she help me with a song I was working on. He was stretching the truth a bit; I wasn't really working on it. But the stratagem served its purpose. She went straight to the piano and we started right in. After my first phrase she stopped me. "Let's go over the poem," she said. "Before you fit the words to the music, you must study the meaning of the poem, the value of each word, each phrase, and the overall line to find the emphasis and the climaxes." She explained that the understanding of the words would give insight into the way the music should be sung. Shades of Ed's Baedeker! (Many years later I asked Frank Sinatra how he prepared a new song. "I study the meaning of the lyric, the value of each word, each phrase, the overall line. . . ." Isn't it interesting, I thought, how real artists all seem to know the same basic principles.)

Carleton sat and listened while I had a full forty-five minutes of coaching, with Lehmann herself singing when she wanted to illustrate a particular line. I was grateful to Carleton for setting it up, and even more to Lehmann for giving me her wisdom and her time.

In Chicago Carleton introduced me to John Alden Carpenter, the American composer, who at that time was hugely successful thanks to an orchestral suite, *Adventures in a Perambulator,* and two ballets: *Skyscrapers,* which had been commissioned by Diaghilev, and *Krazy Kat.* Carpenter, who had written a lot of vocal music, was fascinated by the nightclub world, and he wrote a song for me, called "Blue Gal." He even put in lighting instructions. He wrote me, "If you get around to a tryout of "Blue Gal" in the Great City or elsewhere, do let me know how she behaves." I never did get to sing it. It turned out to be far too classical for a nightclub. Carpenter didn't hold it against me—a few years later he wrote to me on New Year's Day: ". . . If the New Year is really going to bring some happiness, you are certainly one of those who will contribute to it. . . ."

Carleton told me he was a friend of Dr. Robert Oppenheimer, and that I really doubted, because physics was so far from his field of interest. I challenged him. "Let's go see him!" He said, "All right." A week later he called to tell me we were expected for a sandwich lunch with Dr. Oppenheimer at the Princeton Institute for Advanced Studies.

Dr. Oppenheimer's office was an astounding sight. All four walls were made of blackboard, covered with equations and formulas from ceiling to floor. There was a sign tacked to the doorjamb: PLEASE DO NOT ERASE. A cleaning woman could have changed the whole course of science.

The great man was sitting behind his desk. I was anxious to make him like me, because I wanted to be invited back to his house. I had heard he had a collection of French Impressionists.

I remembered that Mother always told me, "If you want to make a hit with Jascha Heifetz, don't tell him what a great fiddle player he is. He knows that better than you do. Tell him he's a great Ping-Pong player (his real passion), and he'll be yours forever!" During lunch Oppenheimer brought out a piece he'd written on Niels Bohr. He said Niels Bohr was like a Rembrandt —illuminated only from one side—while Einstein was like a Holbein, fully illuminated,

I asked to see the piece, and he handed it to me. I read the first paragraph and said, "Dr. Oppenheimer, you are a wonderful *writer!*" And he and his wife, *and* the Impressionists, were mine for the rest of the afternoon.

MOTHER could see that I was beginning to make a life for myself. She started to loosen the bonds. She came down to Baltimore where I was doing *Tonight or Never* in summer stock. We were having lunch when she presented me with an earthshaking gift. "I've found you an apartment on Park Avenue up the street from the Ritz Tower," she said. "You can move in as soon as you get back." I stared at her open-mouthed. *I* never would have had the nerve to suggest it. How simply astonishing that *she* had thought of it! I was filled with a rush of affection. I wanted to hug her. She smiled her beautiful smile, obviously pleased with the role of benevolent parent.

It certainly simplified my relationship with Decio, who by now had come back from Rio. He had engineered a real coup—he got himself appointed Commissioner of the Brazilian Pavilion at the New York World's Fair.

He was in New York over a year, and we saw each other constantly. Unfortunately, after the fair closed it was Rio again for him. This time he said, "We must be married. It's too difficult without you."

I *said* I would marry him, but I never really *saw* myself going to Brazil and living there with him. Unless I can visualize myself in an actual situation, it's not apt to happen. It was wrong of me not to make this clear.

Decio went home assuming that I meant what I said. He alerted the press to the date of my arrival, and there was a lot of interest in the marriage of the diplomat and the movie actress.

Then I told Mother and Ed of my plans. The classic situation is that the mother develops heart trouble when she doesn't want her daughter to marry. The day before I was to leave it was Ed who had a few heart pains—just enough to give me an excuse not to go to Rio.

The timing was bad for Decio. It was too late for him to call off the press. They were all at the airport; I wasn't. Decio was left with a loss of face (and a loss of bride)—wounding for anyone, but for a Latin, intolerable.

Decio forgave me, but I missed him and kept wondering if I would ever find someone else. Eight months later he called to tell me he was getting married, and I had a real attack of dog-in-the-manger. I wailed to Mother, "I'm never going to be married and I'll never have any children!" Mother consoled me: "You wouldn't be satisfied as the wife of a diplomat. By the time he retires, you'll be too old to pick up your career and yet not old enough to be idle. I'm very fond of Decio, but I just know he isn't right for you." "You promise me I'll find someone?" "I promise," she answered.

THE next beau wasn't right for me either. He was the playwright and screenwriter Norman Krasna. I had met him in California the year before. He was cute, rather like a big puppy, and very amusing, and he wrote screenplays and plays, notably *Dear Ruth* (which Moss eventually directed), *John Loves Mary* and *The Devil and Miss Jones.*

Norman admired Moss Hart, a fellow playwright. He talked about him all the time with a kind of hero worship. When Norman came to New York he invited me to go down to Moss's farm with him. Then he called Moss and asked if he could bring a girl for the weekend. "Who is it?" asked Moss. "Kitty Carlisle." "Sure, you can bring her," Moss said. "I know her; she's a nice girl. What's up?" "If I can get her away from her mother," Norman answered, "I think I can get her to marry me."

I wasn't in love with Norman and I didn't want to marry him, but I enjoyed being with him, and I was intrigued by the tales I heard of the highjinks at Moss's farm.

Harpo Marx was a friend of Moss and George Kaufman's. He was a guest shortly after Moss took up residence in Bucks County. One day the local minister came to call. "I don't think we'll have too much to say to each other," Moss said to Harpo, "so after he's been here ten or fifteen minutes, come in on some pretext and interrupt us."

"What pretext?" asked Harpo. "You'll think of something," Moss answered. The minister had hardly warmed a chair when Harpo burst in, wearing nothing but a towel around his middle, brandishing a shaving brush and a razor. "It's time to shave the cat, Moss!" he announced. The minister fled the house, never to return.

Another weekend guest before my time was Alexander Woollcott, critic, lecturer, one of the founders of the Algonquin Round Table.

Woollcott went in for jokes with a cruel twist. He asked if Moss would like to come and hear one of his famous lectures, sit on the platform, and perhaps say something at the end. Moss looked forward to it. Indeed, Woollcott had a chair set up on the platform for him. At the end of the lecture Woollcott said to the audience, "I'm sure you're wondering who this young man is who has been sitting here all evening. Well, so am I." He walked off, leaving Moss still sitting on the platform, feeling utterly foolish.

Woollcott's behavior as a guest was notoriously outrageous. He demanded dinner at all hours; windows to be opened when everyone was freezing; windows shut when everyone was boiling hot. And he left with a parting salvo in the guest book: "This is to certify that, on my first visit to Moss Hart's manor house, I had one of the most unpleasant weekends I can recall having spent." Moss went over to see George Kaufman and told him in detail of the infuriating events of the weekend. He wound up with, "George, if Aleck had broken his leg and I had been obliged to keep him one more day . . ." They looked at each other, and *The Man Who Came to Dinner* was born.

Woollcott, far from being displeased at his unflattering portrait, was delighted to be the subject of a big hit play. He even insisted on playing the part in the national touring company.

I found Moss's place in Bucks County to be a charming eighteenth-century stone farmhouse set in the middle of a cornfield. When he bought it, there wasn't a tree or a bush around the house. Moss was a very impatient man. He planted two thousand fully grown pine trees. George Kaufman came to see what Moss had done with the place. He looked around and said, "Well, Moss, it's exactly what God would have done if he'd had the money!"

George and Beatrice Kaufman had a farm just down the road, and they and Moss shared their guests every weekend. If it was Saturday dinner at the Kaufmans', it was Sunday lunch at Moss's, and the next week it would be reversed. This Saturday we all dined at the Kaufmans'. They had many guests, but I especially remember Edna Ferber, who went out of her way to make me feel at home. It was my one and only meeting with the legendary Beatrice Kaufman. According to Norman, she was the one who took Moss in hand when he began to work with George and taught him the joys of decorating and antiquing. She was hostessy and friendly and seemed to be the leader of the group.

We played word games, and I wasn't very good; I was too self-conscious to concentrate. I didn't know what Norman had told Moss about me, and it made me very nervous. Then I sang, and Moss accompanied me on the guitar. It didn't bring me any closer to him. The whole time I was singing he stared off in the other direction.

I found out later that Moss decided that weekend I would be the wrong wife for Norman. "Norman," he said, "you see Kitty dressed in black velvet, sweeping down the stairs in your house to greet Louis B. Mayer, and she's not that kind of girl at all." (I don't know why Moss didn't think so. Years later I used to sweep down the stairs in our apartment dressed in black velvet to greet people very like Louis B. Mayer.) When Norman protested, Moss ungallantly began to run me down in an effort to win the argument. When Moss and I were married some years later, in 1946, we received a telegram from Norman. It simply said, "Now I understand everything."

LIKE most performers, I spent the war years making propaganda films and entertaining troops. I tried to get overseas—I asked Baruch to recommend me for the OSS; I told him I had friends in France, knew the country well, and was bilingual. But he refused. He said I would be a terrible spy; I'd tell all the wrong things to all the wrong people.

We went on battleships to entertain the Navy. We saluted the thousandth airplane off the Grumman assembly line. We danced with the soldiers at the Hollywood Canteen. I sold war bonds on the steps of public libraries and post offices. I made a movie called *Hollywood Canteen* in which I introduced a lovely song called "Sweet Dreams, Sweetheart," by Ted Koehler and M. K. Jerome.

I made two movies during the war for the Signal Corps. One of them was to cheer up the soldiers who had wives and babies at home. I played the wife left behind, and I had to bathe and put to bed a real infant, all the while singing "Pretty Baby." I not only had my usual stage fright, I was scared to death of handling the baby. The baby was also scared of me, and there was a notable lack of smiling and cooing. But no one seemed to mind.

Traveling around the country was extremely difficult unless you had a high-priority clearance, which entertainers never seemed to have. I spent many a night in an upper berth, sleeping on top of the cardboard boxes that held my costumes. But at least I didn't have to worry about being late. "The Star-Spangled Banner" led off every occasion, and since I always sang it, they couldn't start without me.

War or no war, I had to keep working to support myself and my mother. I got a phone call from George Jessel, who wanted me to do a two-a-day vaudeville show called *Showtime U.S.A.* in California. Jessel was such fun to work with that any time he asked me to join him, I did if it was at all possible. Besides Jessel, there were comedian Jack Haley, singer Ella Logan, the great ballroom dancers Tony and Sally de Marco, Con Colleano and his high-wire act, and Bob Williams with his dog Red Dust.

When we got to San Francisco we were asked to visit the Mare Island Naval Hospital where the worst burn cases from Pearl Harbor had been flown.

There were rows and rows of beds. We tried to stop at each one to speak to these men who were between life and death. I was taken into a small room where a very young boy lay all alone. I wanted to touch him, but I was afraid; he was so badly burned. I couldn't find anything to say, but I couldn't leave him. I just sat there for a long, long time, and all at once I knew that he had died.

A verse from a Brahms song suddenly came to my mind:

> A maiden rose at the break of day
> To wander in the woods so green and gay,
> And as she walked with carefree joy
> The maid discovered a wounded boy.
> His bleeding wounds were gaping wide,
> And as she looked at him, the young man died.

We went to Mare Island as often as we could. Blood was needed desperately. To convince the public that it wasn't weakening, we were photographed giving blood during the intermission of *Showtime U.S.A.* and then performing on stage right afterward. I learned then that women are braver than men. All the women in the show donated blood, but none of the men. Jessel had the best excuse; he said his blood was all brandy and Benzedrine.

Nevertheless, entertainers are the most generous people in the world when it comes to giving of themselves in times of crises. (Vietnam was the exception. I was delegated by the Red Cross to bring celebrities to St. Albans Naval Hospital to cheer up the wounded. Feelings ran so high against that war that it was very hard to get people to come. Jacqueline Onassis came to St. Albans without being asked twice. She understood that the wounded were simply victims.)

Arthur Lyons, by now one of the biggest agents in the business, came to San Francisco to see me in the show. He threw his not inconsiderable selling talent into persuading me to stay in California while he set up a company to make movies for me to star in. I think he was trying to make up for what he considered his failure with my movie career. It seems incredible that I fell for such a scheme. Alas, Lyons was no William Randolph Hearst, and I was no Marion Davies. But there was enough bait for me. I longed to wipe out the humiliation and defeat of Paramount's dismissal. Even though *Showtime U.S.A.* was very successful and went on to open on Broadway, I decided to go to Los Angeles. Mother and Ed wanted me to return to New York with the show. For the first time I defied them and used my own judgment. But I picked the wrong time, the wrong place, and above all, the wrong person.

I was out of work again, so I had all the time in the world to entertain for the Army. A vaudeville unit was formed to go into the Mojave Desert near Indio, where soldiers were being trained for desert warfare in North Africa. They were there for six to eight weeks without being allowed to break training. They were, we were told, in dire need of entertainment and the opportunity to smell a girl. Why smelling was enough I never figured out.

Marlene Dietrich was asked to head the unit, with a comedian, the usual line of girls, and me. We stayed in the barracks and ate what the troops ate: K-rations and powdered eggs. It was a far cry from the steaks, butter, and ice cream we'd had with the Navy.

Marlene was a wonderful troupe mother, ready with the extra pair of stockings, or the needle and thread for a broken shoulder strap. One red-letter day she found some real food, and in half an hour she had whipped up a tasty casserole for us. She was at the height of her glamorous powers—beautiful, and chic, with a reputation for offbeat love affairs. That she turned out to be a great cook with the soul of a German governess was quite unexpected.

IN Hollywood, if you're not working in the movies you're nobody. Two people I knew who either didn't notice or didn't care were Ann (Mrs. Jack) Warner and Slim (Mrs. Howard) Hawks, now Lady Keith. They continued to invite me to their dinner parties, where I met the most intriguing characters. Salvador Dali, who was painting Ann's portrait, was often at the Warners'. He had a stock of wildly improbable pornographic anecdotes, which he trundled out to shock me. He would say to me in French, "Did you know that in Connecticut ladies make love with small garden snakes!" His mustaches, which were at least three inches on either side, would tremble with suppressed laughter at the idea.

Another welcoming house was Eva and Jerome Kern's. Kern was not only one of America's greatest composers, he was also well known as a collector of rare books. He was one of Arthur's biggest clients. He must have been won by my obvious hero worship, because he worked with me on some of his songs, which we performed at parties. Sometimes we rehearsed at my apartment. One day as I waited for him, noodling around on the piano with "Smoke Gets in Your Eyes," I changed one of his harmonies. Kern stalked in and tapped me on the shoulder. "Miss Carlisle," he said sternly—usually he called me Kitty— "I too have that F sharp on my piano, but *I* chose not to use it."

Lyrics were as important to Kern as notes. He told me that one evening he played bridge with Sigmund Romberg as his partner. He wanted Rommy to play his ace, so he hummed the first few bars of "One Alone" from *Desert Song*. Rommy paid no attention. When the hand was over Kern, who hated losing at anything, said crossly, "Didn't you hear me hum 'One Alone?' Why didn't you play the ace?" Romberg shrugged his shoulders. "Jerry," he said blandly, "who knows from lyrics?"

The time passed pleasantly enough, but after seven or eight months of hanging around the Beverly Wilshire waiting for Arthur to set up a movie company that didn't materialize, I became disenchanted.

In the meanwhile *Showtime U.S.A.* was doing very well on Broadway without me. Mother and Ed were I-told-you-so-ing over my bad judgment and stubbornness. They came to California to rescue me and took me back to New York without a peep from me.

I worried that there would be nothing for me in New York, but Mother and Ed were right again. I was asked to sing *The Merry Widow* with Wilbur Evans at the old Boston Opera House. There are certain roles that all sopranos are anxious to sing. One of them is *The Merry Widow*. It's glamorous, romantic, and musically surefire. I couldn't wait to wrap my vocal chords around that Lehár music.

Our notices were so good I decided to send them to Jack Kapp, the head of Decca Records, with the hope that he might let Wilbur and me record our duets. Jack was a man of vision. He decided to make an album of the entire *Merry Widow*. It was the first of such show albums, and he went on to make many others. I recorded three of them, *Desert Song* and *Roberta* with Alfred Drake, and *Song of Norway*. I bless dear Jack Kapp for preserving the original casts of so many Broadway shows.

WHILE I was still in *The Merry Widow,* I auditioned for composer Kurt Weill's *One Touch of Venus.* I didn't get the part—Mary Martin did. So back to nightclubs I went.

I was in and out of New York, and when I was in town I went out with quite a few interesting men: the young publisher Bennett Cerf, tall and handsome, the head of Random House; Tony Bliss, future head of the Metropolitan Opera; producer Alfred de Liagre; and the older director-writer George Abbott. He was a wonderful dancer, but not much of a talker. I would make a list of ten subjects, bring them up one by one, and when they were exhausted I'd say, "George, it's time to take me home."

Kitty's angel, after so many false starts, finally took a hand.

Toward the end of the war there was a big bond rally at Madison Square Garden with all sorts of personalities, from Danny Kaye to Helen Keller. (One of my most treasured memories is of Helen Keller running her hands lightly over my face, then tapping into her companion's hand, saying, according to Miss Thompson, "You're very pretty, my dear.") I led things off as usual with "The Star-Spangled Banner."

I don't like to eat before I sing, so I went home to have supper. At 9:30 Mother called and asked if I was going to the party Lillian Hellman was having for everyone who had entertained at the Garden. I told her I was already undressed and I didn't want to go alone. "I think you should go," she said. Mother believed in circulating. "You don't get married sitting alone in your apartment."

I secretly wanted to go anyway, so around eleven o'clock I got into a taxi. I had heard about Lillian all my life. She came from New Orleans, and our families were acquainted. In a city known for its eccentrics, hers was outstanding. As I reached Lillian's house, my courage was oozing out and I was about to tell the driver to turn around and take me home when a cab pulled up and out came Edna Ferber and Moss Hart. Single girls invent many gambits to avoid the appearance of walking into a party alone. I pretended I was with Moss and Edna and we all went in together.

During the evening I sat on a sofa in Lillian's drawing room. All of a sudden Moss came and perched on the arm. I scrambled around in my mind for something to say that would focus his attention on me—and keep it there, for once. It was a month since he'd returned from the South Pacific, where he'd gone on a USO tour in his play *The Man Who Came to Dinner*. I thought perhaps he'd told all his stories to his friends and might need a new audience. I looked up at him and said, as if it were the most important question in the whole world, "Moss, tell me about your trip to the South Pacific."

When Moss called the next morning I was excited and pleased. "Are you surprised?" he asked. With a little laugh I said, "No, I'm not." I knew that sitting on the arm of that sofa he'd really looked at me for the first time, and he seemed to like what he saw. He said, "Shall we have lunch?" (Where would love affairs be without lunch?) He took me to "21," and the first thing he said was, "I had an extraordinary conversation with your mother. I called her to get your telephone number, and she said, 'Kitty's a very nice girl, and I've done terrible things to her.'" This honesty, the same that had led her to tell her friend in New Orleans that she knew she was affected, impressed him as nothing else could have, and I think that was the beginning of his admiration for her.

At first I was slightly flustered being with Moss at "21." I didn't want to say anything banal or foolish. His reputation as a wit and part of the smart-talking successful theater group made me self-conscious. But in a very short time the tension in the pit of my stomach lessened because he was quite different from what I expected—not brittle, and although the wit was there it was gentle and we laughed a lot. He was a wonderful listener and made me feel that he wanted to know me; he also seemed willing for me to know what he was really like behind those extravagant Sunday *Times* articles. It was a very long lunch, and when it was over he invited me for a weekend at the farm. Of course I accepted, and I was suddenly very pleased with life.

That afternoon I ran into Arlene Francis. Arlene is one of my best friends. I've known her since the days of *White Horse Inn,* when we were both in Benno Schneider's acting class. She was a good actress, and I was lucky to be paired in scenes with her.

I announced rather smugly, "I'm going to Moss Hart's farm for the weekend." She looked at me with amusement. "I bet you think you're going to be there all alone with Moss." "Wel-l-l, I thought—*maybe,*" was my answer. Arlene set me straight: "It's going to be a big weekend. I'm going to be there myself." And when I arrived, there she was, as well as Moss's brother Bernie, his friend and producer Joe Hyman, and both the playwriting Chodorovs, Eddie and Jerry, and Jerry's wife Rhea. There were so many guests that Arlene and I had to share a bedroom.

If I was disappointed at being one of a crowd, I was even more disappointed by Moss's behavior. He was exceedingly cool. When we arrived, he gave a tour of the house, showing everyone some improvements he had just made, pointedly leaving me to trail behind. It turned out that Moss was furious because I had not returned his telephone calls promptly enough to suit him. Moss was a spoiled fellow who expected people to jump at his call, and when I was working with my accompanist, I would turn off the telephone.

I came to bed that night very put out, and went through my nightly routine of putting my hair up with bobby pins and covering it with the brown mesh hairnet that did nothing to improve my appearance. I said to Arlene, "Moss is behaving outrageously. He is deliberately ignoring me, and I don't have to stay here and take it. I'm going to call a taxi and go home." "Are you?" said Arlene. "Where will you find a taxi in Bucks County at two in the morning? Anyway, you can't go back to New York in damp pin curls and that terrible hairnet."

The next morning Moss changed his tune, but I was still vexed. One by one Moss's friends drew me aside and said, "Be patient; you will be so good for each other." I was touched and pleased. I began to unbend and tried to make myself agreeable for the rest of the weekend.

Moss and I saw more and more of each other. We had so much to say that we would stand under the marquee of my hotel and talk so long that the tenants (we all knew each other) would ask me in the elevator the next day why I didn't take that young man upstairs instead of talking all night on the sidewalk. Moss told me about his depressions, and I found I wanted to make up for all his unhappiness. There was something so dear, so childlike, so appealing about him; he touched my heart.

Then it was Moss's turn to be put out. I had been booked to sing at the Mount Royal Hotel in Montreal over the New Year's holiday. He was distressed that I couldn't spend New Year's Eve with him. So the next time I went out of town, to play at the Blackstone Hotel in Chicago, Moss followed me.

He had never bestirred himself to go anywhere to see a girl, and when his valet Charles, who had been with him for years, told his wife that Mr. Hart had asked him to pack a suitcase for the trip to Chicago, she said the jig was up. Travel conditions being what they were right after World War II, anyone who tried to get on a train (planes were still only for VIP's) was embroiled in a nightmare. The crowds were horrendous, people were packed in the aisles like sardines, everything took longer than scheduled, so the trains ran out of water and toilet facilities and the passengers ran out of patience. Moss was not a patient man anyhow, except for his work; yet he put up with an eighteen-hour trip and another three-hour wait in the hotel lobby until his room was ready, and by the time I saw him he was still all sweetness and charm.

There was one hurdle I had to get past, though. I was used to touring and living in hotels, and I had become a gypsy. My suite at the Blackstone reflected this: the wardrobe trunk in the living room had clothes spilling out of every drawer; the piano was covered with sheet music and scores; and in the bedroom, the bed I wasn't using was piled two feet high with newspapers, read and unread. Moss was appalled. I didn't know then that he was the tidiest man on earth.

We walked a lot that weekend, and our steps matched perfectly. I love to walk and could not imagine marrying a man whose gait was out of rhythm with mine.

Next I had a return engagement at the Brook Club in Miami, where I'd had that encounter with the gangster hardware.

Moss was also coming to Miami. Hotel rooms were as hard to come by as travel reservations. He sent a telegram to the owner of the Lord Tarleton Hotel, where I was staying: DEAR MR JACOBS WOULD YOU HAVE SOME WHERE IN YOUR RICH AND CROWDED HOTEL A ROOM HOWEVER SMALL IN WHICH A HARRIED PLAYWRIGHT COULD PUT HIMSELF AND HIS TYPEWRITER. . . . I KNOW THAT MONEY IS LONG THIS YEAR AND ART IS FLEETING BUT THIS COULD BE YOUR GESTURE TOWARDS THE ARTS FOR THE YEAR OF 1946 STOP I WOULD TAKE ANY ACCOMMODATIONS YOU COULD MANAGE TO GIVE ME AND BE A MERRY BUT WISTFUL GUEST THROUGHOUT MY STAY STOP. . . . WILL YOU BE GOOD ENOUGH TO WIRE COLLECT. . . .

Mr. Jacobs replied: YOU CANT TAKE IT WITH YOU and I'D RATHER BE RIGHT and FACE THE MUSIC as MERRILY WE ROLL ALONG the AMERICAN WAY. Can't say GEORGE WASHINGTON SLEPT HERE, but the FABULOUS INVALID had a JUBILEE with the LADY IN THE DARK. So consider it a WINGED VICTORY, AS THOUSANDS CHEER. We've arranged reservations at the Lord Tarleton for the 19th.

Moss wired back: THANK YOU INDEED I AM DELIGHTED AND EXTREMELY GRATEFUL. I CAN TELL BY YOUR WIRE THAT YOU HAVE A SOFT SPOT IN YOUR HEART FOR WRITERS AND SINCE THIS INEVITABLY MEANS THAT YOU WILL END UP IN THE GUTTER I AM SAVING AN ATTIC BEDROOM FOR YOU AT MY FARM IN BUCKS COUNTY. . . .

I didn't have to work at the Brook Club until evening, so we had every day together. Moss had a little terrace off his room, and we sat there and talked and talked and talked. He had a compelling voice of great power and charm—not a tenor, not a baritone, but deep and resonant and theatrical. He *sounded* like a good actor. His pronunciation was cultivated, with occasional tiny overtones of Noël Coward and the Bronx. Professor Higgins would have had a field day with him. Men may fall in love with their eyes; I think women fall in love with their ears. Moss understood me and my small cast of characters wonderfully well. I was discovering what everyone knew about him: he was the best company in the world.

I was quite prepared to fall for him. We were in the same profession, and I admired his work, and I felt I needed a man who was smarter than I was. He was the right age—seven years older than I. I loved the way he looked. He had a circle of friends I longed to know. Bad reasons? Not at all. When he turned the charm on me, my goose was nicely cooked.

When I returned, there was a gathering of Moss's clan at the Plaza after the opening of Garson Kanin's play *Born Yesterday:* George Kaufman, the Chodorovs, Max Gordon, the Harold Romes, and Ruth Gordon and Garson Kanin and Moss. I couldn't go to the opening—I was singing at a benefit—but I joined them for supper. I had the feeling I was being looked over as a possible wife for Moss. I was very tense, but as the evening progressed I thought I was being regarded more and more benignly.

I realized from the very beginning that Moss looked closely at everything I wore. The night he took me to see Laurence Olivier in *Uncle Vanya* I wore my first sable scarf. I was so proud to own a bit of sable that I asked the furrier to leave everything on the skins: little tails, paws, and the heads with their beady little glass eyes. Moss took one look and said, "Darling, have you come right out of the Yukon?"

Going to the theater with Moss was stimulating and enlightening. His comments were penetrating. He was usually on the side of the actor. He said the critics often confused the play with the performance: "They say Miss So-and-So's performance faded away in the last act. It wasn't Miss So-and-So who faded away, it was the last act."

Moss had just finished his play *Christopher Blake*. He went to Hollywood with his agent Irving Lazar to look for actors, and I went off on my nightclub life. Moss loved the telephone. By now we talked all the time and one day he called from California and wanted to chat. I was feeling under the weather, which always makes me cross, and by the end of the conversation I was very short-tempered. He seemed to be talking about marriage, but it sounded offhand. I felt this was no way to propose, casually, over the telephone. He wasn't ardent enough. I didn't want to be married to someone who thought it was time to get married and thought I was available and suitable, even if it was Moss Hart. So I said, "I'm not feeling well and I don't want to discuss it," and I hung up. And then I thought, Oh, my God, what have I done!

But he did propose again, this time in a more appropriate setting. I was doing *Tonight or Never* at the Bucks County Playhouse, near his farm. Moss had offered to cue me. We sat cross-legged at either end of the sofa in the living room with the script between us. The cueing soon began to flag and our own words took over. Moss spoke about his loneliness, his hopes for a family, and he said, "You are The One, the Only One for me." I reached out and took his hand. I said, "I will trust my life to you."

There were four people who were very important in Moss's life. He didn't need the approbation of any of them; nevertheless he wanted them to like me. One was Joseph Hyman; the others were his younger brother Bernie; his father (his mother had died), and his psychiatrist, Dr. Lawrence Kubie. Moss had been in analysis long before we were married. He said that he had started so early in its history that when he went up Fifth Avenue to see his doctor, the Indians were still shooting arrows from behind the trees.

Although almost everyone I knew was in analysis, I was not a member of the club. Whatever I knew about it was from hearsay or reading. When I asked Moss what he talked about with Kubie, he told me that one of the first rules of analysis was that the patient was not allowed to discuss anything he told his analyst. And since Kubie was a rigid Freudian, there was no use asking what *he* said—he didn't talk at all.

I adhered scrupulously to the rules, feeling once in a while like Elsa von Brabant, who was told by Lohengrin not to ask his name. When she disobeyed, he got into the Swan Boat and was never seen again, so I held my tongue.

I didn't meet Kubie until some months after our wedding. When I asked Moss why, he said it wasn't necessary; he had simply announced to him that we were getting married.

Joe Hyman was another matter. He handled all of Moss's finances, and Moss never made a move without consulting him. Joe was not handsome, but if there is a male counterpart of a *jolie laide,* he was it. I was taken to lunch to meet him. After one look I knew that he would either like me or not, based only on his own evaluation of me and my worth to Moss, whom he idolized. I simply presented myself as openly and with as little artifice as I could. He decided then and there that I was right for Moss. I hadn't tried to charm him, but he charmed me for the rest of his life.

Moss adored his brother Bernie, one of the most beloved men in the theater. Bernie was Joe Hyman's producing partner. Moss made other people laugh—Bernie made Moss laugh. He was famous as a punster. My favorites were "Porgie and Bass, an opera for fish," and "Dr. Freud's, a nightclub open only on Freudays, with no tables, only couches." I used to laugh at Bernie's puns with everybody else, but my mind is not attuned to puns, and it took me a while to figure them out. When I told Moss about this, he said, "Never mind all the others; you laugh when you're good and ready."

Moss's father was known as Popsy or the Commodore. He always wore a naval officer's cap in Miami, where he spent the winter. Popsy thought of himself as a songwriter; he wrote songs for every one of Moss's plays. They were naturally entitled "Once in a Lifetime," "George Washington Slept Here," "You Can't Take It With You," and even one called "The Man Who Came to Dinner." They were unpublished and unpublishable.

When I was writing this book I telephoned Irving Berlin and asked him if he remembered the time he and Moss cooked up a scheme to publish one of Popsy's songs as a birthday present from Moss. "Of course I do," Irving said. "Moss brought him to the office, and I had my arranger run through the song. Then I came in, and he played it for me. To make it look legitimate, I said, 'Mr. Hart, may I make a suggestion: if you change these two notes here in the ending, I think we can publish this number.' Whereupon your father-in-law rose to his feet, gathered up his music, and said to me, 'Mr. Berlin, you write your songs and I'll write mine!'"

GEORGE Kaufman was also in the first circle of Moss's constellation of people to be won. Like everyone else, I had a healthy respect for George and I wanted to make a good impression. People were careful of what they said in front of him because he was as quick as the flick of a lizard's tongue to catch any bit of cant or easy sentimentality.

George unwittingly did me a great service. A few weeks before Moss and I were married, there was a big weekend house party at the farm. George and I were playing gin rummy and Moss was kibitzing. At an important point in the game I studied my hand and said, in a terrible baby-talk voice, "I'se a wittle bit wowwied about what to do!" Whatever possessed me? I *never* talked baby talk, not even later to my own children. George looked at me over his glasses and said sharply, "We don't talk baby talk around here." There was a sudden hush in the room. Tears sprang to my eyes. To have George S. Kaufman reprimand me in front of all those people! I held my breath: what would Moss do? I knew what George meant to him—part mentor, part father, and most respected friend.

After what seemed to me an eon, Moss spoke up: " 'Around here,' and in this house, she can say anything she wants!" Oh, my love, I thought, I am yours! And I knew then and there that I was indeed his until death did us part. As for George, he eventually decided that I was good for Moss, and slowly we became truly affectionate companions.

SOON Moss and I began to talk about specific plans for our wedding. I suggested a large room in a hotel to accommodate all our friends. Moss said *"Never!* I don't intend to stand there and shake hands with a thousand people." (He always exaggerated.) "We'll be married quietly in New Hope. Your mother and Ed can come down for the weekend; we'll have George Kaufman and his guests for a wedding supper, and with luck we can keep it out of the papers. And for our honeymoon, we can star together in *The Man Who Came to Dinner* right here at the Playhouse."

"My mother would never consent to that," I said with complete assurance. "I'm her only child, I've never been married, and she'll want a big wedding." Moss said, "Why don't you call her up and ask her?"

I marched to the telephone, and as usual she fooled me. "I think Moss is quite right; it's a fine idea," she said. I was stunned. Moss already knew her better than I did. "You mean you think it's fine for me simply to go from Moss's house to the Justice of the Peace in New Hope and then just drive back again to his house?" "Well," Mother said, "on the way home you *could* ride around the block!"

Moss was determined to keep the wedding secret if possible. On the evening before the ceremony, Rhea and Jerry Chodorov, who had a house nearby, came to dinner. We turned on the radio to hear the seven o'clock news, and at the first turn of the dial out came the "Wedding March," and we said, "Gosh, somebody important must be getting married! Who could it be?" Then came the announcement that the Prince of Broadway, Moss Hart, was marrying Kitty Carlisle. We looked at each other agape, and Jerry said, "It's just like royalty!"

Alas for Moss's hope for a quiet wedding. The next morning the place was awash with photographers. I looked out of the window to see Moss mopping his upper lip (a sure sign of nervousness) and gazing up at my window as if wondering what was keeping me.

What was keeping me was some highly necessary repair work. Faithful to my vow never to be married in white with a veil and a train and an armful of calla lilies, I had decided to wear the red-and-white Valentina print dress and big red straw hat I had worn in the Bucks County Playhouse production of *Tonight or Never*. The theater was a converted barn, and some of its characteristics were still barnlike. The hat had been stowed on a shelf in my dressing room, and the morning of my wedding I was sitting on the edge of the bathtub with the hat in one hand and a pair of nail scissors in the other, straightening the brim where the field mice had nibbled at it.

Finally dressed and hatted, I came down to Moss and the photographers. The photographers followed us to the Justice of the Peace, and as Moss said, so did every stray dog in town. They all sat around in the yard; I don't know what they were waiting for. The ceremony was short and the human audience small—Mother, Ed, Joe Hyman, and Bernie. As we stood facing the Justice, I was thinking, this is for the rest of my life, to love, cherish, and obey; and I felt pure contentment.

I felt Mother was also satisfied. I had married my prince—not of the blood, but of the theater. I had fulfilled her ambitions for me, and she took her hand off the tiller.

WE returned directly to the farm after the wedding (we *didn't* drive around the block), and sat silently in the living room, all of us thinking about what a momentous thing we had done. Mother was the first to speak: "Now, Moss, about the billing in *The Man Who Came to Dinner*—Kitty's name goes first?" (The habit of a lifetime dies slowly.)

Our wedding supper went as planned. George Kaufman, who was writing a musical with Arthur Schwartz and Ira Gershwin, brought his guests and the star of the show, Leonora Corbett. Mother endeared herself to everyone but George. She even won Joe Hyman, and at the end of the evening they were squashed together in the hammock, swinging away and laughing as if they had been lifelong friends.

George made Mother nervous, and in an effort to put her best foot forward, she overdid it. In her defense, he wasn't very nice to her; he tended to ignore her, but the morning after the wedding he showed up at breakfast and deigned to turn his attention to her: "What do you generally eat for breakfast, Mrs. Carlisle?" *"Café au lait* and *matsohs craquerres,"* she said, in an exaggerated French accent. George rolled his eyes heavenward, and the tone of their relationship was set forever. (He always seemed to drive her to excessive theatrical gestures. One of them gave me an unexpected present. A year or so later she came to our apartment one evening. George, Moss, and I were having coffee in the library. When she saw George, she stopped in the doorway, took off a diamond bracelet she was wearing, and tossed it across the room into my lap. "Darling," she drawled, "I always wanted you to have this." George rolled his eyes again.)

Moss, on the other hand, brought out the best in Mother. She hated her name, Hortense, so when I told him that *Hortensia* is French for hydrangea, he renamed her "Hydrangea." Along

with the new name, he invented a new role which she sensed he
wanted her to play. She began to play it to a fare-thee-well: part
outrageous flamboyance, part sophisticated woman of the
world, part smarty-pants, and part the commonsensical creature
that she really was. As Bennett Cerf once said about Moss's
magnetism, "People began living up to Moss's conceptions immediately and saw themselves for the rest of their days as Moss
recreated them."

The idea of doing a play for a honeymoon may not be traditional, but it captivated me. Moss was ever welcome at the Playhouse; he could always fill the theater. He was a wonderful actor,
and I learned a great deal about acting being on stage with him. I
played Maggie, the secretary, and I was pretty good.

Moss insisted on the romantic notion that we share a dressing
room, but after two weeks of watching him wrestle in an un-air-
conditioned dressing room with Sheridan Whiteside's beard I
swore I'd never do it again. The next time we did *The Man Who
Came to Dinner* we had separate rooms. (That time I played Lor-
raine, the temperamental actress, and I was terrible. How Moss
must have suffered over my inadequacy in the role; but good
sport that he was, he never showed his impatience with me.)

Natalie Schafer, who had been in many of Moss's plays, was in
the show with us. Without consulting me, Moss invited her to
stay at the farm, not only for the playing week, but for rehearsals
as well. Having a houseguest at the outset of our marriage created a certain strain. Gypsying around in the theater had hardly
trained me to be a good housekeeper, and I wasn't too sure I was
going to like this new role.

The first morning I came down to breakfast and found Natalie
there ahead of me. "Did you sleep well?" "Just fine, dear," she
said, "but now that you are in charge here, I want to tell you that
there is a special kind of pillow at Bloomingdale's that we're all
mad about." "Thank you," I said. "Is the coffee all right?" "Yes,
dear, but there is a divine coffee at . . ." she mentioned some
French food place I'd never heard of. "They will grind it to your

specification." "Thank you," I said, and wrote down the address, to be polite. A plate of eggs was put in front of her. She looked around helplessly. "The pepper grinder," she cried. "The *fresh* pepper grinder."

After two days I had a long list of items, from pillows to hangers to things to keep the mildew out and electric rods for the piano to keep the humidity in (or was it vice versa?) and I wouldn't have minded an electric rod for Schafer. But I forgave her a great deal; she was very good in the play.

Moss

For what they'd never told me of,
And what I never knew,
It was that all the time, my love,
Love would be merely you.
                    Rupert Brooke

I was once asked on a TV interview what I liked most about Moss. I said everything, and that was the truth. I was so proud he chose me. Whatever réclame I'd had as Kitty Carlisle was as nothing compared to being Mrs. Moss Hart.

I found him endlessly interesting and diverting and stimulating. He was such fun to live with. He made me laugh, which was irresistible. He found *me* funny, which was even more irresistible.

"Forked lightning," George Kaufman called him in the preface to the Modern Library edition of their plays, "only I'm not sure that it plays around his head. I think his head plays around the lightning, deliberately. The prodigality that marks the simplest moments of his life is matched by the prodigality of his mind. Ideas pour forth, and the simplest things of life are highlighted and made interesting. His is an instinctive sense of drama, on and off . . . There are times, I think, when he is not completely sure whether the curtain is up or down."

Moss's theatricality was not limited to the theater. When he went to a restaurant, he didn't just walk in: he made an entrance, his overcoat on his shoulders like a cloak; he looked like a great actor, and every head turned.

His sense of theater pervaded the house and the grounds. One day I looked out of my bedroom window and saw two enormous trucks filled with balled-and-burlapped trees crossing from opposite sides of the lawn. It was like Macbeth—the forest was coming to Dunsinane. I yelled for Moss and asked what was going on. "I didn't like the placement of those trees," he answered, "so I'm moving these over there and those over here."

There was an apple orchard as well, and Moss bought six sheep to crop the grass around the trees. It was a brilliant idea, but unfortunately it didn't work. The sheep refused to have anything to do with the orchard. I was constantly getting calls to bring the station wagon to pick them up from someone's front lawn.

It was a very large establishment, a bit rich for a man who relied on playwrighting for his income. After the phenomenal success of his play *Lady in the Dark,* with Gertrude Lawrence, Moss had added a swimming pool, a tennis court, and what he fondly called the Gertrude Lawrence Memorial Wing, which had a 40 by 30 playroom, a study for Moss, and four double guest rooms. There were five servants at the farm, plus two men to take care of the grounds. On the rare occasions when Moss and I dined alone, as we passed the kitchen windows after dinner he would peer in and say, "Business is better in the kitchen than it was in the dining room."

Although I hadn't thought of myself as a housekeeper, I did expect to be the Keeper of the Flame, there to protect my working genius, taking trays of food up to the door of his study and being the buffer between him and his public. I was in for a shock.

I discovered what all playwrights know from birth: their main objective is to provide legitimate or illegitimate distractions to keep them from work. When Moss was writing at the farm he worked in full view on the lawn, not with his back to the house but facing it, so anyone who went by could be hailed: "Any messages? Anyone phone? Could I have a glass of water?" Company was what he wanted, not solitude.

We had been married about a week when the cook left. Moss said to me, "I think it's time you took over the running of the household." I was horrified.

"Why?" I asked. "You've done it beautifully all these years."

"Did you expect to live in this house as a guest?" he demanded.

"Yes, I didn't expect anything to change."

MOSS

"Well, it's changed," he said. *"You* will take over the household."

Quick to make the best of a bad bargain, I said, "I'll hire the servants if you promise to fire them."

"It's a deal," Moss replied.

I accepted the responsibility of a big household and all the maintenance it entailed, but I was dogged by bad luck, bad judgment, and bad cooks. The first cook I hired served such a terrible dinner that when I put my plate down for our dog Skipper, even he would have nothing to do with it. "Darling," Moss said, "you're going to have to fire the cook."

"I'm going to have to fire her? You said *you'd* do the firing!"

"It's good for your character," he answered. I quickly discovered that anything Moss didn't want to do was good for my character.

I went to the kitchen and had a talk with the cook. When I came back, I said to Moss, "She won't go! She likes it here! *You* must talk to her." He went reluctantly, and so did she.

That summer I hired *nine* cooks. I was in my car all day long going to agencies in Bucks County. Moss kept inviting people and paid no attention to the fact that as the guests were coming in the front door, the cooks were going out the back.

Two guests I always looked forward to and who meant a great deal to Moss were his publisher, my old acquaintance Bennett Cerf, and his wife Phyllis Fraser. Bennett was a great storyteller and much loved as a television personality. But to take the real measure of the man you had to see him in his favorite role of publisher. He cared more about writers and books than anyone I've ever known.

Phyllis had been a movie starlet, but I never knew her in Hollywood. Although she was younger than I, I always welcomed her advice. Her heart-shaped face and wide blue eyes belied the depth of her quick intelligence.

Bennett and Phyllis were a combination of glamour, industry, and civic-mindedness. As far as we were concerned, they were always on the right side of every issue. They took me into their lives with the same love they had for Moss. If one can be "best friends" as adults, that we were.

After the week in *The Man Who Came to Dinner,* we moved back to Moss's New York pied-à-terre. I came with one suitcase, my makeup, and the firm determination not to be in anybody's way, particularly Charles's.

When we married, I never doubted it was forever. But I still kept my hotel apartment with my books and my piano, ostensibly as a studio. I lost three door keys to our apartment the first three months of our marriage, and I begged Charles not to tell Moss, for I knew what that Freudian would think. It takes time for two people who marry at our age to grow into each other in a way that becomes a real marriage.

It's usually the wife who wants a home and household goods to put in it, and the husband who needs domesticating. Mother always spoke of the lady who gave her husband lace curtains for Christmas. But Moss and I were total opposites in the way we had lived. I yearned for hotels and room service, while he loved hearth and home. When Moss went to the South Pacific with *The Man Who Came to Dinner,* he found the perfect solution to the discomforts of living in a war zone. Charles said that all his life he had wanted to try acting, so Moss arranged for Charles the butler to play John the butler. I think Moss was the first person to take his valet to war since Lord Cardigan took his bed, furniture, horses, and French chef to the Crimea.

Charles had many talents. He played excellent croquet, and often made a fourth if we needed one. I would sometimes see a guest looking quizzically at Charles when he was serving dinner, wondering where he had seen that face before. (We all have trouble placing someone out of context. Bennett Cerf said that one day he was accosted on the street by a very well-dressed, distinguished-looking gentleman who said to him, "Bennett! Why don't you ever return my phone calls?" "I'm so sorry,"

Bennett said apologetically; "let's have lunch someday!" "Don't be a damn fool," the man replied. "I'm your dentist!")

Charles was also a very good troublemaker, I found out, as my nine cooks departed in turn. I would be in the swing at the pool during my favorite time of day, in the late afternoon when the shadows lengthened on the lawn, and as Charles passed by, he would drop a bit of poison in my ear: "I think Cook is leaving, madam," he would murmur. Leaping up, I would yelp, "Why, Charles?" But he was already on his way to start another tong war in the kitchen. We never would have fired Charles, but galloping tuberculosis took him from us a year later.

Weekends were spent at the farm. We either had guests or dined out with neighbors every night, and we were rarely alone even in the city. "We've been married three months and I never get *you* anymore. Why can't we have those lovely long days of talk we had on your terrace in Miami?" I asked him. "You're absolutely right," Moss said. He was always very reasonable about everything. "We're going to turn over a new leaf. We'll have long evenings to ourselves, and tonight when we go back to New York, we'll have a quiet evening, just the two of us."

We drove to New York, and when we got to our apartment we came upon a terrible scene. We had been robbed. The burglars must have been there all weekend. I had never seen so many cigarette butts ground into a carpet. Drawers had been emptied in the middle of the floor. They had taken all our wedding presents; there wasn't a spoon left in the place.

By the time the police finally left, it was past 4 A.M.

"Mossie," I said, "you didn't really have to stage a burglary just to prove that we'll *never* be alone!"

There was one wedding present the burglars didn't get because it was in Moss's back pocket. Edna Ferber once wrote, in *Stage* magazine, about Moss's notorious love of luxury: ". . . He is monogrammed in the most improbable places. Just as he stands he is worth his weight in monogrammed gold bullion; gold gallus-buckles, gold belt buckle, gold garters, gold-and-seal billfold, gold pencil, gold pen, gold-and-platinum cigarette case, gold bottle-stoppers."

The one thing he didn't have was a gold tobacco pouch, so I asked Cartier to make me one to give Moss for a wedding present. Moss wanted to wear it in his hip pocket, but he didn't want a bulge under his jacket. Cartier agreed to make a wooden model, and Moss went for a fitting. The salesman brought out the wooden case on a red velvet cushion and solemnly presented it to us. Moss tried it on. "Bulges too much," he said. "It needs hollowing a bit." After two fittings Moss pronounced it perfect. He was the only man in New York to have a bruised hip from a solid gold tobacco pouch.

Moss never forgot the "dark brown taste of poverty." As he wrote in *Light Up the Sky,* some people born poor pinch their pennies "till the eagle flies back to the mint with a double rupture." Not Moss. He lived like an Indian potentate. "Look how it was then, and see how it is now." It was a leitmotif throughout his whole life. The difference filled him with constant wonder. I found his enjoyment of all the good things he was able to provide enormously touching. Going to California in our luxurious drawing room on the Twentieth Century Limited, he would look out of the window when we went through the Bronx and scan the tenements looking for his old house. "There," he'd say, "that's where we lived." I was never quite sure which house he meant, but I got the idea.

Standing in our beautiful swimming pool at the farm on a hot summer day, he would gleefully relive a time, gone but not forgotten. "It's five o'clock," he would fantasize; "I'm getting into the subway on Eighteenth Street. So is the rest of New York, and we're all taking the local. The first stop is Twenty-third Street; the second is Twenty-eighth Street;" and he would name every stop on the way to his station in the Bronx. Then he would describe the next scene: "I am trudging home from the subway, and my mother is hanging out of an upper window, watching for me. 'What's for dinner, Ma?' I call up. 'Lamb stew.' Lamb stew, on a boiling hot night! 'Well, I think I'll take a shower.' 'No,' my mother answers, 'Mrs. Steinberg had to give her cat a bath and the shower's all stopped up.' "

The first winter at the farm I found out how much Christmas meant to Moss. In his autobiography, *Act One*, he wrote poignantly about the time his father took him to the pushcarts in the Bronx to buy him a Christmas present and found, when they got there, that the money he had scraped together was not enough to buy even the simplest toy.

Moss began his preparations around the fifteenth of December; by the twentieth, the presents were piled high under the tree, and the house was decorated with wreaths, boughs, and ornaments. I thought it was beautiful, but Moss said, "There's one thing missing: we need a big snowman just outside the front door to welcome guests, and there's one in the window of that shop in Doylestown. Take the station wagon and get it." "Moss," I said, "it's five days before Christmas; what makes you think that shop is going to dismantle its window display and give me its snowman?" "I know you can do it," he said.

I must confess that if Moss had told me I could jump over the moon, I'd have had a go at it, so I drove to Doylestown.

I don't remember what I said. I don't think I said my husband was mad and if I didn't accomplish what he asked, he'd beat me —I used that gambit another time, when I called up the head of IBM, Thomas Watson himself, and explained that my husband had such an immediate need of the newest electric typewriter that if I failed to get it, he would become violent, and I couldn't answer for his sanity or mine.

This time I think I appealed to their fondness for Moss and the fact that he was a very good customer. Then I paid them an exorbitant price and triumphantly carried my snowman home to Moss.

The privations of his youth had given Moss an obsession for shopping. When he walked into a store, he said, "I feel as if every bit of merchandise on every shelf is trembling with desire to belong to me."

He was as generous to others as he was to himself. Being a writer, he loved to give me presents he could write on. For our first Christmas together he gave me a gold medallion with Rupert Brooke's verse on one side; on the other side were the lines: "To see her is a poem/ to hear her is a tune/ to know her an intemperance,/ as innocent as June." I don't know who wrote the verse. I like to think it was Moss. He had the medallion cut in half. One half went on my bracelet; the other he wore always on a chain around his neck. On Valentine's Day he gave me a gold heart inscribed: "I love little Kitty/ Her coat is so warm;/ And if you don't kick her/ she'll do you no harm." For our sixth anniversary, another gold disc for my bracelet: "What larks, my darling, what larks!"

Moss also wanted to buy houses wherever we went: a cottage in Jamaica, a flat in London, Louis B. Mayer's palace by the Pacific Ocean. As it was, we had a house in Palm Springs, one at the Jersey shore, a farm in Bucks County, and an apartment in New York—once three at the same time. "We live like the Whitneys," I said, "with one difference. Betsey Whitney has stewards and housekeepers; all you have is me."

I was trying to be a good housekeeper, but I was trying harder to be the inspiration, the woman behind the artist. Moss already had a string of successes. Although I didn't say to myself, "I hope I will inspire Moss to write great plays and achieve even more success," nevertheless I think somewhere in my subconscious that's what I hoped for.

When Moss and I went to Boston for the out-of-town tryout of *Christopher Blake,* as the wife of the author I saw the risks and uncertainties of the theater from the other side of the footlights.

Moss had a regular routine for tryouts. He reserved a three-room suite at the Ritz—living room, bedroom, and a room for visiting play doctors and advisers. In those days everyone went out of town to help; friends, knowledgeable professionals, and all those wiseacres from the theater known as the "wrecking crew," who rushed back to New York with malicious glee to report, "The show's in trouble." Moss and George were among the first called to help with a play in trouble, but they never admitted to writing a line of anyone else's script. They were once asked to go out of town to look at Clare Boothe Luce's play *The Women*. Moss said he'd never seen a playwright in trouble sitting in bed with a breakfast tray, wearing an ermine bedjacket, a blue ribbon in her hair, and a diamond clip on her nightgown.

When we got to the Ritz, Moss said, "You call the valet to unpack my wardrobe trunk, and I'll go to S. S. Pierce [Boston's famous grocer] and get something for the room. Tell the hotel to set up a card table in the living room for the food."

When Moss returned, it was like an African safari, with bell-boys marching in single file like bearers, the wooden boxes carried on their heads. The card table I had ordered didn't begin to hold the things Moss had bought—we needed two more.

There had been a triumphant run-through of *Christopher Blake* on a bare stage in front of an invited audience the day before we left New York. I felt my dream of being a part of Moss's continuing success and even greater fame was about to be realized.

In the theater you don't dare count your chickens. The first thing that went wrong was the revolving stage. At the dress rehearsal in Boston something stuck in the mechanism, and the turntable started grinding up the stage. It was a terrible sight; the stage hands stood by as we watched the destruction. Moss knew only too well what this would mean in lost time and money. He ran up the center aisle, and in despair threw himself face down on the carpet, beating the floor with his fists. I ran after him and knelt down beside him. I had never in my life seen anything like it. I had no idea what to do, so I did nothing but pat his shoulder. I felt completely helpless.

Unfortunately, *Christopher Blake* was one of those plays that are swamped by too much and too elaborate scenery. The audience in New York had seen a better play. Sometimes imagination is so much more effective than canvas and wood and paint. Maybe the turntable that ate up the set had the right idea.

After Boston we went on to Wilmington, and it was downhill the whole way. It didn't help that there was a Shriners' convention at the hotel. At night while Moss was trying to rewrite the Shriners were at their rowdy worst, drunkenly running up and down the halls, barging into our suite, and throwing firecrackers into all the bathtubs. However, Moss used the Shriners to advantage in his next play, *Light Up the Sky,* and he drew a devastating vignette of their loutish behavior. But that didn't help *Christopher Blake,* which never recaptured the magic of that last run-through and eventually failed in New York. I didn't tell Moss, but I began to wonder if I was a jinx instead of an inspiration.

Reading your own bad notices is a horrible experience, but when I had to stand by and watch Moss suffer, it was unbearable. I made a painful discovery: in a good marriage, if one partner is hurt, the other bleeds.

Two years later *Light Up the Sky* was ready for its Boston tryout. This time, with more experience as the wife of a playwright, I expected the worst.

The play was a fable about theater people and an opening night in Boston. It dealt with human behavior in success and failure, and the title came from a quotation in "The Idle Jeste," by someone called Old Skroob, thought to be an Elizabethan: "Mad, sire? Ah, yes—mad indeed, but observe how they do light up the sky!" The quotation in fact was made up by Moss, Jerry Chodorov, and me one afternoon over a soda at Schrafft's. Old Skroob was Brooks Atkinson spelled backwards (sort of).

Once we got in front of an audience, it was obvious that there was some trouble in the last act. After the performance, conferences took place in clumps of two or three all over our hotel suite and in the halls, or with everybody all at once in the living room. The suite was filled with well-wishers and not so well-wishers. Moss was not only the author, he was also the director; and when changes were made, he had to write them, give them to the cast the next day, and redirect the scenes that were altered. People came and went, worn out and bleary-eyed, but Moss plowed on and rewrote and redirected an act and a half within ten days. It was an experience that made him swear he'd never again be both writer and director of the same play.

On opening night in New York we went to the theater and stood in the back as we always did. Moss said that fifteen minutes after the curtain goes up a silent bell rings in the audience, and they either know what the play's about and they like it, or they don't know what it's about and even if they did they wouldn't like it. This time the play started to catch fire. As the curtain came down, Moss did what he always did when he was sure the play was some kind of a hit. He took me by the hand and we went down the side aisle and stood where we could look back at the audience. They were all smiling and applauding.

Light Up the Sky was a success. Finally I felt that I might bring Moss good luck.

With the unpredictability of the theater, the next play, *Miss Liberty,* was a failure, even though it had everything going for it: Moss as director, a lovely score by Irving Berlin, and a book by one of our best playwrights, Robert Sherwood.

But there was one good and lasting result. Ellin Berlin and I formed an instant bond. She is a marvelous friend, loyal to the point of ferocity. She is one of the few women I have ever known who have an original turn of mind, and I love her. Our friendship never wavered, and a few years later she became godmother to my daughter Cathy.

WE didn't want to wait to have children. Moss was forty-one, and I felt time was nipping at my heels, so he and I set joyfully about starting a family. I was almost three months along in my first pregnancy when Moss decided we would have another honeymoon, in Palm Springs, visiting Darryl and Virginia Zanuck.

When I was in California making movies, I was so insulated that I knew less about Hollywood life than any teenage reader of *Photoplay*. But when I went there married to Moss, I had a passport to movie moguldom. Darryl Zanuck was the head of Twentieth Century-Fox.

We went out on the Superchief, and I quickly realized that "order," Moss's watchword, also applied to trains. Five minutes after we boarded, our compartment was a home away from home, the cushions arranged just so on the seats, books on the table, and Moss's pipes lined up in perfect symmetry on the windowsill.

The train was a moving house party. The club and dining cars were the focal points for socializing. Tycoons, actors, and writers made deals and dates for dinner, and one and all played gin rummy. At dinner we were offered *specialités de l'* Atchison, Topeka & Santa Fe—steaks, well-aged, out of Kansas City, and trout fresh from the Rocky Mountains.

The second night on the train we dined with the screenwriter Nunnally Johnson, a raconteur and wit. Knowing Nunnally was happily married, Moss confided to him that his biggest worry in marriage was not running out of conversation or sexual interest; his greatest fear was telling the same story in front of the same audience—me. It violated his sense of drama. "Had the same trouble when I married," Nunnally told him, "so to amuse Dorris I vary my stories each time I tell them." Moss followed his advice, and the first story he changed he completely ruined. "Darling," I said, "it may violate your sense of drama, but it doesn't bother me a bit. I love to hear you talk, and you could read from the telephone book as far as I'm concerned." I begged him to go back to the original version, which he was only too happy to do. (Years later, on Edward Murrow's show "Person to Person," Ed asked Moss if I was a good audience. "She's great," Moss said, "she listens to every anecdote as if she's never heard it before!")

We arrived in Palm Springs on a Saturday. There was a star-studded group staying at the Zanucks', and that evening more guests were coming to dinner.

We were dressing for dinner, and suddenly I felt very strange. Then I was aware that something terrible was happening. "I'm losing the baby," I said to Moss.

My body, which had always been my instrument, my means of support, and my joy; which had always done my mind's bidding, was playing me false. I was betrayed inside my own skin. I was in a rage.

I heard a tough, sullen voice issue from my lips: "Get a doctor; and don't take me to a Palm Springs hospital, I'll die there!"

Poor Mossie, he was a new bridegroom, with no experience of marriage, much less a miscarriage. He called my mother in New York, who said, "Don't be an ass; call an ambulance and get her to a hospital."

When the ambulance came, my worst fears were realized. Instead of paramedics, the attendants were two Palm Springs policemen in cowboy boots and hats, with guns strapped to their hips. By now the cocktail hour was in full swing in the Zanucks' huge playhouse, through which the cortège—Moss, cops, stretcher and I—would have to pass, and I balked. "I will not be carried out past Merle Oberon, Joan Crawford, the Louis Jourdans, and all the others." So Moss and Darryl arranged for me to be carried out in solitary splendor.

I was able to leave the hospital three days after the miscarriage, and Darryl invited us back to his house to stay for as long as we liked.

Virginia Zanuck was a sweet and gentle hostess. Darryl wanted Moss around not only for his charm and verve, but because he was a champion croquet player.

Croquet was an important part of the life of our friends in the East. The Long Island group was headed by Herbert Bayard

Swope, Averell Harriman, and Mrs. Emerson of Bromo-Seltzer fame, who had her croquet turf imported from Ireland by the square foot. The Bucks County contingent was headed by Moss and George Kaufman. Our croquet sets came from England, and it was no children's game—the wickets were wicked, and the games went on for hours. It was chess on the lawn.

Croquet spread to California and was played with the same seriousness. One day at the Zanucks', Virginia and I were sitting at the pool when the maids came running: "Come quick, Mr. Hart and Mr. Zanuck are going to kill each other!" We rushed to the croquet lawn, where Moss and Darryl were shaking their mallets like fists over each other's heads. The fight was over who had hit whose ball last. After that a blackboard was set up to keep the record straight and avoid murder.

Hollywood was a purdah-like society. Darryl never spoke to me except when my seat at the dinner table was at the other end. Then he figured that by addressing me from that angle he commanded the attention of all the guests. Women were regarded as commodities rather like cotton futures or pork bellies. They were not invited to play croquet, except *in extremis;* only two were really welcome, Dorothy Rodgers and Minnie (Mrs. Vincent) Astor, and they played better than the men.

Darryl had more than croquet on his mind when he invited us to stay. He wanted Moss to write a screenplay based on the first bestseller about anti-Semitism, Laura Hobson's *Gentleman's Agreement.*

The book and its subject fascinated Moss. He told his agent, Irving Lazar, not to argue about the money. This was an issue of burning importance.

Moss was quite unprepared for the pressure from some of the Jewish studio heads to scrap it. He received phone call after phone call urging him to give up the project. "We're doing okay. Why not let sleeping dogs lie?" they said. "Let's not stir up a lot of trouble."

Moss went right ahead with the screenplay. He had a real

stubborn streak when it came to resisting pressure he felt was either unfair or unethical. For him it was a labor of love. The movie won many Academy Awards and had the success it deserved. The studio underpaid Moss so badly that to assuage their consciences, when we left Los Angeles they gave him a whopping big wooden-bodied Chrysler station wagon as a bonus.

By the time Elia Kazan, who was directing the film, and Moss had to start work together, I was well enough to leave the cocoon-like existence we had had in Palm Springs. We were going to Hollywood to stay with Otto Preminger. I thought I was looking forward to it, but my apprehension of going back to a place where my career had fallen apart was so intense that I was seized with a thundering headache. I never have headaches, and certainly not psychosomatic headaches. Even when my troubles with my mother were at their worst, I didn't retreat into illness; but the day we left for Hollywood, I was blinded by pain.

Through his analysis, Moss had great knowledge and feeling for other people's psyches. That night at Otto's he talked to me with all the compassion and sensitivity that he could always muster for someone else's problems. He made me dredge up my failure in Hollywood; the humiliation of being paid off and sent home by the studio; the feeling of being pushed and pulled and manipulated by Mother and Ed. He tried to explain that I had created a great cloak labeled Kitty Carlisle, which I had wrapped around myself because I believed that the real me, underneath, Catherine Conn, was nobody. He said there was someone under that cloak worth knowing, who didn't have to *try* to be somebody, but who *was* somebody. "You cannot depend on wrapping yourself in another cloak labeled Mrs. Moss Hart. You don't need to do that either."

We talked all through the night, and I understood what he meant. Moss said I made great psychic leaps. As dawn was breaking, he said, "Tomorrow night we're going to a big party, the first of many here, and I will not stick to you as if we were joined at the hip. You're going to do fine. Besides, you must swim off on your own, or we'll have nothing to talk about when we get home." It may sound like oversimplification, but I began to believe in who I was, and I started enjoying Hollywood. I met new people with no self-consciousness, and I stopped worrying about what they thought of me.

My acceptance of California and what it had to offer brought me the friendship of the grandest of Hollywood's *grandes dames,* Irene Mayer Selznick. She was Louis B.'s daughter and David O.'s wife. She is a fascinating woman, a rare bird. The day she asked me to go for a walk I told Moss I felt I had come of age. I loved her from the start. Her counsel and unfailing encouragement all these years caused me to say to her, "With your head on my shoulders, I should go far."

WHEN Moss finished writing *Gentleman's Agreement,* we returned to New York, and I was pregnant again. This time I grew bigger and bigger and happier and happier, and when I could no longer tell the front of me from the back, and I was filled with the future Christopher Hart, I was also filled with joy. I loved being pregnant; I felt I was was doing something terribly important without the slightest effort on my part. For the first time in my life, all I had to do was just sit there, while a baby was being made.

Once I was married, Mother didn't attempt to run my life, but that's not to say that the umbilical cord had snapped. There was "that twitch upon the thread," via the daily telephone call. If I didn't call her, she called me. She sometimes reduced me to a tearful five-year-old within minutes over some imagined slight.

It wasn't always on the telephone; occasionally it was face-to-face. Mother and Ed came to the farm one weekend when I was big with Christopher. She started in on me just after dinner, for what transgression I cannot remember, but I stood in front of the fireplace crying while her words poured over me like hot glue. When she got wound up she could go on and on like a political rabble-rouser. I couldn't answer her or defend myself; I just wept and wept. Moss and Ed were speechless. She finally flounced up the stairs to bed.

"I'm going up to talk to her," Moss announced. "Don't, don't, I beg of you," Ed pleaded. "Don't interfere between those girls. You'll only make matters worse."

Moss didn't stop to argue. Half an hour later he returned and said, "She's coming down." Why didn't I ask what he said to her? I'd give anything now to know, but he didn't tell me. When Mother came back it was as if nothing had happened. "Deal 'em up, let's play some gin," she said.

I finally had a champion who could take her on, and I was free to love her without resentment.

Mother and Ed were with us for all the usual holidays, and they were included in opening nights and all celebrations. But by now they lived their own life. They shared friends, bridge, music, and fishing, which Mother, ever surprising, adored. Ed would pick her up at 6:45 in the morning in front of the Ritz Tower. She'd be standing on the curb in her fishing outfit— pants, shirt, and cap, a sight that none of her friends at the Regency Bridge Club would have conceivably recognized, and off they'd go for a day's fishing.

He must have loved her very much. I knew he wanted to be a judge, like his grandfather, but he sacrificed his ambition because of their relationship, which was of course well known.

With a baby on the way we couldn't stay in the pied-à-terre, it was too small. Moss asked me if I'd like to live at the farm. I said I was too young to live in the country, and when I got old I'd be too old to live in the country. So he set out to get an apartment with two bedrooms. He found one in the old Pulitzer house on Seventy-third Street. He took it without showing it to me. It was still too small, but it was beautiful. Moss began decorating with a vengeance.

Moss had a lot of nice things, but we were short on good paintings. I knew why.

George Gershwin had said to Moss one day in the early thirties, "My-Cousin-Botkin-the-painter is going to Paris and says that for ten thousand dollars he can put together a fine collection of pictures. I'm going to give him ten thousand dollars and if *you* give him ten thousand dollars, he'll do the same for you." This was at the beginning of Moss's career and he didn't have ten thousand dollars to spare. Apparently My-Cousin-Botkin-the-painter knew what he was doing. George wound up with a stunning collection of Impressionists: Pascin, Modigliani, Rouault, and Picasso ("The Absinthe Drinker").

Now the time had come to give up my apartment, and I moved my books and my piano to Seventy-third Street.

The first of the only two fights Moss and I ever had was over that piano. It was installed in the living room, and Moss proceeded to adorn it with an enormous, heavy, five-branched red Bohemian glass candelabra with five glass globes and dangling ornaments. I took one look and said, "You can't put that thing with all those prisms on my piano." "It's always stood on *my* piano," he said. *"Your* piano," I said scornfully, "was an old spinet, an ornament. Mine is my work area, and I've never allowed anything on it, not photographs, not even a Spanish shawl" (not since I got rid of the one my mother used to put on every piano in every house we ever had). "Anyway," I went on with great assurance, "when I play it will tinkle."

When Moss was decorating he hated being thwarted. His nostrils flared, and he looked for all the world like an angry thoroughbred. We were standing on opposite sides of the piano, with the candelabra between us, and I was panting with fury. "Try it," he said. We looked at each other, and each took a deep breath. Then I said, "I don't care who is right, I love you." I sat down at the piano and played a few arpeggios, and the damned thing never tinkled one tinkle.

That became our watchword: "I don't care who is right, I love you."

On January 14, 1948, Christopher was born. He took his time coming, about twenty-two hours' worth. Mother wanted to be kept informed, but after the fourth phone call her fear expressed itself in anger, and she said, "For God's sake, don't call me again until the baby is here!" There was no natural childbirth then, and husbands were kept out of the delivery room, so Ed came to the hospital to keep Moss's mind off what was going on in the next room. He chose to tell him a story whose length was appropriate, but whose content was outside Moss's field of interest. Ed was a passionate Wagnerite, and he felt that interest or no, Moss should be educated in the lore of the Ring. He went nonstop from the beginning of *Das Rheingold* to the end of *Götterdämmerung*. By the time Chris was born I don't know who was more exhausted, the father or the mother.

The next summer I did a week of *O Mistress Mine* at the Bucks County Playhouse. Moss loved to invent instant theatrical tradition. This time he said theater families always presented their firstborn child to the audience at the Saturday matinee. He even wrote a little speech for me: "Ladies and gentlemen: will you indulge me in an old theatrical tradition? It is the custom, among theater folk, to have their babies take a bow with their mothers in the sentimental fashion of the stage. Will you allow me to present Christopher Hart to you for his first bow? Thank you." It was a bit long-winded, but heartfelt, and I dutifully presented Chris—in arms—to a cheering public.

Pregnant again—we had to move again. Moss said he'd look, but he promised he would never take a place that I hadn't seen.

Soon after, he came home and announced in dramatic tones that he had to sign up for an apartment right away. Moss always had to sign "right away." I never knew whether it was because he had to own whatever it was "right away," or whether it was because he always walked into an either/or crisis "right away." I got dressed and off we went to 1185 Park Avenue.

It was the antithesis of cramped quarters. There were fifteen rooms; a curving staircase leading from a solarium (perfect for trailing black velvet); a bedroom which could have accommodated our whole former apartment; terraces big enough to bicycle on; and above all Irene Selznick's dictum: "a wing for the children." I fell in love with it at first sight, and Moss signed the lease. Our financial status hadn't changed—Moss was just doing what he always did, acquiring what he wanted and then trying to earn the money to pay for it. I was no more help decorating this one than I had been before. I had to take to my bed to save the child we were awaiting. Once again Moss took charge, and after Catherine Carlisle Hart's birth I walked downstairs to a fully furnished apartment.

(Moss's predilection for decorating hit a new high some years later when he went to London for rehearsals of *My Fair Lady*. He arrived at the Savoy Hotel early in the morning. Herman Levin, the show's producer, had reserved a suite for him. Moss had not stayed there before, and he was expecting something very elegant and grand. He took one look around, turned to the morning-coated assistant manager and said, "It won't do. Get your decorator and your painters." The manager protested: "Mr. Hart, it's terribly early." "The earlier the better," Moss said. The hastily summoned decorator realized immediately that she and Moss were kindred spirits. She took him right down to the storeroom to pick out the furniture. The only complaint she uttered was, "Don't you think you're getting a bit *lampy*, Mr. Hart?" Moss said Americans like lots of light. The entire suite was refurnished and repainted within twenty-four hours, and was long known as the Moss Hart Suite.)

The months I had to stay in bed before Cathy was born were some of the happiest I have ever spent. I could live my whole life in bed like Proust and Elizabeth Barrett—read, receive friends, telephone, love—and the best part was that Moss was there in and out of my room all day. We did the *Times* crossword puzzles together, and we finished them, which I'd never been able to do. I knew mythology and foreign words, while Moss knew everything else. At night he had his dinner on a tray with me. I begged him to go out to dinner once in a while to bring me some new gossip, but he said he really would rather stay with me.

We even had breakfast together in bed at first, but Moss decided it might be dangerous to our health because of the telephone. We had incoming calls at breakfast, and as we passed the receiver back and forth, the cord would become entangled around Moss's neck and mine. I don't think he really liked to eat in bed anyhow; most men don't.

I suppose to some women having a husband who works at home is difficult. "How can you stand a man who's around the house all day?" Mother asked. I adored it. I resented every moment that he wasn't with me.

Moss liked my company so much that I complained once, half seriously, to Lillian Hellman, "I love Moss working at home, except that it cuts me out of giving ladies' lunches." "You're crazy," she said. "Ladies' lunches are the worst form of entertaining!"

Even though I disagreed with Lillian, she was dear to my heart. After all, it was at her house that Moss's and my romance had begun. Lillian was quarrelsome, but she never fought with me. My guess is that she didn't think I was worthy of her steel.

MOTHER wasn't at all grandmotherly with our children. She called them "my little relatives," and they in turn called her Heidi (short for Hydrangea). When they were infants, if it was feeding time when she came to visit me she'd stand over me or the nurse, take the bottle, and shove it into the baby's mouth. She never sat down and she never took off her black suede gloves or the bracelets she wore over them. I shuddered, but of course I never said a thing, and it did the children no harm.

Moss, who used to go to the farm in a car encumbered by nothing more than a briefcase, was now surrounded with cribs, potty chairs, and baby carriages. Life had changed radically since his bachelor days. Far from feeling burdened by the role of pater familias, he gloried in it.

With the huge apartment and two children to take care of, I had to look for some proper household help. I got a couple that came from England.

We nearly didn't keep them. John couldn't seem to remember anything, even forgetting to put the bell on the dining room table, and Moss would say every evening, "John, I'm giving you the No Bell prize." After about ten days we decided we'd have to let them go. "Let's wait until after dinner to tell them," I said.

That night we had guests. In the middle of an anecdote about Ivor Novello, the English playwright and composer, Moss called down the table to me, "What was the name of that friend of Ivor's?" I had no idea, but John, who was passing behind my chair, whispered, "Bobby Andrews, madam." "Bobby Andrews," I piped up. Later that night Moss said, "How can you fire a man who comes up on cue with a name like that?" John and Ruth stayed with us for years.

In New York we were busy every night, either giving parties or having dinner with friends. Moss had many more friends to present to me than I had to introduce to him. We went through the usual stages until "yours" and "mine" became "ours."

I nearly lost two at one clip because Moss could be quite outrageous. Some friends of mine came to New York from their country place to have tea and meet Moss. They arrived with a station wagon full of pheasants they had shot, and their conversation about great houses and shoots and beaters and the sport in general went on a bit too long for Moss's taste. When they finally ran out of steam, Moss said, "When I lived in the Bronx we used to have the same kind of sport. It was called a relative shoot, and we used to beat the relatives out of the tenements." It was quite a while before I saw those friends again.

Two of Moss's friends who quickly became "ours" were Leonora and Arthur Hornblow. Of course I'd heard about Arthur when I was at Paramount, but I'd never met him. He was a producer/director (*Witness for the Prosecution* and *Oklahoma*), one of the most urbane and cultivated men around. Leonora was a novelist, and Moss thought her writing reflected her own grace and charm. We and the Cerfs and the Hornblows loved to take trips together. I discovered that Leonora had total recall, and I nominated her our group's historian. The six of us seemed to have more fun and laugh more together than at any other time.

Moss and I also did a lot of play-hopping, which meant popping into a theater where we'd already seen the play, and taking in a special musical number or scene. It was like being part of an elite club.

Moss directed my clothes the way he directed a play. I happily followed every one of his notions. He was always getting people to dress me up. He had Bill Blass design me wonderful creations, and the milliner Mr. John created elaborate tulle and jeweled headdresses. Costume jewelry adorned even bathing suits. I had to pass inspection when I was dressed. If I had my jewelry on crooked, he'd say, "Back to wardrobe, you're antisymmetrical."

Mother said I had such faith in Moss's taste that if he told me to walk down Fifth Avenue with a mud pie on my head, I'd do it and feel I was well dressed.

As for me, I was living within a circle of people who created an atmosphere of excitement, whose imagination gave rise to spur-of-the-moment doings just for the fun of it, who turned ordinary life into wild hilarity by simply looking at it from a different point of view. Work was serious, and they worked very hard, but life was merry.

One of the circle was Edna Ferber. She had already written *So Big*, *Show-Boat*, *Cimmarron*, as well as plays with George Kaufman:

Dinner at Eight, Stage Door, The Royal Family. She had never been married, and her friends discussed her sex life quite as freely as if they were talking about Elizabeth, the so-called virgin Queen. Was she or wasn't she? Had Edna tried it at least once, back when she was a reporter in Chicago? Moss wasn't sure she could have written the way she did without experience.

The first time Moss took me to Edna's house for the weekend he made up one of his scenarios to amuse me. "She will greet us. I will put out a cigarette in an ashtray. She'll wait two minutes and then she will get up and take it to the kitchen and bring it back clean. Then she'll show us to our room, saying all the while, 'But Moss will hate it; it's too pink, too feminine, oh dear!' No amount of reassurance will help. She's house-proud and a very persnickety housekeeper. She'll tell you to take a shower if you're going to swim in the pool. 'I am a writer,' will be the start of many sentences. She'll want the weekend guests out of the house by Sunday afternoon so she can get to work Monday morning. When we come down to breakfast on Sunday, she'll be standing at the bottom of the stairs with a sheaf of letters in her hand. 'Will you mail these in town after lunch?' If we don't take the hint to leave right after lunch and we go back to our room, we'll find the beds stripped." Moss wasn't just being funny; it was exactly as he said it would be.

I loved Edna; her eccentricities amused me, and I admired her work, which I think has been underestimated. She treated me with unfailing courtesy and affection.

Edna's fame was not diminished by the length and the intensity of her feuds. Many years earlier, when they had had a fight, she hadn't spoken to Moss for six months. After they finally made up, he took her out to dinner. As he deposited her on her doorstep she said to him, "It's always nice to have dinner with an attractive young man, but you realize Moss Hart died for me six months ago!"

Another feud was brewing. Edna wanted to make her book *Saratoga Trunk* into a musical, and she asked Moss to work on it

with her. She was determined to have Rodgers and Hammerstein write the score. Moss knew that Rodgers and Hammerstein
already had three projects lined up, so he recommended Harold
Arlen, who might be available. But Edna closed her mind and
preferred to live in her hope, however unrealistic.

A script was posted to Rodgers and Hammerstein. They called
very quickly and said exactly what Moss had predicted: thanks
but no thanks.

Moss called Edna to tell her of their decision and said: "Now
let's get on with Harold Arlen." "Who?" said Edna. "Who is this
young man? Have I ever heard anything he's ever done?" Considering that she was talking about the man who'd written "Over
the Rainbow" and "Stormy Weather," Moss lost patience.
"Edna," he said, "I've been talking about Arlen for months and
now you pretend you've never heard of him." He left the telephone and said to me, "I simply cannot work with her."

Moss went to see Edna to tell her this and came home shaken
by her fury. Because of her faulty recollection of Moss's words at
the height of their interview, Edna harbored deep resentment.
She insisted he'd said she was an old granite-face; what he really
said was that she was as stubborn as a piece of granite.

The *Saratoga Trunk* fight went on for years. In the middle of
this imbroglio, Moss took our daughter Cathy, age five, to *Peter
Pan*. They went backstage to see Mary Martin, and in the corridor they had the ill luck to run into Edna. They passed each
other without a word, but Cathy must have noticed something
about the way they looked at each other, for she said, in that flat,
penetrating voice that small children sometimes have, "Who
was that?" Moss, without missing a beat, said, "That, my child,
was Captain Hook!"

What Moss said about Edna was just as bad as her description
of Alexander Woollcott. At the height of one of their battles she
called him "that baby-faced New Jersey Nero who wears his
pinafore like an imperial toga."

There were quotable phrases about her too. She threatened to sue a friend who said she looked like a buffalo. "How will you defend yourself?" the friend was asked. "That's easy," he replied, "I'll simply bring a buffalo into court!"

In spite of their rifts, Moss and Edna missed each other so much that they were obviously looking for an excuse to make up. One day they both went to have tea with Rebecca West. Within the time of their handshake four years of silent anger were swept away.

If Moss had known how Edna really regarded him, he never would have fought with her, and he never would have allowed *her* wrath to harden.

Edna made her feelings about Moss quite clear at his memorial service: "When I first met Moss Hart he had just been discovered hidden in the bulrushes. A year later, a tall gangling youth, stunned by his own spectacular success, possessed of an extraordinary zest for life, he had been turned loose on the slippery race track that was Broadway and New York and the world of creative writing. To his amazement he found himself one of a hardworking, realistic, laughing, talented group made up of people such as George Kaufman, Lillian Hellman, Marc Connelly, Aleck Woollcott, Dorothy Parker, Herbert Swope, Helen Hayes, George Gershwin and many others. Moss was like a young spindling colt turned out on the track to compete with Sea Biscuit and Man O' War. He promptly surged ahead and outdistanced many of them. He was younger than most; much younger than some. For me he was, I suppose, the son I'd never had—you know, mine son de doctor."

I felt I was in a continuous drawing-room comedy. Conversation was an art, and people sharpened their epigrams ahead of time. Once in a while I would hear Moss muttering to himself while he was shaving. I'm convinced he was orchestrating the conversations for our dinner party that evening.

In the beginning I wasn't quite ready for the high-powered cast. Moss's friends were the crème de la crème of the theatrical and literary world. At the first really important dinner party we gave in New York, just after Chris was born, our guests were Noël Coward, George Kaufman, Edna Ferber, and Laura Hobson. It was fast company even for champion talkers. I enjoyed listening, but I couldn't seem to get into the conversation. Nobody spoke to me except Laura Hobson, who tossed me a conversational bone. "How's the baby?" she asked, as if that were my only interest in life—and without waiting for my answer, she quickly turned back to the others.

After they left I said to Moss in high dudgeon. "I will not sit through another dinner party at my own house feeling left out!" Moss looked at me coolly. "My dear," he said, "if you think that at some point every head at the table is going to turn in your direction and someone is going to say, 'Your turn, Kitty!' you're quite mistaken. You have to push your way into the conversation like the rest of us."

There was one occasion where the conversation got away from Moss. There was another impressive group: Aldous Huxley, the Richard Rodgers, Edna Ferber, Irene Selznick, Garson Kanin, and Ruth Gordon. Huxley started telling us about his experiments with LSD and the effect it had on his heightened perception of color and light and shadow. This led to a discussion of other chemical substances—namely, sleeping pills.

Everyone started talking at once: "Which ones do *you* take? The red? The yellow? The white with the blue band?" Moss rapped the table for attention. This obviously was not one of his planned topics. "Do you realize there are youngsters who dream of New York, going to dinner parties like this to listen to profound talk of the theater, the world and the hereafter, and all they hear is, 'Are the yellow ones better than the red ones, and do you prefer aspirin to Bufferin?' "

That certainly stopped the conversation. As the hostess, I was frantically casting around in my head for something to fill the silence when someone mentioned Virginia Woolf and *Orlando*. I knew about Virginia Woolf, but the only Orlando I'd ever heard of was in Florida. So I said, "What or who is Orlando?" and all heads swiveled in my direction to tell me. I learned a good lesson: don't stay silent or pretend you know. Ask! Everyone will want to enlighten you.

Moss encouraged me to keep my hand in as a performer. He told me, "You don't marry one kind of woman and try to turn her into another, because the woman you loved disappears and you wonder what happened to her."

I was moseying along at an antique show one day when a woman came up to me and invited me to speak at her ladies' club in Bryn Mawr. I went looking for Moss, who as usual was buying everything in sight, and asked his advice. "You must do it," he said. "You're a creature of routine, a terrible stick-in-the-mud. If it were left up to you they'd never have invented the wheel. Anyway, George Bernard Shaw said everyone should shake up their lives every seven years."

"Well, that's all very well for you and George Bernard Shaw to say, but what on earth would I talk about?" Moss said, "No one is dull if they talk about something they know, and there is one subject to which you have given unfailing and flattering attention all your life, and that's yourself." I had to laugh.

At first it seemed a bit presumptuous to talk about myself, but I thought if there was something of value in telling my story, perhaps for women whose daughters were casting a lingering look toward the stage, it might be worth a try. Also, I am always interested in knowing how people got where they are in their lives when I meet them.

For the first lecture, I didn't do enough homework. I didn't even have a cue card or notes, and in the middle of my talk I suddenly went blank. A great wave of fright overwhelmed me. I couldn't remember who I was or why I was there. I tried to rescue the situation, but I finally gave up, and in despair leaned over the platform and in a stage whisper hissed, *"Moss! Help!"* That got a big laugh. Moss came up on the platform and finished the talk with me. But going back in the car he said, "My dear, you can't take money for doing *that!*" and he wrote me an outline with a beginning, a middle, and an end.

He launched me on a career that has taken me from Fargo, North Dakota, to Biloxi, Mississippi, and countless towns in between, in forty-seven of the fifty states, and I've loved it all. It's the only kind of theatrical work I know where they pay you, thank you for coming, and you never get bad notices!

I had no pressing need to earn a living, so I was able to take on projects that were artistically satisfying.

Sometimes unexpected bounty falls from the sky, rather like what Harry Cohn said about talking pictures: God was looking for someone to give the Vitaphone to, and when He threw it down, it hit Harry Warner on the head. In 1948 I was asked to sing Benjamin Britten's *The Rape of Lucretia,* produced by Giovanni Cardelli, the husband of my old Paris friend Jacqueline Stewart. It was to run as a Broadway show eight times a week.

The Rape had been done in London with the glorious Kathleen Ferrier in the title role. In New York my former dancing teacher Agnes de Mille was the director. The New York cast included Giorgio Tozzi, Brenda Lewis, Robert Rounseville, and Marguerite Piazza. Moss and I felt it would be a *succès d'estime* that would run only three weeks and wouldn't disrupt our lives.

For me it was difficult modern music, which I could only learn by drilling. Agnes took no notice of singers' insistence on standing still to sing high notes. We had to accommodate the singing to the acting. In the rape scene, Tarquinius had to kneel on the stage and catch me as I tried to run past him; and then, with me draped over his shoulder, rise and throw me on the bed. Giorgio Tozzi was tall and strong, and we were both happy to try anything Agnes wanted, but neither of us realized that the bed was made of wood and that the set designer thought that Etruscans never used mattresses. The first time we did it, I nearly broke my back.

Opening night I was so nervous (it never gets better) that when Moss came backstage to wish me well, he took one look at me and said, "Let's play the Alternative game. If I could wave a magic wand and this whole production would disappear, would you ask me to do it?" "Of course I wouldn't," I said. Moss smiled at me. "Well, then," he said comfortingly, "remember eleven o'clock *will* come and then I'll take you home."

Mother and Ed would never have allowed me to take such a chance; the idea of a starring operatic role on Broadway was too risky. But they had surrendered their authority to Moss, and *he* said I could do it.

It was worth all the anxiety. Olin Downes, the music critic of the New York *Times,* said: ". . . and how admirable, here and all through, was Miss Carlisle, beautiful in her plastique, rich-voiced, tragical in the color of the tones, as well as the treatment of the text. A figure like Niobe at the end. . . ."

As we had predicted, *The Rape* ran exactly three weeks.

The following year Maurice Abravanel invited me to sing *Carmen* with him in Salt Lake City.

Pasteur said, "Fortune favors the prepared mind," so I worked for months and months with that meticulous conductor and coach Jean Morel. The actress Margo offered me some words of wisdom: "Even cigarette factory workers in Spain have enormous personal pride—they would always wear clean petticoats." Clean petticoats might seem a small point, but to an actress, pride was the key to Carmen's whole physical bearing, down to her walk.

Moss also gave me a piece of overall advice: "When you come

on in the first act, remember you don't know you're going to die in the fourth act. Most Carmens come on so filled with doom and gloom they have nowhere to go."

After the pickup bands of my nightclub career, singing with Abravanel and a symphony orchestra was a musical treat, and it was *fun*. The setting was perfect—outdoors in the football stadium, with the mountains as background. In the smuggler's scene in the third act, even the summer lightning obliged: it flickered on cue.

The production pleased the audience. Moss and Irving Lazar, who came to see a performance, gave me good marks, but I don't remember anyone suggesting that I might give Risë Stevens a run for her money.

That was the beginning and the end of my operatic career for twenty years. I continued doing summer stock, including one glorious four-week run with *Lady in the Dark,* which Moss directed.

Lady in the Dark was the first play about psychoanalysis. It broke new ground in the theater. Moss had written it in 1940 during his own analysis, and it was an enormous hit, with music by Kurt Weill and lyrics by Ira Gershwin. Gertrude Lawrence was the star. Moss had come through on his promise to Sylvia and Danny Kaye, and Danny was featured in the production, and opening night in Boston both Gertie and Danny made history, each in his own way.

Gertie hated the song "Jenny Made Her Mind Up." During rehearsals Moss, Ira, and Kurt reassured her. "We'll have another number by the time we open in New York; just do this one for now." So Gertie walked through it the way actors do when they want to show the author and director how bad they think the number is.

By the time of the Boston opening there was still no replacement for "Jenny," which came directly after Danny Kaye's "Tchaikovsky." Danny was a new face in the theater and he burst on the scene with such force that the applause at the end of his song stopped the show cold.

Moss, standing in the back of the theater, was at first delighted by Danny's reception. Then, as it went on and on, he realized with icy panic that the leading lady herself had to follow this wild enthusiasm with a number she not only hated, but had barely rehearsed. Knowing the ways of leading ladies, Moss was afraid Danny's number wouldn't stay in the show. So he began to try to quell the ovation, shushing the audience, to no avail.

When Danny finally returned to his place after his song, Gertie, who had been sitting onstage on a swing during the whole scene, hopped off her perch, tossed Danny a snappy salute, and swung into a "Jenny" that no one had ever seen before. She danced, she sang, she did bumps, she did grinds, she brought the house down. She topped Danny—and both numbers stayed in the show.

Moss took infinite pains when I was in the summer stock production of *Lady in the Dark*. He coached me in every scene, he chose costumes and went to fittings, and he even prevailed on Gertie, who was then in *The King and I*, to take time out to teach me her routine for "Jenny."

Lotte Lenya, Weill's widow, came to see the show, and afterward she wrote me a letter that I treasure;

> ". . . I didn't tell you enough how much . . . I enjoyed the evening. I thought it an excellent production. The play is as fresh as when it was written and the music is one of Kurt's best scores.

The week we played Dennis, on Cape Cod, Elliot Norton, the dean of all the critics, re-reviewed the show. "Kitty Carlisle, who has not been seen or heard on the stage here for a few years, is the lady in the dark in this summer theater production. She plays Liza Elliott, a confused career woman, with direct simplicity and sings the songs in fine voice. She is lovely to look at and immensely appealing, which is fine from all points of view, including the sentimental. Her husband, Moss Hart, wrote 'Lady in the Dark.' "

But what pleased me even more was Norton's feeling that the pared-down version, without the three revolving stages and the whole glittering theatrical Broadway production, let Moss's book, the play itself, come through: "Whittled down to summer theater size, with one piano in place of the full orchestra for which Kurt Weill's music was written, this 'Lady in the Dark' . . . gains a kind of simplicity and its story is strong enough and entertaining enough to withstand the compression."

Moss needed an English cast for his play *The Climate of Eden.* He said the streets of London were paved with first-rate character actors, so in 1951 we sailed on the *Queen Elizabeth.*

Just as Mother's bridge had opened many doors for her, Moss's expertise at croquet procured us an unexpected dividend. Robert Sherwood was a friend of the Earl of Warwick, who was a croquet buff, and when Bob and Madeline went to Warwick Castle for a weekend, they asked the earl to invite us. It was a very moving experience for both of us. When we were ushered to our bedroom, Moss leaned out of the window overlooking the Avon and was thrilled to think that he was so close to the birthplace of William Shakespeare. I couldn't get over the fact that I was a houseguest in the very castle where as a little girl I had paid two shillings and sixpence to be shown the public rooms.

In England there was still austerity and practically no meat to be had, even in the great houses. At lunch Sunday afternoon, the dining room door opened and a ravishingly beautiful angel of mercy appeared, bearing the ultimate house present. The angel was Pamela Churchill, later married to Governor Averell Harriman, who had just arrived from Paris, where food was plentiful. Tenderly cradled in her arms was a large roast beef, wrapped in brown paper. Moss and Pam and I took an immediate liking to one another. I have learned through the many years of our friendship that she's always there, at the right time, with far more than roast beef.

When we returned to London after the weekend, Moss found out that the character actors he wanted for *The Climate of Eden* either couldn't or wouldn't come to New York. However, he made one lucky discovery. He went to the Birmingham Rep to see an ingenue whom he brought to New York to be in his play. She made a brilliant career on both sides of the ocean, and she makes a point of mentioning Moss in every Playbill bio. Her name is Rosemary Harris.

Even her brilliance couldn't save *The Climate of Eden* that first time around. Before the New York opening the show went to Washington in late August. Almost no one in Washington wanted to see *The Climate of Eden*—there were fifty people in the theater that afternoon, and we were worried about paying the actors. After the matinee, Moss and Bernie and I sat in a sad, dusty little park opposite the theater, terribly dispirited, staring at the ground. Bernie, who had a wonderfully calming manner, broke the silence. "Don't worry, Moss," he said. "We got out of Egypt—we'll get out of Washington."

A year after that first production, *The Climate of Eden* opened off Broadway. If Brooks Atkinson, of the New York *Times*, had given the Broadway production the kind of notice he gave the show the second time around, it would still be running.

Moss always said that the fiscal year wasn't made for the playwright: "It takes a year to write a play. It fails. Another year to get an idea, pluck up your courage, and write another play. A year to get it produced; it fails. Two failures in a row (and there could be more) and there you have six years of no income."

We were running short of money. Even though *Light Up the Sky* had been a success, it had not sold to the movies, where the big money was. *Christopher Blake* and *Miss Liberty* had not brought in very much. So it was time to head for Hollywood. Irving Lazar arranged with Sam Goldwyn for Moss to write *Hans Christian Andersen* for Danny Kaye.

Moss wanted to spend the summer in California anyway. We rented a nice house on the beach and moved in with Chris and Cathy.

Moss had already demonstrated that he had a divining rod where Danny was concerned. Now, for *Hans Christian Andersen*, he tapped into all the pools of Danny's talent: his empathy for children; his singing (Frank Loesser's score was delicious); and his elegance of movement. (Watching him cooking in his Chinese kitchen, I've often thought he was a combination of a great surgeon and Baryshnikov.) The pairing of Moss, the prince from the Bronx, and Danny, the prince from Brooklyn, was a natural.

The summer ended, the movie was finished, and after the first preview we went back to New York. *Hans Christian Andersen* was wonderful, but Sam wanted some rewrites. Moss said this time we were going to stay at the Goldwyns'. "For goodness' sake, why not a hotel?" I asked; "Sam'll roust you out of bed at seven A.M!" "No, the reverse," Moss said. "You see, Sam is a great gentleman, and in his own house he won't disturb me—whereas if we went to the Beverly Hills Hotel, he'd call at dawn." Moss was right.

Sam, of course, was famous for his Goldwynisms. "I ran into Moss Hart the other day," he said to Sylvia Kaye. "Where?" asked Sylvia. "At my house," Sam replied.

Sam was different from most Hollywood tycoons. He did not consign women to the seraglio, and he and his wife Frances worked together (but she kept an eagle eye on him). When Sam and I played gin rummy, Frances would call out from across the room: "Watch him—he's cheating again." But he gave an honest accounting in business, and Moss never found him anything but honorable.

THE following winter Irving Lazar tempted Moss back to California to write *A Star Is Born* for Judy Garland. Moss couldn't resist. He was crazy about Judy.

We decided to rent Frank Sinatra's house in Palm Springs for a few months. It was a ranch-style house, spread out and comfortable. Harpo Marx had a house down the road, and he invited us to dinner, along with my old beau Norman Krasna.

The second and last fight Moss and I had was precipitated inadvertently by Norman. He had been living in Switzerland, and he boasted about his children's ability to speak French, German, Italian, and English. As Moss and I walked home, I said, "Why don't we go to Europe to live? You can write anywhere, and Norman's kids speak four languages. I'd settle for ours speaking two." The argument became more and more heated. I suppose my voice did rise a few octaves, and Moss said, "Darling, you're getting shrill." "Shrill!" A red rag to a bull is nothing compared to "shrill" to a singer. I greeted this low blow by running into our room and slamming the door. I flung myself onto the bed. Moss followed me, knelt beside me, and said, "Darling, I don't care who is right, I love you. But you must know I could never live anywhere but in America. Just the sight of the Statue of Liberty from the Staten Island ferry brings tears to my eyes!" And of course I knew he was right. Aside from his love for his country, Moss, whose musical ear was incredible, had no facility for languages. He could never have lived in any country where English was not spoken.

Here was a man who could go out of town to fix a musical, watch the performance, change the running order in his head; and at the conference after the show it would still be so clear to him that the director would never have to say, "That won't work, Moss; the chorus can't make the costume change." But in a foreign country, he would go mad not knowing what was being said. In Paris my simple request to a porter to get us a taxi would start Moss plucking at my sleeve: "What are you saying, what's he saying?" "What *could* I be saying? Get us a taxi! He's not asking me to elope!" Moss's linguistic ability was limited to learning one song in French. I translated "I'm Just Wild About Harry" to sing at a party for the screenwriter Harry Kurnitz. Moss wanted to sing it with me, but the party came and went without his help, because it took him six months to learn the lyric:

> Moi, j'ai un béguin de Harry,
> Et il est fou de moi;
> Mon coeur se casse quand il m'embrasse
> Mais il se casse de joie.

A Star Is Born took longer to write than Moss expected. In the late spring we left Palm Springs to go to the beach and rented Norma Shearer's house in Santa Monica. We saw quite a lot of Judy Garland. She was lovable and funny and able to laugh at herself. We both adored her. But there were difficult times during the filming when Judy got too fat to photograph.

There were also marvelous times when we heard her sing "The Man That Got Away" with the composer, Harold Arlen, at the piano. One always recognizes a hit song immediately—except of course when one doesn't. It took four years for Cole Porter's "Begin the Beguine" to become a hit.

The Shearer house was the same one Oscar Levant had taken me to with the intention of getting me the part in *A Night at the Opera.* Irving Thalberg had died, and Norma was living at the Beverly Hills Hotel. The idea of staying in that house suited my sense of history.

It was a big old place, with an indoor basketball court, a walk-in doll's house by the swimming pool, a projection room, and something quite unusual in beach houses—an attic. Shearer said she had many things stored in the attic and she would keep it locked. "Then we won't take it," I said. "I won't live in a house with two small children and a locked attic, in case of fire." "Well," she said, "I'll leave the key on a nail at the top of the attic stairs," with the implied understanding that I wouldn't use it; but to tell the truth, the first rainy day I scampered up the stairs and opened the door.

I expected at the very least Aladdin's cave, and in a way it was: beautiful antique gold snuffboxes; clothes on racks; brocade coats with fur trimmings; rows and rows of shoes that had never been worn; pale blue leather-bound volumes of still pictures from Shearer's movies; broken children's desks; crystal radio sets; the detritus of a lifetime.

Norma was a most generous, if peculiar, landlady. Every week she came with a carload of fake flowers—in California!—and changed the arrangements. The minute she left I put them away until the next week when she arrived with a new batch.

A novelty for us was the projection room, and we showed a lot of movies. One night Marlene Dietrich, Cole Porter, Irving Lazar, Moss, and I were watching *Morocco,* which starred Marlene and Gary Cooper. In the middle of the movie I saw the butler come creeping in. I followed him into the pantry, where I found firemen coming up from the basement with ropes and hoses. Outside the back door the highway was blocked with fire engines, all flashing red lights. Oh my God, I thought, I'm being punished for going into the attic! "Madam," John said, "there is a fire in the air conditioner in the basement. I got the children and Ruth out of the house. They are next door at the neighbors'."

I went back to Moss and the guests and said, "There's a fire in the house, but it's under control. Do you want to stop the movie? It's exciting out there with all the trucks and firemen." Nobody wanted to stop the movie, least of all Marlene. We watched her contentedly watching herself as she walked after Gary Cooper, in her high heels, into the North African desert. By the end of the movie the excitement was over. The road was quiet.

I never went back to the attic again.

A Star Is Born was such a success that the studio persuaded

Moss to take a five-package deal, but the idea of having five movies hanging over his head was so burdensome that he fell into a deep depression.

Moss handled his depressions extremely well and tried valiantly not to take them out on his family and friends. He believed that if you're at a party, you have an obligation not to impose your misery on the company. I tried to help him find his way out from what he called the black umbrella of despair. I would suggest we not go out, so that he wouldn't have to make a continuing effort to spark the party. But he would answer, "You don't escape *from* life, you escape *into* it." So off we'd go to one of the never-ending tent parties. He did it so well that no one except me ever knew the effort it cost him.

That summer Cole Porter was the other big social star, and no one ever knew the effort it cost *him.* He was in great pain because of his riding accident and needed crutches. Hollywood was the capital of the endless cocktail hour and Cole couldn't stand around. He had a secret pact with hostesses. When he arrived at a party we knew that dinner was about to be served at last.

Cole was a painstaking worker and perfectionist. Before rehearsals of *Jubilee* started, he and his wife Linda spent a weekend with Moss at the farm. During a walk in the country, Moss told him he felt they needed a big song for the second act and he hoped it would be ready for the third week of rehearsal. Cole's face darkened at the suggestion, but he said neither yea nor nay. The next morning when Moss came down to breakfast Cole beckoned to him from the music room. There was a scribbled sheet of notepaper on the piano, and he sat down and played and sang "Just One of Those Things." He had written it overnight; it was just as you hear it today, and it was perfect.

At the same time he was a spoiled dilettante. Moss told me that during rehearsals of *Jubilee,* Cole would appear at the theater around noon with a group of friends. They would sit in the front row and discuss in loud voices where they were going for lunch. This conversation was accompanied by Cole's valet rattling a large cocktail shaker full of martinis and the jangling of the ladies' bangle bracelets. The cast was terribly disturbed by the din, but Moss could hardly order the composer/lyricist out of the theater. He told the actors to whisper and mumble so that no words would come across the footlights. Very soon Cole and Company got the message, and when he came back he was sans friends and sans cocktail shaker.

Many years later when Cole was in the hospital for one of the countless operations on his legs, he asked me to come and see him. When I got there, his valet had set out hors d'oeuvres on a radiator in the corridor of the Harkness Pavilion, and Cole, sitting in his wheelchair, served the same Taittinger champagne he always had. He made it seem like the most elegant occasion. But I knew, despite his gallantry, that I would probably never see him again.

Moss and his agent Irving Paul Lazar had the best possible basis for friendship—mutual gratitude. *Winged Victory* was the venture that brought to Moss enormous satisfaction and to Irving a place in the sun.

Moss and Irving met in 1942. Irving had been a minor night-club agent. Now he was a second lieutenant in the Army. He came to Moss with a proposition to write a play for the Air Force. The idea was that it would do for the Air Force what Irving Berlin's *This Is the Army* had done for the Army. By some sleight of hand, Lazar had obtained a telegram from General Hap Arnold, chief of the U.S. Army Air Force, inviting Moss to come to Washington. Moss went there in a high pitch of excitement. He had been turned down by the Navy for lack of education and by the Army because he was overage. At last it looked as if he could use his professional abilities to do something for the war.

After two minutes with Arnold, Moss could see that the gen-

eral hadn't the faintest idea who he was or why he was there;
mortified, Moss rose and said he wouldn't take up any more of
the general's time. At that, Lazar, who'd been relegated to a seat
by the door, got up, saluted smartly, and said, "Sir, have I
permission to speak?" He then produced a book with Moss's
credits, photographs, and notices, accompanied by a professional spiel. At the end of his speech the general said, "Mr. Hart,
you can start to do your research right away. I'll put a plane and
a typewriter at your disposal. You can write your play and tour
the bases." Moss turned down the offer of the typewriter, saying
he wasn't going to write the play in the air, but he accepted the
plane. He also went through basic training. He said he was the
oldest trainee in the Air Force.

Winged Victory was sold to Twentieth Century-Fox for
$1,400,000, which Moss turned over to the Air Force Benevo-
lent Society. Irving was promoted to captain, and became
Moss's lifelong friend and agent. Moss advised him to go to
Hollywood, where he was a huge success.

Irving always had his eye on the main chance. When Moss
asked him what he wanted for Christmas, Irving, who knew
which side of his bread his clientele was buttered on, answered
"Cole Porter," and Moss delivered the goods.

We traveled a lot together and Irving unknowingly arranged
one of our strangest experiences.

It began as an ordinary weekend trip. A group of us went to
Las Vegas to hear Frank Sinatra. On the plane I read in the paper
that an atomic bomb would be exploded at 4:48 A.M. at Yucca
Flats, seventy miles away. In the clear desert air it would be
visible from Las Vegas.

I showed Moss the paper and said: "The Sinatra show will be
over around two-thirty. Let's stay up and watch the explosion,"
as if it were another show. It's hard to believe how cavalier we
were about seeing an atom bomb go off, but in the early days,
before we were aware of the dangers of fallout, tests were not
unusual.

The casinos are very clever at turning night into day, and by the time we finished discussing the show over drinks and a bit of breakfast, it was already 4:30. I said to Moss, "Let's go and see the atomic bomb."

No one else was interested; they all went back to the gambling tables. Moss and I walked outside in the gray desert dawn. The garish lights of the gambling joints looked rather sad at that hour. The street was empty. There were only eight or nine of us, a few tourists and one or two bellboys, a motley crew to witness such an earthshaking event.

No one spoke. Suddenly, off in the distance, a column of smoke appeared; then the mushroom cloud rose and billowed out, majestic and inexorable. When the shock wave reached us some seven or eight seconds later, it was not the blast that the newspapers had warned could shatter glass doors, it was just a puff of hot air.

We stood on that Las Vegas street looking at something beyond our comprehension. At least we had the sense to be silent. We all filed back into the frenzied atmosphere of the hotel, with the sounds of slot machines clanging in the air, croupiers calling the numbers, and waiters hurrying by with trays of food, in stark contrast to what we had just seen. I wasn't smart enough then to know that we were all fiddling while Rome burned.

Marlene Dietrich was also in Las Vegas that weekend, and we met for an early dinner before we all went back to Los Angeles. "I'm not going with you," she announced. "My astrologer says it's not safe for me to fly tonight!" My heart skipped a beat. "What about us?" I demanded. "What's your sign?" Marlene asked. "Moss is Scorpio and I'm Virgo." "I'll find out if it's safe for you," she said. A phone was brought to the table and she dialed her astrologer. "How is the eight o'clock plane for the Scorpio? Good? Good. And the Virgo? Oh. *Very* bad?" Irving plucked at her sleeve. "How about me, Aries?" "Aries is all right," Marlene said, "but not the Virgo." Irving pushed his steak away and ordered some soft-boiled eggs, which he couldn't eat either. Moss remained calm. "How can it be all right for us and not for Kitty?" It did seem odd, but I suddenly recalled a news item I had seen recently: "Do you remember that freak accident when a woman went to the bathroom in a plane and fell out the back door twenty-eight thousand feet over the Atlantic?" I asked. Moss looked at me disbelieving. "No, it's true," I protested; "it was in the paper." "If you ran your life by astrology, as Marlene does, I could understand your staying behind," Moss said, "but since you don't, you should come with us." Whereupon Marlene went out and bought me a gold Saint Christopher medal; then she took us to the plane, with admonitions to me not to go to the bathroom.

Epilogue: Three days later at a dinner dance we saw Marlene floating by in the arms of a handsome young actor we had seen in Las Vegas. "It wasn't the astrologer that kept Marlene from flying," Moss whispered; "that young man was the star that crossed her chart!"

That summer Moss asked Marlene if I could copy two of her dresses. Marlene leaped at the idea and took charge of the whole operation. One dress was pink satin; that was easy—we only needed to match a swatch from her dress. The other was beige chiffon, and she insisted on going with me to choose the material. She held every bolt of beige chiffon in the shop to my face to make sure the color was good for my skin. Her dressmaker was next. Marlene went with me to every fitting, supervising the placement of every pin. She was the same German governess I had known during the war. The dresses were a huge success, and I wish I had that beige chiffon right now.

Moss told me that Samuel Johnson said, "No man but a blockhead ever wrote, except for money." But of the five pictures Moss had agreed to do, he only completed one, *The Prince of*

Players, with Richard Burton. Irving and I watched Moss struggle with his depressions. Irving saw that Moss was not able to fulfill his contract. "Don't worry," he said to Moss. "I'll get you out of it." He forfeited his own commission, and Moss was eternally grateful. We went back to New York, and once again Moss had to rely on the theater for our livelihood.

While Moss was trying to find an idea for a play of his own, his best friend Jerry Chodorov and Joe Fields read him a play of theirs, *Anniversary Waltz,* and asked him to direct it. Moss liked it and thought there was a good part for me in it. I had to audition twice. Joe Hyman, who was the producer, was very doubtful about me. Finally he gave in. (He was a good loser. When I left the show after a year, he and Jerry and Joe gave me a gold bangle for my bracelet, inscribed "To the rock.")

Anniversary Waltz opened on Broadway in 1954. MacDonald Carey was my co-star, and Mollie Parnis made me the prettiest clothes. It was the only straight play I ever did on Broadway.

Every interviewer asked me how I liked being directed by my husband. "It's just like home. I do exactly as I'm told," I replied. The problem was that this time, unlike *Lady in the Dark,* Moss had told me very little except some general moves. The opening loomed closer and closer. I hesitated to ask for help during rehearsals, because I knew the cast believed Moss gave me private direction at home. And of course the last thing Moss wanted to do when we got home was to start directing *me.*

I cornered him one morning while he was shaving: "I really need some direction on lines and timing, so if you'll read through the part aloud, I'll simply take your readings and be quite happy." That is exactly what I did. I had no compunction about imitating Moss. Anyway, by this time it was too late for the actor's usual germinating process.

Moss was already working on a new musical with Harold Rome and Jerry Chodorov. After *Anniversary Waltz* opened he went to the country for a few weeks, taking the children with him. I went down on the train every Saturday night after the show and came back to town on Monday.

On Saturday of the July Fourth weekend, I made sure to call Penn Station to check on the holiday schedule. "Yes, there's the eleven-fifteen train to Trenton on Saturday night." Our curtain came down just before eleven. I grabbed a cab and went to the station, to find it completely deserted. Not a ticket taker, not a porter, no travelers, not even a bum asleep on a bench. I spotted a cleaning man and ran to him. "Where's everybody?" He looked at me blankly. "Where's the stationmaster?" (How did I think of that?) He pointed across the station: "Up those steps." I started to run; I can still hear the sound of my high heels on the marble floor. Up the steps and through the door, there was the stationmaster. "Sir," I gasped, "I was given wrong information —there was supposed to be a train to Trenton, and my husband and children are waiting for me, and tomorrow's my only day off!" "Lady," he said, "there is a train pulling into the station, but it's a sleeper from Montreal to Miami, and it doesn't stop at Trenton." Distress made me overly dramatic. "What will I do?" I cried. "I must be there tonight!" Why was I so determined to get to the country that evening? Was it stubbornness? Was it my usual insistence on getting something done that I had promised to do? Or was it some premonition of how crucial it was for me to be with Moss?

The stationmaster saw my distraught face and tear-filled eyes. He said, "The train's about to leave, but I'll run you down and get the porter to let you on board. He'll tell you when the train's coming in to Trenton." Then he spoke the magic words of everyone's secret desire: "Pull the emergency cord; the train will stop, and you can get off." I shook his hand and suppressed a desire to kiss it. "Thank you," was all I said as we dashed down to the platform. The porter handed me in, showed me the emergency cord at the entrance to the Pullman car, and I stood there clutching the handle. At Trenton I pulled it with a vengeance. To my delight the train really stopped. I got off, waved to the porter, and arrived at the farm after midnight.

The children were asleep. Moss and I were happy to see each other. Everything seemed peaceful and in order, and I wondered what had caused me so much urgency and inner turmoil.

Sunday was a lovely, uneventful day, but Monday morning about six o'clock I awakened and discovered Moss pacing the floor, looking miserable. "What on earth is the matter?" "I have a terrible pain in the top of my head," he said. I said I'd call the doctor. "No," said Moss, "it's too early; maybe it'll get better." By seven o'clock it was worse, so I called the doctor in the village. He asked all the usual questions, and none of the answers fit. In desperation I called our doctor in New York, who told me to lay Moss down on blankets in the back of the station wagon and bring him immediately to Columbia Presbyterian Hospital, where he would meet us. John drove and I rode with Moss in the back. The trip was awful. I didn't know what was wrong and I didn't have anything to give him to help his pain.

Once settled in the hospital, Moss insisted that I go to the theater that night, not because the show must go on (he didn't believe in that), but because it would be better for me. I couldn't stay in the hospital with him, and his tests would not be ready until the next day.

In the morning Moss was feeling a great deal better. His doctor came in and announced immediately: "Mr. Hart, you've had a heart attack." It was the last thing in the world we expected to hear. I didn't want to accept it. I asked angrily, "How is a pain in the top of the head connected with a heart attack?" "It's most unusual," said the doctor. "The pain never goes above the lower jaw—but Mr. Hart is unusual." I hate doctors who are jocular, and I hated him at that moment, but there was no mistake. Moss had had a heart attack.

Slowly one adjusts, and slowly he recovered. He'd already stopped smoking his three packs a day and his pipe, because one morning there had been a piece on the front page of the *Times* about smoking and what it did to the heart and arteries. I had called Moss at the farm, and he'd said, "Good morning, darling." "Don't good-morning-darling me! Have you read the *Times?*" "Yes," he said. "You've had your last cigarette, and so have I," I told him. Moss was surprisingly docile. We promised each other not to smoke till we met Saturday night. He told me later that if he hadn't promised and we hadn't been apart all week, he never could have kept the pact. I was hard put to keep my end of the bargain with the pressure of playing in the theater. But I did. And now I made another pact, with the good Lord: I would never smoke again as long as He kept Moss with me.

I continued to perform in *Anniversary Waltz.* My routine was: the hospital in the morning; my afternoon nap on Moss's bed with him; supper with him, and at 7 P.M. I left for the theater. Then his guests would arrive: Jerry Chodorov with the latest theatrical gossip; Joe Hyman with gloomy predictions about business at *Anniversary Waltz,* and as many others as the hospital would allow him to see. Marlene showed up with a gramophone and records from her latest act at London's Café de Paris to entertain him. All singers play their records too loud, and she was no exception; they nearly threw her out of the hospital.

After four weeks Moss came home. I took over a lot of the things that he would have done with the children; while he rested in the afternoons I went to Central Park and played baseball with them. I didn't know how to play baseball, but *they* didn't know I didn't know, so they happily accepted my rules. We ice-skated, and I wasn't too bad; we went bowling, where I never managed to get my ball out of the gutter.

Moss never enjoyed batting balls around with the children in the park, or fastening their skates, or steadying their bicycles. He played board games of all kinds with them—dominoes and back-gammon—and taught them cribbage, a very grown-up game. What he really liked was taking Chris and Cathy to rehearsals, the theater, the movies—into *his* world of make-believe.

Once Moss recovered, he recovered completely. He seemed

to have no fear of the future. He wanted to live his life as he always had, with no reminders, no drugs that required monitoring, no restrictions on his activities. I went along with him in all things but his diet. I bought all the low-fat cookbooks and eliminated soufflés and fried chicken from our menus, though Moss would slip in the frankfurters over my protests and, before I could stop him, eat the rich desserts I had provided for our guests.

We went along pretending it was life as usual. Of course it wasn't—I never let him carry a suitcase, push up a stuck window, or do anything that might be a strain—but it was never mentioned between us.

IN spite of Moss's promise not to take a house we both hadn't seen and liked, he did it again. He had sold the farm after his heart attack. I persuaded him it was wrong for a writer to try to keep up real estate by doing work he didn't like and which made him ill.

We were looking for something for the summer. He found his Elysian Fields one dismal February day, on a drive with Joe Hyman to Long Beach Island, New Jersey, where Joe had an apartment. There were no fields, Elysian or otherwise, on the sandy wastes—just cottages lining the treeless streets and long cattail reeds waving in the ocean breeze. Moss came back ecstatic. He'd rented a house across the reeds from Joe's little place. I never saw it until we arrived on the first of June with cook, butler, nurse, and two small children.

It was a cute little cottage, built and owned by a childless couple who obviously had no live-in help. We shoehorned the servants into unsuitable spaces, and the children had a room across the narrow hall from our bedroom. It had bunk beds and a swinging barroom door. They woke up at 6:30 and made

enough noise to awaken a regiment, much less a playwright with
insomnia.

Moss appropriated the top of the garage for his studio. It was
a spacious room, and he furnished it from the five and ten. The
faithful, for whom Moss was a Pied Piper, rented houses of their
own on this sand spit. The Chodorovs and the Romes had come
to work with Moss on their musical, and the Axelrods and the
Goetzes to work on plays of their own. Augustus and Ruth Goetz
were established playwrights—authors of *The Heiress* and *The
Immoralist*—and old friends of Moss. The Axelrods were new
friends. George Axelrod had just flashed on the Broadway scene
with *The Seven Year Itch*. He and his wife Joan were great additions
to our circle. Almost every evening we congregated in Moss's
garage. The talk was mainly about the theater, and occasionally
it was very heated. Ruth had decided feelings for everything,
both pro and con. If she liked a play you couldn't wait to see it. If
she didn't, she let you know it. Gus was a balance wheel for all of
us.

Beach Haven, windswept and lonely, had eighteen miles of
almost empty beach with the Atlantic Ocean on one side and
Barnegat Bay on the other. It was paradise to Moss. I think he
loved it so much because when he was growing up in the Bronx,
the family's two-week vacation started with a trip on the subway
with the pots and pans and the cat, and wound up in the over-
crowded Rockaways.

By the end of that August Moss had found a big, comfortable
house, with every room facing the ocean, including bathrooms
and kitchen. He bought it, and we lived there for seven sum-
mers.

That first year, in the little cottage, Moss retired to his garage-
top every morning and left me to run the household. I spent an
awful lot of time on the beach with Chris and Cathy, who were
only five and two and a half. I knew the ocean was treacherous,
and I didn't trust nurses, who might fall asleep, or lifeguards,
who were more interested in pretty girls. There were plenty of

children for Chris and Cathy to play with, and on rainy days I invented games that they all loved but which caused their parents to accuse them of fanciful fibs. One of them was, "Let's clean Mrs. Hart's jewelry." I set out toothbrushes and little bowls of water and ammonia on tables in the garage, and I brought out all my jewelry, both fake and real, which they scrubbed happily until it was time to go home or the rain stopped.

After a few weeks of tight communal living, I began getting depressed. One day I found myself at eleven in the morning, hiding in a corner of the kitchen with my back to the door, a big jar of cookies clasped in my arms, stuffing one cookie after another into my mouth as fast as I could. It was compulsive and unattractive.

Better *do* something, my girl, I said to myself, and I remembered that the grocery man had told me his daughter wanted to learn to sing, so I decided to start a singing class.

I found a piano across the weeds in the house of two spinster ladies who ran the kindergarten in the winter months. It was a big upright with missing ivories and the worse for wear from years by the sea, but it served my purpose. My pupils were diverse in talent, interest, and age. Besides the grocery man's daughter, there was a little boy who confided to me that his ambition in life was to sing in the choir at school. They told him he was a monotone, and it seemed to symbolize all his rejections. I also had an actor or two from the summer stock theater.

At the end of the summer, I was very pleased with them all. My young monotone got into the school choir; the grocery man's daughter developed a very pretty coloratura, and the actors had improved their speaking voices.

And then that miserable piano was elevated to an instrument of historic importance. Alan Lerner and Frederick Loewe came down to the beach to persuade Moss to direct their new musical based on Shaw's *Pygmalion*.

The minute I heard Fritz Loewe play the first two songs, "I

Could Have Danced All Night" and "Why Can't the English," I looked at Moss, and I knew he felt that no matter what was at stake, he had to do that show. It had the inevitability of a great love affair.

The musical Moss was doing with Jerry and Harold was in its preliminary stages whereas Alan and Fritz's show was almost ready to go, and Rex Harrison and Julie Andrews had been signed. Moss went to the Chodorovs and the Romes and threw himself on their mercy. Never have friends been more generous in their understanding of Moss's having to postpone their project, even though it meant that it might never come to pass.

The new musical didn't have a title. One after another had been discarded. At the eleventh hour, in desperation, Fritz and Alan and Moss settled on *My Fair Lady*.

Moss and Alan went to Atlantic City for a week to work on the script. (Later on, when I asked Moss why he didn't get credit— the wife is always more royalist than the husband—he said he was hired as the director, and the fact that he was a writer-director didn't make any difference. After Moss died, Fritz and Alan and Herman Levin, the producer, gave me a small percentage of the royalties for both *My Fair Lady* and *Camelot,* in appreciation of Moss's work. This is an example of generosity quite rare in the theater, or anywhere else for that matter.)

Moss always asked me to come to rehearsals. He also arranged for me to come to the first reading of the play, which was trickier —outsiders were not welcome; they made the actors self-conscious. Moss knew I loved every aspect of the theater, but the best part was watching the pieces of the mosaic put into place and seeing the whole picture emerge. To me the empty theater with one work light on stage was wonderfully romantic. I loved sitting there in the dark, watching the actors fumble their way to perfection, or as near to it as they could get.

Rex Harrison was born to play Henry Higgins. He was the Compleat Perfectionist. He walked around with a Penguin edition of *Pygmalion* in his pocket and referred to it constantly, interrupting rehearsals to powwow with Moss and argue every point. Julie Andrews, nineteen years old, was being entrusted with the starring role of Eliza Doolittle. Even though she'd been singing in vaudeville since she was twelve and had the voice of an English lark, she had been in only one musical, *The Boy Friend,* and her inexperience showed.

After the first three or four rehearsals, on the way home Moss was unusually silent. Finally he said, "What do you think of Julie?" "She needs a bit of help," I answered. "Yes," he said and then, as if he were musing, "If I were David Belasco I would take Julie to a hotel for the weekend. I'd never let her out; I'd order up room service. I'd keep her there and *paste* the part on her."

Moss swore that I said, "Why don't you do it?" Of course he didn't do it. But he did dismiss the company for forty-eight hours and worked alone with Julie at the theater.

In a *Playboy* magazine interview, Julie talked about those first rehearsal days: ". . . I knew I was the worst, and if not for Moss Hart . . . I'm sure I would have been sent back to England. Talk about Pygmalion and Galatea; Moss was my *Svengali!* . . . I knew it was going to be agony, and I also knew it was now or never—if I couldn't cut it, I was going to be fired. . . . Moss was offering me a lifeline, and it was the most wonderful thing he could have done. . . . Moss really wanted me to succeed, and so did I. . . . I knew where I wanted to go with Eliza, but I didn't know how to get there; Moss *showed* me how to get there . . ."

For about three weeks I could hear every inflection of Moss's voice in Julie's reading of the lines, and then she had the wit and the talent to make the part her own.

I never hesitated to give Moss advice, because he went ahead and did exactly what his good judgment told him to do. But I unsettled him one day when he described the scenery Oliver Smith had designed. "But you've swamped the play!" I cried, remembering *Christopher Blake.* "All that scenery will ruin it!"

Moss turned quite pale, but luckily it was too late for changes, and Oliver's sets were perfect.

Cecil Beaton, who was a minor genius, did the costumes. He was arrogant and snobbish, and although criticism is something none of us craves, he brooked it with less enthusiasm than most.

At the dress rehearsal I was sitting with Oliver Smith when Julie came out in her dress for the ball. It was most unbecoming, and I opened my mouth to say so when Oliver whispered urgently, "Don't even shake your head—Cecil is right behind us."

When Cecil asked me later if I liked the dress, all I said was, "No, Cecil." He designed another dress, a very successful one, but he didn't speak to me for three days.

Cecil's costume sketches for the Ascot scene broke completely with theatrical tradition. No one had ever done a whole scene in a musical in black and white and gray. Moss liked the sketches immediately. Selling them to Fritz and Alan was another matter. They demurred loudly, but when Moss was in one of his moods of exhilaration, he was irresistible.

My Fair Lady was Rex's first musical, and I felt there was something I had to warn him about most urgently. "Rex, at the first orchestra rehearsal you'll be quite disoriented. It's a terrible hazard even for experienced performers. So far you've only sung with piano, and you can always hear the melody. With full orchestra, you'll hear everything *but* the melody. You won't even find your first note, much less anything else. Don't panic. It will eventually sort itself out."

The company went to New Haven for the first performance and I went to bed with the flu. The rest of the story was told to me. As I had predicted, the orchestra rehearsals left Rex up that well-known creek without a paddle. In spite of my warnings he did panic, and at four in the afternoon of the opening he sent word from his dressing room that he would not perform that night.

Everyone went to talk to him, but he was adamant. "I never

liked musical com," he called it disparagingly, "and I won't *do* musical com!" So Moss had to dismiss the company and crew.

The weather, which had been threatening, turned into a blizzard. At five o'clock that afternoon, when the manager of the Shubert theater found out that there would be no opening performance that evening, he was beside himself. He met with Moss and Rex's agent in the theater lobby, along with Alan and Fritz and Herman Levin. He started in high gear: "There's a raging blizzard outside; people from miles around have already left their houses to mush through to the theater. I can't head them all off even if I get on the radio now. There will be a riot in this lobby at seven-thirty when I announce that there won't be any performance. You people leave here next week and move on, but I have to face this same audience every week, and I depend upon them to fill my seats. I have no choice but to announce that there will be no performance tonight, and the reason is that Rex Harrison refuses to go on."

The house manager's threat stiffened Rex's spine, and he had a sudden change of heart. Now the trick was to get the company back. My brother-in-law Bernie, one of the stage managers, was dispatched to round up as many players as he could find. He went to all the nearby movie houses, asked them to interrupt the film and turn on the lights; then he yelled: "Everybody from the *Fair Lady* company back to the theater; we're opening tonight!" He went on to the health clubs and made the same announcement. People were jumping off massage tables, flinging their sheets onto the floor, and heading for the theater. By the time the curtain went up, not one member of the company was missing. Rex gave a performance that made theatrical history.

In my bed I watched the clock and waited for word. About 12:30 Moss phoned. "How did it go?" I held my breath waiting for the answer. "It's some kind of a hit," he said; "I don't know how big."

A hit of the proportions of *My Fair Lady,* of which there are very few, has a built-in rocket that goes off after a week or so and propels it into the stratosphere. Tickets became so scarce that crooks enticed people to the theater by sending them a pair of seats, and they then proceeded to rob their houses. When Moss let Mother have our house seats, it gave her power, prestige, and pleasure. She could bestow four seats for every performance on whomever she wished, becoming a dispenser of unheard-of largesse.

For me, the moment in the play that gave *My Fair Lady* its unique position in the annals of the theater was when Julie, as Eliza Doolittle, got "The rain in Spain stays mainly in the plain" right. As the song started, the audience took a deep breath and was lifted two feet in the air. It was an act of levitation, and everyone just stayed suspended in magic for the rest of the show. (It didn't happen only with the original cast. A few years ago I saw a school performance in Harlem with teenagers. The same phenomenon occurred at exactly the same point in the show.)

Even a great success creates tremendous strain, and Moss badly needed a vacation. Right after the opening, we went to Barbados to stay with Ronald Tree, a former British M.P., and his beautiful American wife, Marietta. Marietta was a friend of Moss's and I didn't know her very well, but I admired her. (Now I admire her even more because I know her very well, and she's become a cherished friend.) Marietta came from a distinguished family, the Peabodys. Her mother was deeply involved in the civil rights movement. Once when the Queen of England asked, "And how is your dear mother?" Marietta replied, "She is well, ma'am; she's in jail in Miami."

The Trees had built a most elegant and romantic Palladian house around a huge courtyard filled with orchids and tropical trees. When Moss and I arrived, the first thing the house party wanted to hear was the songs from *My Fair Lady*. We had just gone for our first swim, and they couldn't wait till we got out of the ocean, so we sang the entire score standing waist-deep in the Caribbean. It was the first and last time that we came face to face with anybody who had never heard at least one song from *My Fair Lady.*

Moss was an insomniac, which was well known because he complained about it all the time to everyone. When he felt a restless night coming upon him, he would put his head on my shoulder and say, "Tell me the story of your life." I felt like Scheherazade, spinning tale after tale. He said I was a witch because I always knew the exact moment when he fell asleep. I never told him how I knew; it was so simple—when he was awake, he blinked, and his eyelashes brushed against my skin. The moment he fell asleep he stopped blinking.

After a while I ran out of stories, so I said, *"You* tell me the story of *your* life." His stories were so touching and so funny that I laughed and I cried and one night I said, "You must write them down!" Moss dedicated *Act One* to me with the words: "To my wife, Kitty Carlisle Hart—the book that she asked for."

Moss had terrible ups and downs about the fate of *Act One. My Fair Lady* hadn't come along yet, and he was really worried about money. One day he'd say, "It's going well. It will make our fortune." A few days later he'd say, "This book won't pay the grocery bills. It's an indulgence on my part." "Never mind," I told him; "I'll go to the Silver Dollar Café in Montana and sing to support you, but you *must* finish it." (To Moss, the "Silver Dollar Café" stood for the last stop before the poorhouse.)

Every evening Moss read to me what he'd written during the day, which he had never done with his plays. For a play he needed a wider audience, but for *Act One* he seemed to need only my ear.

Just once did he read any part of it to others. We had gone on a holiday with the Cerfs and the Hornblows. Moss read several chapters to them. Their reaction was enthusiastic, but in no way prepared us for the wild and lasting acclaim the book received when it was published.

Moss waited until the book was in galleys to send it to George Kaufman. George was an important part of the book, and his approval meant a great deal to Moss. But Moss had written at some length about George's idiosyncrasies. He also wrote with considerable heat about the lunches George had provided during work on their first play together, *Once in a Lifetime.* Moss, who had had a long subway ride from Brooklyn to Manhattan, was starving. He considered the meal a snack; it was just a small plate of tiny thin sandwiches of the watercress-and-cucumber variety, and George's own homemade fudge, which Moss said was terrible.

When George called, we were on our way out of the apartment and Moss had his coat and hat on, but he rushed to the phone. He came back a moment or two later, much too soon for a long dissertation from George. "Well? What did he say?" "All he said was 'I did *not* make bad fudge!' " This was George's way of saying "Well done." Moss was jubilant.

George hated sentimentality, but he cared so much about Moss as a writer that he said to me, with more emotion than I'd ever seen him show over anything, "Moss must not waste these precious years directing plays. He must use the time for writing." George was closer to prophecy than he knew; Moss didn't have all that much time left.

Moss had an ingenious way of making anything *he* wanted seem good for me. In one instance he was absolutely right.

We were at Beach Haven for the summer when Mark Goodson called. Mark and his partner William Todman had practically invented the television game show. They produced "What's My Line?," "I've Got a Secret," and "To Tell the Truth." Mark asked me if I'd like to go on "To Tell the Truth," which had been on the air, live, once a week for about two months. He asked me if we would look at it Monday night and tell him what we thought.

After watching it I said, "I don't think it's such a much—what do you think?" "I think it's wonderful," Moss said. "You can go into town once a week. It will give you a change from the beach, and you can bring back the mail, the knackwurst, the cleaning, and whatever the household needs." So every Monday through the summer I went to town on the bus, did the show, and came home afterward in a limousine with "whatever the household needs." The show that I thought wasn't such a much lasted upward of twenty-three years, and it created an army of friends for me.

"To Tell the Truth" always played to an audience in the studio. Bud Collyer, the first moderator, sat at a desk center stage. The four panelists sat on one side, and on the other, facing us, sat three contestants: one "real" person and two impostors. It was our job to figure out, through questioning, which one was the "real" person. After the question period was over and our choices had been recorded, the moderator would give his well-known instruction: "Will the real Whoever please stand up."

Among the original panelists were Polly Bergen, Tom Poston, Ralph Bellamy, Bill Cullen, and Orson Bean. Peggy Cass became a regular, and she and I were quite different in our approach to clothes on the show. Peggy favored sweaters, skirts, and Peter Pan collars, while I was generally trailing around in chiffon and feathers. One day we met in the hall outside our dressing rooms. "Hello, Madame Butterfly," she said. "It doesn't look like we're going to the same party!"

To be a good panelist, you need a wide range of information, a feeling for show business, the sense not to step on a colleague's joke, and the ability to make a joke of your own. Every once in a while, though, I gave my fellow panelists a laugh where none was meant.

Kitty, Moss, Arlene Francis, and George Jessel at the opening of
A Star Is Born

Judy Garland,
Moss., George
Cukor during the
filming of
A Star Is Born

Leonora and Arthur Hornblow, Bennett and Phyllis Cerf, Kitty and Moss caught in a lighthearted moment in Jamaica

Moss, Alan Lerner, Frederick Loewe during rehearsal of My Fair Lady *(Gordon Parks, Life Magazine, © 1956 Time, Inc.)*

*Kitty and Moss in
Times Square (Alfred Eisenstaedt,
Life Magazine, © Time, Inc.)*

Kitty and Moss in Rome

Kitty in London on opening night of My Fair Lady (*London* Daily Mail)

The casts of "To Tell the Truth" and "I've Got a Secret"—(standing) Steve Allen, Bud Collyer, Betsy Palmer, Bill Cullen, Bess Myerson, Henry Morgan; (seated) Tom Poston, Peggy Cass, Orson Bean, Kitty

Kitty and Moss in the South of France

Moss and Kitty Hart with Somerset Maugham at the Villa Mauresque

Kitty and Moss in Jamaica after publication of **Act One**

Kitty and Cathy at the Valley Ranch
in Wyoming

Danny Kaye and Sylvia Fine Kaye

Backstage at the Met (Louis Melançon photo, Metropolitan Opera House)

Kitty as Prince Orlovsky in Die Fledermaus *at the Metropolitan Opera (Louis Melançon photo, Metropolitan Opera House)*

Kitty and Tom Dewey

*Changing the name of the
Empire State Mall to the
Nelson A. Rockefeller
Empire State Mall: Kitty,
Governor Rockefeller,
Governor Carey,
Mrs. Rockefeller*

With Lady Bird Johnson at the White House. President Johnson is in the background (The LBJ Library)

Singing in the East Room at the Carter White House with Joseph Moon, accompanist (The Carter Library)

Chris (© 1988 by Jill Krementz)

Cathy (Cecil Beaton)

Anne Kaufman Schneider and Kitty

*With President Reagan at the
White House*

*Governor Michael Dukakis and
his wife, Kitty Dukakis,
who is named for Kitty Carlisle*

Dear Kitty – As always it was wonderful to
have you here in the White House. Every
good wish & Warmest Regards Ron

Governor Carey, Governor Cuomo, Kitty, and Mary Hays

Kitty and Matilda Cuomo

With Woody Allen (Brian Hamill/Photoreporters

*Getting an honorary degree at Amherst
(Frank Ward, Amherst)*

I should be so lucky —
Woody Allen

Mark and Cathy Hart Stoeckle

Christopher Hart

With James Hart Stoeckle

One day we had three champion women bowlers on the show. I tried to figure out why the fact that they were women was being stressed, and what was the important difference between men and women bowlers. Suddenly I had a thought. "Number Two," I asked, "how heavy are the men's balls?" A howl went up from the audience; I looked around for my fellow panelists, but I was sitting there all alone. They were laughing so hard they had slipped right under the table.

Around the time of the remake of *King Kong* we had three men on the show in gorilla suits. I *really* didn't know what to ask a man in a gorilla suit, but something came to me, and I asked, "Number Three, how do gorillas breed?" And I stressed the D. Number Three must have been a true Brooklynite, because he answered, "Troo de nose!"

One memorable day many years later there were three men, all claiming to be decoy cops. The first was dressed like an old lady, with a gray wig and a shopping bag. The next was an elderly man on crutches, with white whiskers and a black homburg, a sort of European-professor type. The third looked like a Bowery bum, with a cap, a rheumy eye, a face like a battered pugilist. When Garry Moore, the new moderator, said, "Will the real decoy cop please stand up," it turned out to be the old lady. He swept off his wig, and we applauded a good-looking New York policeman. Then Garry said to the old professor, "Number Two, what is your name and what do you do?" And the old fellow rose and said, "I'm Christopher Hart, and I'm Kitty Carlisle's son."

I couldn't believe it. Chris had been coached until there was no trace of my son in voice, manner, or looks! Joe Garagiola, the sports announcer, who was next to me on the panel, put his arm around my shoulder. "You poor kid," he said, "you didn't even know your own son!" Big laugh.

Then Garry Moore said to the old bum, "Number Three, what is *your* name and what do *you* do?" and the bum replied, "My name is Joe Garagiola, Junior!"

KITTY

We were together for so many years that we were like a big family, and we were all a part of one another's triumphs and woes. We suffered with Garry when his wife died; we saw Peggy Cass through five years of work for a B.A. from Fordham and we surprised her by presenting her with her diploma on the air; and everyone, from cast to crew, helped me through some rough times when I came back after Moss died.

Arlene Francis and I are always getting mixed up with each other, and the reason is that we were both on game shows. People often mistake me for her. *She* says it's the other way around. I think she's only being kind—her show, "What's My Line?," had a longer life and was better known.

I bow to no one in my gratitude to Goodson-Todman. Because of them strangers smile at me on the street, and when I go out of town to give my lectures, I not only have a ready-made audience but every city becomes a small town full of welcoming faces. One Christmas Eve I got on a Madison Avenue bus, and as I fumbled for the fare the driver said, "Don't bother, Miss Carlisle. You've given me a lot of pleasure through the years. This ride's on me!"

Moss always complained that when we went to the theater he spent most of the time searching under the seats for my gloves. (He mentioned it to Alan one day, and it wound up in *My Fair Lady* as a part of the lyrics of "I'm an Ordinary Man": "You want to talk of Keats or Milton;/ she only wants to talk of love./ You go to see a play or ballet,/ and spend it searching for her glove.") I do lose things occasionally—plane tickets, jewelry, and even a gold inlay for my tooth—and they turn up in the strangest places.

One evening we went to a big dinner at the Plaza Hotel. We were seated on the dais and as we got up to leave, I looked down at my dress and saw with a terrible pang that a ruby and diamond clip that Moss had given me was gone. Determined not to leave without it, I dived under the table and searched the floor. There was nothing there. I crawled on my hands and knees the length of the dais, every so often sticking my head up from under the tablecloth like a turtle from its carapace to ask, "Has anyone seen my clip?" No one had, and we went sadly home.

The next night, about eight o'clock, the phone rang; it was Mrs. William Randolph Hearst. "Mrs. Hart," she said, "the most extraordinary thing just happened. I was dressing tonight, and as my maid put the dress over my head, your clip fell off and hit me on the nose. It must have caught on the lace last night and I carried it all the way home." I was effusive in my thanks and sent her flowers, but I couldn't help thinking poor Mrs. Hearst, having to wear the same dress two nights running!

There was one occasion when as usual I was trying to do three things at once. I was taping "To Tell the Truth" at NBC; there was a fashion show I very much wanted to see, and I had an appointment with my doctor, who gave me some pills for hay fever that were then available only in England. I didn't have time for lunch, so I brought along a sandwich in a brown paper bag, and I put my pills in the bag with the sandwich.

After the fashion show Mary Lasker offered to send me back to NBC in her car. On the way, I ate half my sandwich. I didn't want to leave the rest in the car, so I asked the chauffeur to throw away the paper bag. It wasn't until I got on the set that I remembered that my precious pills were also in the bag. I immediately called Mary, explained what I had done, and asked her to find out if the bag was still in the car.

That evening Mary called to tell me what had happened. The chauffeur had thrown the bag into a trash basket in front of the Public Library on Forty-second Street. When he heard about the pills, he drove back to the Library. To his horror, he saw a tramp scrabbling in the trash basket. He came up with my brown paper bag. The chauffeur jumped out of the car and tried to grab it from the poor tramp, who had seen the uneaten half sandwich inside and wanted it. It became a tug-of-war between the tramp and the Rolls-Royce's uniformed chauffeur. A crowd gathered and started to cheer the tramp. The chauffeur, dreadfully embarrassed, said, "Keep the sandwich; all I want is the bag." The tramp let go, the chauffeur climbed back into the Rolls and drove off. It was a perfect subject for a Charlie Chaplin movie. I wish I had seen it.

BEFORE Moss went to London to direct the English production of *My Fair Lady,* I was told that my strong, indomitable mother had cancer of the lymph glands. Her doctor promised me she would have no real pain. She had already become quite frail and had lost some of her stubbornness. When Moss left for England, she let me have my way and stay behind with her—contrary to her usual edict that Moss's needs were never to be sacrificed for her comfort, or anyone else's, for that matter.

Her health improved a bit, and I decided to spend a few days in Tangiers with Moss, who had a break from rehearsals and wanted a change from the chill of February in London. We went on to Madrid. As we arrived at the hotel the phone rang. My mother had been taken to the hospital and was asking for me. I called her doctor, and he said I should come home immediately, but he wasn't sure she would still be alive.

Moss and I and a bellboy from the hotel piled into a taxi and headed for the airport. There was a plane ready for take-off. I had no ticket and no Spanish, but the bellboy explained, and a bus took me onto the field. I ran up the steps and we took off almost before I sat down.

At eight o'clock the next morning I walked into the hospital straight from the airport. My mother was in an oxygen tent. "Mama, I'm here," I whispered. She looked up at me with all the old fire in her eyes and said, "Get me out of this goddamn thing."

We got her out, and for a day or two she seemed to be getting stronger. As her doctor had promised, she was in no pain. I spent every day at the hospital. I brought food from home, a pearl necklace I had bought for her birthday, and my needle-point. She played with the pearls on the blanket, and she tried to eat the food. I did the needlepoint while she slept. We talked and talked and talked, about the excitement over the *My Fair Lady* opening in London and all the parties for it; about our lives; about my children. She was delighted to have Chris, then nine, visit her. He would sit by her bed and they would discuss base-ball scores by the hour—another unexpected facet of her char-acter.

Ed came every day, and every day he was quieter and more distressed. He made no decisions—he left everything up to me. Her doctor asked to see me. He said there was one thing left to do for her: another course of chemotherapy. It was the only hope. I felt there was no choice; she must be given the chance.

She weathered the chemotherapy and she fought gallantly, but she was losing the battle. One day she suddenly said to me: "When does *My Fair Lady* open in London?" "What does it matter, darling?" I said. "We're talking quietly and uninterrupt-edly for the first time in our lives. It's a great joy for me just to be with you." "I want to know," she said. "In ten days," I told her. She was silent for a moment. "You're going to the opening," she said. "You're going if I have to die to get you there."

Mother hadn't lost her gift for gallows humor. "No funeral!" she admonished. "Don't spend any money on ceremony, just wrap me in a sheet and put me in the incinerator, and above all, no notice in the New York *Times!*" "But Mama, I'll be walking down Madison Avenue next year and I'll meet one of your friends who'll ask, 'How is your dear mother?' then I'll have to say, 'She's no longer with us!' " Mother laughed. "That's *your* problem!"

The next day she looked up at her doctor and said quite clearly, "I've had it. Let me go." By then the doctor knew her well; there were no heroic measures. He just let her slip away. Late one afternoon she opened her eyes and said, "Where's Ed?" I went to the bed and held her hand. "He just left," I said; "he was here all afternoon." "Get him back!" It was like old times—Mother was giving orders.

Ed came back and stood at the foot of her bed. He looked at her lovingly. "You've done everything you wanted to do in your life," he said to her. "You made a success of your daughter; she has the kind of life you dreamed for her . . ." He couldn't go on. I watched them and I thought, he's saying goodbye to her and speeding her on her way. She smiled one of her sweetest smiles for him. A few hours later she died.

I obeyed Mother's wishes. There were no ceremonies. But I did feel it was wrong for Chris and Cathy to let their grandmother fade out of their lives without marking the occasion in some way. Before I went back to London I took them to Temple Emanuel for the Friday Service for the Dead. I explained that would be our way of saying goodbye.

The atmosphere in the temple was somber and imposing. There were three rabbis dressed in black robes at the altar. The children sat down solemnly, and I whispered to Chris, "This is the house of your forefathers." Chris looked around, counted carefully, and said, "I only see three."

Mother didn't live to see all the lovely things that happened to me. So many of them were the result of her plan. Certainly Moss was; whatever he saw in me was the sum of my schooling, my experience, the life my mother had made for me. Her struggle for upward mobility—long before the phrase was coined—had been only for me. She was glad to play bridge in the daytime at the Regency Club with the likes of Lady Ribblesdale and Miss McKay Twombley, but she refused their dinner invitations. She would rather have dinner with Ed and go to a concert or the theater with him. Once I was where she thought I should be, she dropped the social game forever.

It was not until she began living up to the larger-than-life personality that Moss had created for her that I was able to appreciate her ability to laugh at herself. I particularly liked the story she told about the time we were in a taxi and she had dropped me off. "Is that Kitty Carlisle?" the driver asked her. "Yes. She's my daughter," my mother said. "Is she Jewish?" asked the cabby. *"She* may be," she answered blithely, "but I'm not!"

After Mother died, Ed seemed to lose the mainspring of his life. He was like an old clock which simply didn't want to tell the time anymore. For thirty years Mother had been his life, and without her he lost his way. I looked after him until he died. I had been his child, and he became mine.

FIVE days after Mother died I went to England. It was a difficult trip, but somehow I felt she was with me. She had so much wanted me to go to Moss.

In London everyone was in a fever of excitement. The British felt that it was Shaw and Eliza Doolittle coming home. Queen Elizabeth herself had chosen the first Monday after the opening for a gala command performance.

Everything had to be planned to the nth degree. Moss worked with Her Majesty's equerry on the evening's protocol—who was to present the bouquet at the door; who was to make the little speech to the Queen at intermission. The presentation of the cast and crew was of prime importance. They were there in serried rows, and each row had to know when to about-face so that as the Queen walked down the ranks, nobody's back was turned on Her Majesty.

The little speech fell to me, because Alan Lerner's fourth wife, Micheline, who was French, said, "No, no, darrling, I do not make ze speech, my Eengleesh eet ees not good enough." The equerry suggested that I inquire about the health of Princess

Anne, who had gone into a public hospital that morning, the first time any member of the royal family had done so, to have her tonsils out.

The night of the gala the theater was awash with white ties, tails, decorations, and tiaras. The royal party filled three boxes. The Queen wore a white beaded dress, long white gloves, and the tiara with the diamonds all going straight up and down. Around her neck was a simple necklace, three strands of diamonds on a platinum chain, each diamond as big as my thumbnail.

At intermission we were all escorted up the winding staircase to the antechamber behind the royal box and stood bunched up at the landing. Two footmen in powdered wigs and white satin knee breeches were pouring champagne. I was so nervous I spilled some down my new blue peau de soie dress. I was about to meet the Queen of England, and Mother would have been so pleased, bless her ambitious heart!

The Queen was standing with her hand resting lightly on a small table; Prince Philip was two paces to her left. I made the court curtsey I had learned at Princesse Mestchersky's, and shook hands with the Queen. Moss came forward, bowed, and shook hands. She looked at us and we looked at her. There was a long silence. The equerry at Moss's elbow said in a whisper you could have heard in Trafalgar Square, "Don't you wish to speak to Her Majesty?" "Should we?" Moss asked in an equally loud whisper. "Go ahead," said the equerry, shooing us forward. I said, "Ma'am, I'd like to inquire about the health of Princess Anne." The Queen smiled and said in her lovely, lilting voice, "How very kind of you. We went to see her in hospital today, but she was sleeping, so we let her be." There was another long silence while we smiled at each other. Moss, who had never in his life been at a loss for the *mot juste,* was standing there as if he were *stuffed.* I know you're not supposed to ask royalty personal questions, but my mother told me never to leave a pause unfilled. All I could think of was tonsils, so I said, "Ma'am, did *you*

ever have your tonsils ou . . ." She bailed me out: "I had my
tonsils out when I was very small, but all I really remember is
buckets and buckets of ice cream." We smiled at each other
again. We had very little in common, the Queen and I, and I had
run out of conversation. Again she bailed me out. This time she
simply shifted from one foot to the other, and we got Prince
Philip and the Lerners got the Queen.

When we boarded the *Queen Elizabeth* to come home, I feared
that the sudden quiet after the unprecedented success of London would destroy Moss's mood. But there was another sugar-
plum awaiting us on the boat: on the desk in our stateroom was
the first review of *Act One.* Bennett had gone to great trouble to
get it there. It was on the front page of the New York *Times* book
section, it was by S. N. Behrman, a distinguished fellow playwright, and it was an absolute rave. I have never seen Moss so
elated about anything as he was about that review.

Bennett and Random House gave a huge party for *Act One*'s
publication. It was the hottest ticket in town, a real show, which
Moss of course planned and directed. Mel Brooks wrote a skit
based on Moss's early life; Harold Rome wrote songs for the
male chorus: Moss, Bennett, Martin Gabel, and Adolph Green;
Betty Comden and Adolph wrote lyrics for the female chorus:
Arlene Francis, Florence Rome, Phyllis Cerf, and me. Arthur
Schwartz and Howard Dietz composed a twenty-minute musical
comedy based on *Act One* for the grand finale, with a lovely song
for me to sing to Moss called "Once in a Lifetime."

Life with Moss was like living on a high mountain range,
jumping from peak to peak. The depths were always below; they
were Moss's depressions, and I never knew what would trigger
them. This time it was the success of *Act One,* which was an
immediate bestseller.

As soon as the book was published we went to Jamaica with
the Cerfs and the Hornblows. Moss went into one of his fanta-
sies: "As we walk up the steps of the plane, every passenger will
have *Act One* under his arm; and as we walk along the beach,

everyone will be reading *Act One.*" That was exactly what happened, but instead of making Moss happy, he woke up the morning after we arrived with the glazed eyes that I knew by now meant "the black umbrella of despair and anxiety" had come down once more on his head. We started our walks on the beach again.

I asked Moss how it could be possible that he was so miserable when his dreams had come true. He said he felt that each success had been sleight of hand, dust in the eyes of the audience and the critics, and he'd gotten away with it again. "You strive for success, hoping it will change your life and change you. Then you achieve it; but you wake up the next morning to discover that nothing is changed. You're that same old fellow you were before."

I simply couldn't understand it. I'm happy with success and unhappy with failure. When I'm depressed—which is not very often—my cure-all is sleep. Once, after an unsuccessful audition, when the weather was as bad as my performance, I came home and hopped into bed still wearing my fur coat, galoshes, hat, gloves, and umbrella. I pulled up the covers and went fast asleep.

All those walks and all those talks failed to pull Moss out of his misery. I think I understand now. I was being realistic, telling him to count his blessings, to look at his successes, what he had made of his life, how much his friends loved and admired him, how much *I* loved and admired him. I knew my words were bromides; nevertheless, they were true. But they never reached him. It was as if we were in different countries, speaking different languages. I was in a bright, sunlit land, and he was in some dark, stormy region with leafless trees and scorched earth. There was nothing to do but suggest he go back to the analyst.

The analyst was not always a panacea; sometimes quite the contrary. Moss hadn't been sleeping for several weeks, and I was apprehensive about his health. One morning in Beach Haven I woke up early and found the bed empty. I looked out of the window and saw a lonely figure walking way down the beach. I pulled on some clothes and ran and ran and finally caught up with him. He turned, put his hands on my shoulders, and leaned heavily on me, his beautiful eyes veiled with misery. "I couldn't make it without you," he said.

That evening I called Dr. Kubie and told him Moss needed a prescription for sleeping pills. "I won't give Moss a sleeping pill," Kubie said; "it will mask his symptoms." "Mask his symptoms!" I cried. "This man has been in analysis for fifteen years; he's had a heart attack, and what he needs is a good night's sleep. If you don't call the local drugstore immediately and give them a prescription, I'm going to come to New York this minute and snatch you bald-headed!" I don't know what dredged up that expression from my childhood, but I was beside myself. In any case, I got the prescription.

My Fair Lady lifted the burden of financial worry from Moss's shoulders. (*Act One* eventually made a fortune, but not for us. Moss gave the copyright to the children and immediately started calling them King Lear's kids. He would complain to Bennett: "You dog! You told me it would never be a real bestseller! Now look! The Lear kids are getting all the dough!")

Then came *Camelot*.

Camelot was beautiful but flawed; for some of us it was tragic. When T. H. White's *The Once and Future King* was first mentioned, Fritz Loewe said that the best and perhaps the only part that was workable was the first book, *The Sword in the Stone.* The betrayal of King Arthur by Guinevere and Lancelot was a sticky wicket for a musical. He was overruled, although I think in the end he was right.

This time Alan asked Moss to write the script with him as well as direct. Moss was delighted with the idea.

We were in Jamaica again, on a winter holiday, hoping for some sunshine. The weather was terrible, but Moss was in a jubilant mood. He wrote to Alan:

Dear chap,

    I am a true friend. The vrai! I could tell you it has been marvelous. But it would not be the vrai. Wretched is the word for Mossie! We arrived in a downpour and it has been torrential ever since. Only one thing has dissipated the gloom for me. In yesterday's local newspaper there occurred a glorious—a collector's item—typo error. They were reporting a wedding and went into great detail on the bride's costume. Then, the last paragraph read: 'and the groom, not to be outdone, wore a large red carnation in his bottomhole.' If the rain keeps on, I may stick one in mine.

Your dolorous friend.

Then a letter arrived from Alan, a herald of troubles to come. Moss, looking stricken, brought it to me. Alan had changed his mind; he wanted to do *Camelot* alone. He didn't want Moss to write it with him, he wanted him only to direct it.

Moss was bitterly disappointed; he had looked forward with so much pleasure to this collaboration. I knew I had to find something to say to soften the blow. To play for time, I suggested we go for a swim. Standing in the warm Caribbean, I told him, "You're well out of that. There's no way *Camelot* can ever be as good as *Fair Lady,* and you'll be the one who gets the blame. Just do what you did on *Fair Lady:* direct it, and help as much as you can."

The arrival of Alan's script was the faint sound of a distant bell —and it was tolling for us. We were back in Beach Haven. Moss came into the bedroom and tossed the play on my breakfast tray. "Read it," he said without preamble. When I finished it, I said, "Fritz was right. The first part is delightful, lighthearted and charming, but there is no second act. I don't see how you can even put it on the stage." His answer was: "Let's go for a walk on the beach."

As we walked, we discussed the lack of drama in the second act. "There's no menace," I said; "you'll have to use Mordred as the villain to create the tension." I proceeded to ad-lib a whole story line for him. Moss stopped dead in his tracks: "If anyone knew that *you* were fixing up a major Broadway musical—" He left the sentence in mid-air and we started to laugh. We laughed so hard we fell into each other's arms and rolled down the dunes together. It was the last laugh we had over *Camelot*.

No doubt Alan would have come to this by himself, it was so obvious. But it pleased me to think that Moss had liked my idea well enough to pass it on.

That summer Alan rented a château in Antibes and asked Moss to come for a few weeks to work with him. When we arrived, Alan had gone off on his yacht to Capri, and Fritz and Moss were left with nothing to do but wait. Moss called up Somerset Maugham, whom he had met some years before, and Maugham invited us to lunch at the Villa Mauresque. Moss asked Fritz if we could borrow his car and chauffeur. On the way to Cap Ferrat Moss was exultant. "Imagine!" he said, "I'm riding in a Rolls-Royce along the Côte d'Azur to have lunch with Somerset Maugham, with my own autobiography under my arm to give him because *he* asked for it!" For Moss the trip along the Corniche in the Rolls was a long way from the trip to the Bronx in the subway. As we drove along, we sang a little song from a Noël Coward revue that Bea Lillie had sung, dressed in full regalia for a presentation at court:

> I've traveled a long long way;
> The journey hasn't been all jam;
> I must admit the Rolls in which I sit
> Is one up on the dear old tram.
> I say to myself each day
> In definitely marble halls:
> Today it may be three white feathers,
> But yesterday it was three brass balls."

Moss had always admired Maugham, and he was extremely interested in his writing habits. "How do you work?" was his burning question. "When I first started, I just wrote William Somerset Maugham, William Somerset Maugham, William Somerset Maugham, over and over and over, until finally something started to come. Now I sit down at my desk at nine A.M. and write till twelve every day." This revelation didn't change Moss's habits one bit. He never did anything at 9 A.M.

Lunch with Maugham was disappointing, at least for me. He stuttered so badly I couldn't understand much of what he said. But it didn't matter anyway; he was only interested in Moss.

Alan continued rewriting *Camelot*. Early the next summer he invited Moss to come to his house on Long Island for a few days. It was apparently difficult to work with Alan's wife, Micheline, around. She would waltz into the room where he and Moss were working, saying, "I want to lerne about ze zeatre." Then she would sit there, pasting photos into an album, making the kind of rustling noises that are just loud enough to be maddeningly distracting. With Fritz she was even worse. One day he and Alan were working on a melody at the piano when she called out from the next room, "Oh, zat sounds just like ze leetle Frrench folk song I used to zing!" Micheline hadn't exactly started off on the right foot with Moss and me either. It was reported to us that shortly after she came to New York to marry Alan she said, " 'Oo *are* zees pipple, ze Mosses?"

The writing of *Camelot* progressed slowly. The play got bigger and bigger and longer and longer. Casting and rehearsals were like a roller coaster, up one minute, down the next. Moss couldn't find a Lancelot. Late one afternoon, after a day of fruitless auditions, an agent brought in a young man named Robert Goulet. He was en route from Bermuda to Canada, where he had a radio show. He was still dressed for Bermuda in white ducks and a T-shirt. Moss, Alan, and Fritz were about to leave the theater, but when Goulet started to sing, they stopped in their tracks. The young man was then asked to read some

Shakespeare. On the spot he was hired to play Lancelot. That may happen in romantic movie musicals, but it is rare in real theatrical life.

Richard Burton as King Arthur was a director's dream, prompt and willing, no matter how late he'd been out the night before. And of course Julie Andrews, serene and undemanding, was an ideal Guinevere. Roddy McDowall rounded out the cast. He was a charming villain.

All of this was the best of *Camelot*. The worst was to come. Our old friend Adrian had retired from M-G-M, where he'd been the star costume and set designer. He wanted to get back to work. Moss asked him to do some sketches for the costumes. Alan and Fritz were very enthusiastic, and Adrian was signed. He never even had a chance to finish his sketches; he died of a heart attack before rehearsals began.

Camelot was the first show to play the 3,000-seat O'Keefe Center in Toronto. Toronto was chosen because it was thought that if we got far enough away from New York, the "wrecking crew" wouldn't come. We had reckoned without the O'Keefe Center's publicity department. They brought two planeloads of people up from New York to publicize the new theater.

Moss always said that his wickedest wish for his worst enemy was to be out of town with a big musical in trouble. *Camelot* was in *deep* trouble.

Opening night Moss and Alan and Fritz went to the theater very early in case of last-minute catastrophes. I was to escort Micheline. I waited quite a while for her, and when she didn't show up I was afraid I'd be late, so I went off to the theater alone.

I went looking for Moss. He was backstage with Fritz and Alan and Micheline. She had found her way to the theater by herself. She was berating Alan unmercifully in her strong French accent: " 'Ow could you let me walk zroo ze strits of Toronto in zis beautiful dress all alone? 'Ow could you be zo zoughtless?" She was working up to hysteria over the lack of escort, which had been her own idiotic fault. Poor Alan was distraught. She was not a theater person, and she had no idea how nervous creative people are when their work is viewed for the first time. What is needed is a clear head focused on the play and not on a woman and her dress, even if it is from Yves Saint Laurent. I had to get her away from Alan. I grabbed her hand and pulled her down the corridor. I didn't know where I was going, but I opened a door and there we were on the fire escape.

Micheline's ravings were out of control, so I did the only thing I could think of. I hauled off and smacked her.

She was so shocked she stopped crying, shook her head, and said sweetly, "Ees my drress rreally all rright? Do I look prreetty?" "Yes," I said sincerely, "really lovely." "But," she said, "ees too many petticoats, no?" I said no, but she was now implacably on another track. "Oh yes," she said, "you help me take one off?" I said, "Sure." So we went into an empty dressing room. I got down on my hands and knees and burrowed up through the petticoats and unhooked one. "Step out of it," I said. I rose to my feet and held it out to her. She looked at it and said, "Zat ees ze wrrong one."

Camelot on opening night was chaos. The average musical runs three hours. *Camelot* ran over four. The music and lyrics were fine, but Moss and Alan and Fritz had to work around the clock to rescue the book. Nevertheless, Moss wanted me to bring the children up for the weekend. He had been feeling a little poorly the day before I left. He had a mild toothache, and ever since his heart attack any pain in his head alarmed me. I had insisted on a cardiogram. It was normal, so I flew to New York and the following morning returned with the children.

On the trip in from the airport, Chris had turned the radio on to a music station. There was a sudden interruption, and a voice said something about Moss Hart and a hospital. Then the music resumed.

I knew Alan had been in the hospital with a bleeding ulcer, and I thought maybe the announcer was saying that Moss had gone to see him. But Alan was recovering, and it was hardly newsworthy that Moss was visiting him in a hospital. I asked Chris if he had heard anything about Daddy a minute ago when the music stopped. He said he didn't think so. I'm sure he did hear something, but children tend to deny anything unpleasant when they're frightened, hoping the trouble will go away. Panic began to rise in me.

At the hotel I bundled the children into the elevator. When we reached our floor, I began to run. Our suite was at the end of a long corridor, which seemed endless, like a tunnel in a nightmare. I had a feeling of impending horror. Our door was wide open. Something was terribly wrong.

There was a big man sitting squarely in an armchair facing me. It was John Bassett, a friend of ours, and I knew he was going to say something ghastly. "Moss has had a heart attack, and I'm here to take you to the hospital. Bernie" (who was assistant stage manager on *Camelot)* "is on his way over to stay with the children." All I could think of was that I had to get to Moss.

At the hospital Fritz and the doctor were waiting for me outside Moss's room. The doctor mumbled unintelligible phrases, out of which I distinguished a few reassuring words: "Mild . . . no fear . . . a few weeks."

I went in. It was not like a hospital room. It was very small and dark, and the bed was so low it was almost as if Moss were on a stretcher on the floor. He looked awful. He'd had the aching tooth pulled, and there was blood at the corner of his mouth. I knelt down on the floor to be nearer, and murmured words that were really just cooing noises. Moss took my hand and held it with surprising strength. "Go immediately to Alan's room and tell him to take over the direction of the play until I'm well enough to come back, and not to look for anyone else." I hesitated to leave him, but he said, "It's important. Go now."

The atmosphere in Alan's room was quite different—he was getting ready to go home next day, and Micheline was packing for him. After I delivered Moss's message, Micheline said she was taking Alan's things back to the hotel and offered me a lift. "Thank you," I said, "can you wait? I must go back to Moss."

I went to Moss's room, but he wasn't there. Oh God, he's dead, and they've taken him away. I'll never see him again! I ran out into the hall. "Where is Moss? Where is my husband?" Someone calmed me and took me to a proper hospital room, where Moss was lying asleep in a proper hospital bed. The nurse said he would probably sleep for quite a while. I should go home to my children and come back early the next morning.

In the car Micheline chattered away about nothing in particular. At the hotel she got out at her floor and said casually, "I zink you want to be alone," and she left me. Alone was the last thing in the world I wanted. The suite was empty; Bernie had taken the children to the theater. I walked up and down the living room with sounds coming out of my mouth I didn't know I was capable of. It wasn't weeping, it wasn't sobbing, it was a kind of primal keening and howling.

(I later discovered the real reason for Micheline's abandoning me at the elevator. It wasn't lack of consideration or revenge for the slap I had given her. She went to her room to call Irene Selznick. "Moss has had a heart attack," she said. "Who can we get to direct the show?" She obviously didn't trust Moss's judgment or Alan's talent as a director. She thought she knew more than she did about theater matters and was not hesitant in voicing her opinion. Fortunately Alan didn't listen to her.)

When the children came back that evening they looked so pinched and frightened I had to soothe their feelings instead of giving way to my own.

The next morning, after making sure that Moss was in no imminent danger, I took the children back home, and I returned to Toronto with our New York doctor.

Moss spent three weeks in the hospital in Toronto, while *Camelot* was on that juggernaut to Boston, Philadelphia, and inevitably New York. I took him home, but he still was not well enough to go to the opening. He wanted me to go, and I came home and reported that the music and lyrics were poetic and imaginative, the work of two geniuses, and the people in the show were engaging beyond words; it was a majestic musical-cum-operetta. When Moss was able, he went to the theater and did a major job of cutting and rehearsing. His work, plus an hour on the Ed Sullivan TV show, turned *Camelot* into a hit.

Camelot may not have been the perfect musical, but it has had a long afterlife. It became a symbol of the Kennedy years; no one can fail to be moved by the words King Arthur sings, just before the final curtain, to a little boy who had run away from home to join the knights of the Round Table:

> Don't let it be forgot
> That once there was a spot
>   For one brief shining moment that was known
> As Camelot.

THAT year in New York Moss wasn't up to an awful lot; he couldn't walk in the wind, he grew tired easily, and worst of all he was frightened—I could see it in his eyes. New York is not for those who must step aside after having been the grand marshal of every parade.

Fritz Loewe had been begging Moss to come to Palm Springs. He'd been living there ever since he'd had a massive heart attack some years earlier. Moss and I liked Palm Springs, and I encouraged the move. I thought it might save his life.

We decided I would resign from "To Tell the Truth"; we'd sell the apartment, go to California a few months of the year, and live and travel in Europe the rest of the time. Moss said the children would learn French and German and Italian, just like Norman Krasna's children.

Now that we were leaving New York, Saint Genesius, the patron saint of actors, decided as a parting shot that this year I would be offered two musicals.

One of them was Noël Coward's *Sail Away*. I had always wanted to do a Noël Coward show, but when he offered it to me, I knew in my heart I couldn't do it—it would mean months of separation from Moss. But I did not say No, I said I'd think about it. Actresses like to toy with offers. Once you've said No, the fun of calling your friends and telling them you're up for a Noël Coward show is over. Three days later Noël called and asked for my decision. "Noël, darling," I said, "I'm going to have to make the sacrifice." He said, "That's my girl! One should never play the sacrificial lamb; one always ends up angry and resentful over the sacrifice."

I was horrified. We were talking at cross purposes. He thought I was going to sacrifice Moss to be in his play. "Oh, darling," I said, "I meant I was going to make the sacrifice *not* to be in your lovely play!" There was a terrible silence on the other end, and then Noël said, "My heart is broken!" I ran to tell Moss, and he found the perfect thing to comfort me. "You've had the best of it; Noël has just given you your finest notice. No critic could ever top that!"

In the fall of 1961 we moved to Palm Springs with the children and Ruth and John and Rusty the cat. Just before we left, I heard Moss telling Jerry Chodorov about it. "Kitty's lived in a fifteen-room Park Avenue apartment, and she's giving it up to move to a Palm Springs house with a swimming pool, guesthouse, playhouse, rose garden, and a beautiful view. I'll say this for Kitty: she's stuck to me through thick!"

Many friends came to visit us. Irving Lazar was a permanent weekend guest, always welcome except for his insistence on our changing his sheets twice a day, in the morning and after his afternoon nap. I knew about his cleanliness fetish, but this was too much. "Come as often as you like, Irving," I said. "But bring your own sheets. We'll change 'em, but you bring 'em."

Chris, who was of an age for boarding school, went to Cate, a prep school in Santa Barbara. Cathy went to a one-room school in Palm Springs, where she was the only child in the sixth grade. Our governess, Ruth, who had ridden to hounds in England, taught her to ride, and she had her own horse called Chester. Moss said she loved him so much that if she ever met a man named Chester, she'd throw a blanket over his back and marry him.

One day Moss came home and said he'd bought a monkey. He said it would live in a cage on the terrace. I had visions of an ordinary small cage and started feeling sorry for the monkey. I should have known better. At our front door was a truck with an enormous circular cage, eight feet tall and at least eight feet in diameter, with a beautiful black-and-white-striped canvas curtain to roll down at night against the cold desert air. Inside was a small Capuchin monkey with bright eyes and a mean little face. "Whatever do we want this for?" I asked. Moss took my hands and put on his most appealing look. "Darling, all my life I've wanted a monkey." I knew exactly what had happened. Moss had gone to the pet shop that morning to buy a collar for the cat, and the pet shop man sold him the collar and an eight-foot cage with a monkey to boot. "What's his name?" I asked. "I don't know yet," Moss replied.

The next morning when I came to breakfast Moss said, "Monkey is called Max J. Monkey." "What's the 'J' for?" I asked. "He's Jewish," Moss said, "loves matzos."

FIVE days before Christmas Moss awoke very early and he said he had a toothache. All the alarm bells went off. I reached the dentist on the phone, and he said he'd meet us immediately in his office, which was not too far from our house. We dressed quickly, and I went to get the car out of the garage. Moss stood waiting outside. As I backed out, I heard a terrible thud. Moss was lying on his back on the grass. I jumped out of the car, never stopping to put on the brakes or turn off the motor, and as it rolled backward I thought, "Please don't let it roll over him, and please God don't let it be a stroke." I ran to Moss and screamed for help. People came out of the house, and we carried him into the living room and laid him on a sofa. Someone went to call the doctor.

Moss was gone, and with him went the joy, the excitement, the fulfillment—everything that he had brought into our lives that had been part of his genius, his imagination, his sense of drama, and his ability to make a trip to Trenton, New Jersey, seem like a journey to the Taj Mahal. I knelt by him and kept repeating, "I know it's over, it's over, everything is over."

My memory of the next moments has fearful holes in it, as if I had had a blow on the head and was drifting in and out of consciousness. They tried to take me away from Moss, but I felt in some animal-like way that as long as I was near him, he was still there. I was like a dog guarding his master's body. I was afraid to get up off my knees, afraid to let go his hand, afraid to stop stroking his forehead, afraid to be alone. This was the day I had been dreading for the past seven years.

The doctor came and acted out all the futile gestures, passes of hands and rituals that doctors must perform even when they know that they are helpless in the face of death.

Chris was home for the holidays and he came out of his room and stood silently by my side, holding my hand. When I went in to Cathy's room, Ruth was with her. Cathy was sitting rigid, bolt upright in her bed. How does one know what a child is going through at a moment like this? All I knew was that when my father died I was horribly frightened. I wanted to say something to Cathy for her to hold on to. I said Daddy was gone, but he had left her a heritage to be proud of that would be with her for the rest of her life. It may not have been suitable for the moment, but it was all I had to give her.

People came and went. The first to arrive was Fritz Loewe. I was still huddled in the coat I'd worn to take Moss to the dentist. I was so cold. I didn't want to let the world in, I didn't want to share my grief. I wasn't ready. All that was for later. I didn't cry. Tears were for pinpricks, not for tragedy. I was dry-eyed and empty.

The sight of Fritzie affected me deeply, for I remembered that he was to leave that morning on an extended trip to the South Pacific. We sat together silently. I reached for a cigarette. He said sharply, "Don't." He knew I'd given up smoking, but he didn't know about my pact with God. It didn't matter now, the pact was over. Moss was gone, really gone—someone had taken him away, and I was staring at the empty sofa where he had lain. I smoked the cigarette.

Irving Lazar took charge of all arrangements. I wanted a traditional service. I believe in ceremonies hallowed by time and custom.

The house was full of people; I was never left alone. I don't remember much, but my mind has preserved pictures, like a stop-camera: Christopher, aloof, very dignified, alone in the garden; Cathy a little ghost among the guests.

The Christmas tree was already up and the pile of presents was extravagant. Happy holidays have no place in a house of mourning. Take down the tree, store the presents for the children, and try not to think of other Christmases.

The first thing people tell widows (why is that word so awful?) is to make no decisions for at least a year. I knew I didn't want to stay in Palm Springs alone. But I couldn't leave until the school year was over. Then I had to sell the house and go back to New York.

I tried hard to follow some of the precepts Moss had taught me, most of all that you can't escape *from* life, you escape *into* it. I went back to singing lessons; I tried to learn Spanish.

Our friends were an essential part of the road back to life. They came and went from New York, from Los Angeles. Bennett and Phyllis Cerf came immediately. So did Sylvia Kaye, who stayed with me for days. Danny came in his airplane to take us for Sunday rides. Chris and Cathy were thrilled, and I remembered that in my day, the Sunday ride in the family automobile was considered a great treat. To entertain the children (and to scare me), Danny said, "I'm going to cut one engine so you can see how safe this plane is." I was terrified and frantically begged him not to, and the children shrieked with pleasure when he did it anyway. They adored him. He had great sweetness, and he helped them over some hard moments with his antics. When Cathy fell and skinned her knee, he painted faces with iodine on the other knee as well. He told both children wild and wonderful stories about the days when he'd run away from home to the Orient.

Phyllis knew that work would be the best healer, so she persuaded Mark Goodson to take me back on "To Tell the Truth," and I flew to New York every other week to do the show. She asked me to stay at her house, and she and Bennett treated me like a favorite child. Marietta Tree took me and the children off to Barbados for a holiday. No one ever had more tender or loving friends.

At the end of the school year I carried out as best I could Moss's plan to show the children the West. Max J. Monkey was sent to an animal farm. I bundled Cathy and Chris and Ruth and John into our station wagon and we set out, up the coast to Vancouver, across Canada, and to a ranch near Cody. The children and I stayed there for six weeks.

The ranch I chose was a working ranch. By that I mean they worked the guests. In our cottage we stoked our own pot-bellied stove and played chase-the-mouse with wire coat hangers. We saddled our own horses, and the first hurdle for me was getting my own saddle from the tackroom—I never could tell one saddle from the other. Luckily I made a new friend, Virginia Krementz, who told me to put a dab of nail polish on the underside of my saddle. I was so slow saddling up that I was the last one out of the corral. The rest of the group was usually far ahead. Virginia would wait for me, and rescue me from the humiliation of constantly getting lost.

I have done many things for and with my children that they may have construed to be for my benefit, but not the ranch. That was for them all the way, and they loved it.

We came back to New York the last week in August; there was a pall of heat over the city, and a pall of misery over me and the children. George and Joan Axelrod were the kind of friends everyone needs in a crisis. George had to move to California to write movies, and Joan decided that their apartment would be perfect for us. Fritz Loewe lent us his apartment in the Hotel Dorset until we could move in.

My new apartment was located in midtown, and it had Irene's famous decree, "a wing for the children." Joan Axelrod had moved us in with a minimum of fuss and a great deal of thoughtfulness, down to bowls of flowers on the tables and sheets on the beds.

There were no guidelines to follow in New York. Moss had been the focus of all of our lives: the household, the children, and above all, me. Now everyone was drifting away from the center, and there were the children, looking at me, saying wordlessly, "Mommy, make a life." I didn't know how to make a life.

I was painfully aware that for the fifteen years of my marriage I had lived Moss's life completely and exclusively. True, there had been the television appearances and the occasional theatrical performances, but the prism through which I saw the world and everyone in it was Moss.

I set about finding schools for the children. Cathy was easy; she went back to Spence. Chris wanted to go to boarding school. The Millbrook School was the perfect solution. It had an exceptional headmaster, Edward Pulling; a wizard biology teacher; and a small zoo, which delighted Chris, and we both loved it.

But the bitterness of my loss was constant, and at moments unbearable. The worst was the morning when I woke up and Moss's black umbrella of despair opened over my head. Then there were months I thought I caught sight of him in the street—the back of a head, a half-glimpsed profile—and my heart leapt; but it wasn't Moss, and even though I knew he hadn't simply vanished to turn up on a city street, the pain was so sharp that I would have to stand quite still to catch my breath. I thought of suicide. I once confided my thoughts to Irene Selznick, who said, "No, I don't think you'll do it; by the time you write all the goodbye notes and decide what to wear, you'll be too tired to jump!"

She was trying to make me laugh, and she succeeded, but what she was really saying was that I had to pull myself together.

And then came Mama's voice, back from the grave, clear and unequivocal as it had always been: "Use your gifts; don't turn down any opportunity; don't sink into oblivion. Get going!"

After Moss

Time does not bring relief; you all have lied
Who told me time would ease me of my pain!
Edna St. Vincent Millay

THE traditional mourning period of a year is a mirage. The second year is worse because one is supposed to feel better. Holidays, as everyone knows, are the hardest to bear. Everything points up the loss. There is a spotlight on the empty seat at the dinner table.

My diary says: "I forgot my birthday. Wanting to blot it out because of my age? No. Without witnesses I am nothing, my life slips away unrecorded. I miss Moss terribly; his enormous presence such a void. I'm looking old and worn and I'm so tired by the thought of the coming year. It's all too much of an effort."

In the hope of some relief from misery, I turned to a friend who enmeshed me in a form of Zen which employed self-hypnosis. We drew circles of Moss and me and Chris and Cathy. The purpose was to pull Moss into our circles to be a living presence in our lives. I was to concentrate on the circles for long periods each day, and I dutifully tried to do it. But this summoning of a spirit gave me terrible nightmares about Moss, and I began to imagine I was hearing and feeling things in the night. I thought I was going mad. Thank heaven my inherent drive to health took over; I told my friend I had better stop trying to reconstruct my life with ghosts. Mother had been right—I had no business with the supernatural.

Camelot again, and that not-so-distant bell was tolling once more. In 1963 Fritz Loewe asked me to come to London, where *Camelot* was set to open, directed by Robert Helpmann and with Laurence Harvey as King Arthur. On the plane I was overcome by a dreadful sense of foreboding. When I arrived in London, there was a message that Moss's brother Bernie had died. In the space of four years I had lost my three closest relatives.

Bernie had tried, after Moss died, to be a good uncle to Chris and Cathy, but as he explained to me, he would be much better with them when they got a little older. Alas, he didn't live to have them know the gentle, comedic spirit that was his.

Bernie had never married; he eschewed any form of responsibility. Vincent Sardi had begged him to go into the restaurant business with him, but he refused, even though Sardi's was his home away from home. It was typical of Bernie that when he died he left some money for a party at Sardi's, and all his cronies, which meant literally the whole theatrical community, came and drank to his memory. Sardi had a plaque embedded in the bar where he had stood holding court every evening after the theater, with the inscription "Bernie Hart shlept here."

Work was the best antidote. I was glad I hadn't lost the habit. I continued "To Tell the Truth"; I played in summer stock—I toured in Mossie's play *Light Up the Sky,* and I did quite a few seasons of *The Marriage-Go-Round.* Claudette Colbert, who had created the part, was generous with her time and her expertise. She read the play through with me two or three times (I hope the audience couldn't hear her readings in my performance the way I could hear Moss in Julie Andrews's). The producers wanted me to sing, so I went to Sylvia Fine Kaye. Sylvia's lyrics are so brilliant that her work as a composer, which is equally fine (no pun intended), has never had the recognition it should have had. She wrote a delightful song, a kind of round, only it was sung by just one person: me. It suited the play perfectly.

I ran faster and faster to stay in the same place. I said yes to anything anyone asked me to do. I accepted every invitation that came along—sometimes I ate two dinners in one evening. I went back on the lecture circuit. I was asked to serve on boards. I had never been on a board, but I think most Americans have a built-in feeling for public service. I went on the Red Cross board, the

Visiting Nurse Service, the Girl Scouts, the Third Street Music School Settlement, the Manhattan School of Music, the Theatre Development Fund, the Empire State College, and I became an Associate Fellow at Yale. John Loeb asked me to join the Overseers Visiting Committee at Harvard and Gardner Cowles put me on the music committee. I learned a great deal about handling boards from those two men, and it was a good thing, because I was on more boards than you could shake an agenda at.

I was just beginning to try to breathe again when my tax man called to say that California was claiming Moss as a resident; therefore I would have to pay huge death duties. It was necessary that I go to California to be examined in court and explain that Moss had no intention of being a California resident. Moss was a true-blue New Yorker, and I should bring along *Act One* to prove it.

In Los Angeles I was met by our Palm Springs lawyer. He took me to the State Building but left me at the hearing room door to face it alone. Inside there was a pleasant-looking young man at a large table. We shook hands and sat down. I put my copy of *Act One* in my lap, and he started right in with questions:

"Mrs. Hart, did you not put your children in school in California?"

"Yes."

"Did you not buy a house commensurate with a domicile you might have had in New York? In other words, it was not just a weekend cottage."

"Yes."

"Did you not switch all your magazine subscriptions to your California address?" I wasn't sure of the significance of that, but I was beginning to feel that he had me dead to rights.

Then he produced the coup de grâce. "I have here a newspaper clipping written when Mr. Hart arrived in Palm Springs: 'Moss Hart says "This is where I want to reture." ' "

"Oh, I can explain that. My husband was like Madam Schumann-Heink, a famous diva. On her 'positively last' farewell concert tour from Tasmania to Lapland she said at each stop, 'This is where I intend to retire!' She had no intention of retiring at all but was trying to charm the natives, and she had genuine enthusiasm for wherever she was. Just like Mr. Hart!"

My examiner seemed amused enough by my outburst for me to feel the moment had come to produce *Act One*. "My husband was a true New Yorker; he could never, never have lived permanently anywhere else. Now I have a favor to ask of you. Would you read his autobiography? That will give you a better picture of Moss Hart than anything I could tell you."

He agreed to read it; we shook hands, and I went back to New York to wait it out.

A lot of money was at stake, and I worried that I had depended too much on *Act One*. Could it convince, or would it simply provide the court with some pleasant hours of reading?

The wait seemed endless. Finally my lawyer called: "We've had word from California," he announced. Why don't people tell you right away what you're waiting impatiently to hear? "Well? Well? What happened?" "They decided in your favor!"

Act One had saved the day in a way Moss would never have dreamed of, but I am sure it would have given him a certain amount of ironic pleasure.

ONE of the nicest legacies that Moss and George Kaufman left is the custodianship of their plays. George's daughter Anne and I control the plays, and she and her husband Irving Schneider take care of the business details. That's a big job, because the plays are done all over the world. Fortunately, Irving is most knowledgeable about theatrical matters. Moss and George would be enormously gratified, and perhaps surprised, to know that they are now considered classic American playwrights. They had pleasure in their friendship and in their work; and so it is with Anne and Irving and me.

Now the time had come for me to start entertaining again. I was scared, but I simply had to take the plunge. A dinner party seemed impossible; it would go on for hours. I didn't think anybody would come without Moss. But perhaps I could get people to come to me for lunch. It's not such a serious commitment.

Remaking your life takes an enormous amount of energy. The writer Irwin Shaw came to see me one afternoon and found me very depressed. "Why don't you come and visit Marian and me in Klosters this winter?"

Klosters is a skier's paradise, but I hadn't skiied since schooldays in Switzerland, when I had worn a woollen skirt and bloomers because we couldn't afford ski pants. The Shaws found a walking companion for me, Salka Viertel, the mother of Peter and mother-in-law of Deborah Kerr. She had been a writer at M-G-M in the early days. Her stories were endlessly diverting, and I invited her to stay with me when she came to New York for a short visit.

There was a bonus for my hospitality. The day Salka arrived, she received a huge box of flowers. She looked at the card and said "Garbo." "Garbo!" I echoed. But I was not surprised. I knew Salka was Garbo's trusted adviser and had written scripts for her at M-G-M. Salka asked me if she could invite Garbo to tea. "Yes, please," I said. "Every day!"

Garbo was no stranger in my life. I had known her casually for many years. I had even taught her some exercises for her back, explaining that orthopedic surgeons were getting rich on the kind of stretches she was doing with her knees straight. She had been very grateful.

She did indeed come every day that Salka was with me. She was easy and simple. She told me of her life in New York: she got up early and walked and looked at antiques; then she cooked her little steak and went to bed at 8:30—no reading or television. I asked if she was still doing the exercises. "Yes," she said, "on the days when I'm not walking."

To be truthful, her conversation wasn't terribly interesting; her fascination lay in her looks. And standing in the doorway when she was about to leave, she smiled her smile—the smile of the world. Her beauty was so breathtaking that it made me gasp.

Sometimes the fates give us a chance to retrieve what might have been. I hadn't seen Decio de Moura in years, when one morning he called from the airport. His wife had died, and he was on his way to Brazil from his post in Japan. We agreed to meet for dinner.

But the enchantment was gone. We were like two people washed up on an empty beach—gasping for breath and unable to reach out even to touch each other's hands. I took him back to the airport and he said, "You know, we could never be married now. It's too late." And I said sadly, "I know." I watched him go through the gate and disappear forever.

The children were settling down pretty well, Cathy at Spence as if she'd never left (though riding in the park began to pall after riding the range). Chris was happy at Millbrook. Both children made another stab at pets. I am not a passionate lover of animals, but I have a strong feeling of responsibility for anyone or anything under my roof. Cathy had a rabbit called Betty that some misguided friend had given her when it was a tiny bunny-in-a-basket. I didn't have the heart to take it away. It lived in her

bathtub, surrounded by a wall of books, until it grew big enough
to leap out and leave a trail of pellets all over the Aubusson rug.
We finally took it to Irene Selznick's house in the country and
released it. We hoped that it still had enough instincts to survive
in the wilds of Connecticut.

The snake never had a name. It was a large black king snake
that lived in the little zoo at Millbrook. Chris, who loved snakes,
was allowed to bring it home for the holidays.

That evening I went with some friends to see Elizabeth Taylor
and Richard Burton in the movie *Cleopatra*. During the scene
with the asps, my mind went to our snake at home, safe (I
thought) in its box.

After the movie we came back to my apartment for a drink.
When I walked in, I saw Chris and Cathy at the end of the hall
leading to their bedrooms. They were on their hands and knees
in front of the open door of the linen closet. "Why aren't you in
bed and what are you doing there?" Two white, stricken faces
turned to me. "The snake got out." "How?" I demanded. "I
thought it needed some air," Cathy whimpered, with an implor-
ing look at Chris, "so I slid the top of the case back just a
smidgin . . ." "Never mind," I said hastily, my mind racing to
first things first. "Chris, go and close the door to the cook's
room. Then go to bed, both of you." I returned to the living
room and made the drinks, all the while wondering where the
snake was. Eventually I said goodbye to my guests at the elevator.

I hurried to the kitchen to make sure the cook hadn't seen the
snake. Just then John came in from his day off, looking ashen.
"What's the matter, John?" "Oh, madam, Chris's snake must
have gone down in the elevator with the guests. The doorman
said he'd never seen a snake on Madison Avenue so he killed it."

Poor Chris—how could I tell him. I felt so guilty. Could I have
prevented it? Was it a mistake to have gone out?

There were so many decisions to be made, how could I tell
which was right and which was wrong? Bringing up children

alone in the sixties was not easy. Of course it wasn't easy for them either, but at least they had me to turn to. I had no one. When I yelled at them (and I did yell), hearing my mother's angry voice coming from my lips made me wonder if *her* rages weren't partly due to being left alone to bring up a child, with all the worries and responsibilities that come with the job.

Mother said one should be able to play children like a bridge hand: try the finesse both ways, and then you'll be sure which is the correct move. I only wish it were so simple.

LITTLE by little my life began to take shape again. "I've come a long way since the last entry," I wrote in my diary in 1966. "I'm more peaceful (sleeping better); contented? Yes. Happier? Well . . . Chris got into Harvard; he's directing his first play and he's developing a graceful pen. His notes to me are charming. Cathy is blooming in every way. I have given up smoking for the very last time."

I was even giving dinner parties again. One of the first ones brought me the star on the Christmas tree of my career.

Garson Kanin and his wife Ruth Gordon were the first arrivals. I don't remember anything else about the evening because Garson said, almost before he took off his coat, "I'm directing a production of *Fledermaus* at the new Met at Lincoln Center. We're opening on New Year's Eve. How would you like to sing your old part of Prince Orlovsky?"

Anyone who has studied singing seriously dreams of the Met. But I had long ago put those dreams aside; I told Garson he must be mad. "No," he said, "I want to see you in those black tights again up to here." He gestured to under his chin. Then he added, "Of course, you'll have to audition for Mr. Bing." My heart turned over. Rudolf Bing to a soprano was like the Big Bad Wolf to Little Red Riding Hood. He ate sopranos for breakfast.

So I said, with as much composure as I could muster, "May I let you know?"

Of course I thought of nothing else for days. Finally I decided to sing for Mr. Bing.

My audition was in the old Metropolitan Opera House on Thirty-eighth Street and Broadway where the company was still performing. Every time I had crossed the stage on my way to a friend's dressing room after a performance, I had had a wild temptation to stop, look out into the house at the diamond horseshoe, and sing one "Ah" just to hear how I'd sound in that revered auditorium. Of course I'd never dared do it. Now I was being asked to sing a whole song on that stage.

I thought I'd better not sing an aria. Mr. Bing had heard arias sung better than I could sing them; so I chose something I knew how to do, a musical comedy number, "Falling in Love with Love," by Rodgers and Hart. It was short and sweet, and certainly nothing Mr. Bing had ever heard before as an audition piece. I decided that if he interrupted me in the middle with the traditional "Thank you very much," I would pretend not to hear him and sing my one song straight through.

My accompanist Joseph Moon and I stood in the wings and waited for our turn. Then I started, and it sounded pretty good to me. What was terrible was the piano. Joe and I were shocked to see a battered old upright on stage. We expected at the very least a baby grand in that house. But it didn't matter. Win, lose, or draw, just as I had dreamed, I was singing on the stage of the Metropolitan Opera House.

When I finished, Mr. Bing called out, "Did you bring something from *Die Fledermaus?*" "No, Mr. Bing, it's been quite a while since I sang *Fledermaus.*" I didn't tell him how long. "Well, did you bring something else?" Already it was a triumph. Two songs! "Yes, I brought *'Wien, Wien, nur du allein.'*" "*Wien, Wien*" is a popular Austrian song, and I heard the amusement in Mr. Bing's voice as he said, "All right, go ahead, sing it."

When I finished, the stagehands, who were waiting to strike

the set after the matinee, all applauded, and I was floored.
Stagehands are not generally the most enthusiastic audience.
Mr. Bing called out, "Thank you very much."

Outside I said to Joe, "I'm satisfied. I've sung not one but two
songs at the Met." But I wasn't satisfied. I wanted that job.

The same evening I'd been invited to dinner at the Lunts'. In
the morning I had received a note from Lynn Fontanne saying,
"Darling, dress up this evening, we're having a real dinner
party." I came up the steps of the Lunts' house in drifts of green
chiffon and all the jewelry I could wear. Lynn was receiving her
guests in the drawing room, and next to her was—Rudolf Bing.
"Darling Kitty," she said in her beautiful voice, "I want you to
meet our dear friend Rudolf Bing." Mr. Bing turned pale. He
hadn't bargained on meeting an aspiring soprano who had auditioned for him that afternoon, much less finding her as his
dinner partner. We were both very guarded; neither of us mentioned the audition. It was not until I was leaving that I said what
was in my heart: "Oh, Mr. Bing, I *did* enjoy this afternoon." He
did a funny little double take. Then he said, "Me too!"

For ten days I practically held my breath until Mr. Bing's
assistant called and said, "You've got the job."

I told my children that if I could make my debut at the Metropolitan Opera at my age, they must never despair, because anything could happen to anybody.

The road to opening night was rocky. The part of Prince
Orlovsky is usually played either by a soprano with a real operatic voice or by a "personality" who can sing "a little." The
powers that be decided I should combine the two, with *Sprechstimme,* "talking-voice," because they didn't trust my singing. I
didn't blame them; musical comedy is one thing, but opera is
something else.

The only person in my time who ever did *Sprechstimme* success-
fully was Rex Harrison in *My Fair Lady,* and he did irreparable
harm to the musical theater because he made it look so easy that
all actors think they can do it. I tried, and I certainly couldn't. I

did it for Garson and he quailed. So I asked if I couldn't just sing it straight for the conductor, Franz Allers, who was an old friend. After he heard me, he said, "Forget about the *Sprechstimme*. You have a few months before New Year's Eve. Keep working on it and you will be all right."

The next crisis occurred during rehearsals, when Garson came up to me and said quite casually, as if it were a trifling thing, "I want you to cut your hair for the part, short like a man." Oh God, how could I cut my hair? Hair is a touchy subject with me, and I think I'm not alone. Why did boys leave home over long hair in the sixties? And shaving a woman's head, except for nuns and Hasidic women, was the ultimate humiliation.

Garson's request set off every feeling of inadequacy and anxiety I'd ever had. I left the rehearsal hall in tears and was wandering aimlessly around backstage when I ran into a small blond woman who asked, in a soft burry Scottish voice, "What's the matter? You look so upset!" I told her what Garson wanted. She said, "I'm Nina Lawson, and I just happen to be the chief hairdresser! Come with me." She led me to her office, where she proceeded, with bobby pins and her own magical fingers, to turn my hair into a man's haircut with nary a snip of the scissors.

I went back into the rehearsal hall. Garson glanced at me and said, "Good, you've cut it, looks fine." I ran back to Nina and hugged her. "He thinks I cut it!" I've remembered her in my prayers ever since.

Tales of jealousy, backbiting, and dirty tricks abound in the theater; just as everything in opera is larger than life, the tales are more horrendous. Not so in this all-American group. There was a camaraderie and mutual helpfulness which I never expected. Roberta Peters gave a party for me, to introduce the cast; Donald Gramm took me under his wing and became a close friend; Phyllis Curtin showed me some useful vocalises and even did them with me. Garson was an expert director. He knew exactly what he was after, especially since we were singing his and Howard Dietz's new English version. Rehearsals were exhilarating, and working with all those fine singers boosted my capabilities into another dimension.

To one who had played plain old Broadway theaters, the dressing rooms in the new Met were like the Ritz Hotel. Each room had a full bath, and a piano, in tune. (After we opened, before every performance a rehearsal pianist would come in with the score and ask if there was anything I'd like to run over. "Yes, please," I'd say, "my entire part!" Sometimes Mr. Bing himself would stand in the doorway "conducting" as we were going through the scene, a mark of approbation, I was told.)

On Christmas Eve, after rehearsal I stayed behind when everyone left. I walked out onto the stage. The curtain was up and it was dark except for a few work lights on stage. There was no one in the house. It was an eerie feeling. I stood on the stage and sang through my whole role *a capella* to hear how I'd sound. If only my mother could see me now, I thought, a part of this great opera company. I walked to the edge of the stage and held my arms out to the empty auditorium. "Mama," I cried out to her, "I'm here! I made it, I made it!"

We opened on New Year's Eve. There was a wide red carpet from my dressing room to the stage, and as I slowly walked along, all I could think of was The Last Mile.

I loved the whole experience. It gave me a confidence I had never had. I went with the opera company on the spring tour, and when we did the concert version in the summer parks series, I sang my part and narrated the story as well.

I had never taken a chance all on my own in a big way before. Now my success opened the way for future chance-taking. So far, at least, most of it has paid off.

KEEPING an engagement can be a double-edged sword: what you gain on the swings you lose on the roundabouts. Sarah Caldwell asked me to play the Duchess of Crakendorp in Donizetti's *The Daughter of the Regiment* with her opera company in Boston. The part is small but showy; it comes at the very end of the opera, and it's usually played by a well-known personality. One of my reasons for accepting was that Beverly Sills was singing the lead. I was a great admirer of Sills, and I jumped at the chance to listen and watch her in rehearsals.

A week before I was due in Boston, Jackie Onassis invited me to fly to Dakar to meet her and Ari and travel back across the Atlantic with them on their yacht, the *Christina*. I told her I would let her know. I was caught between Sarah and literally the deep blue sea.

In Boston I met Beverly for the first time, and it was instant friendship. She was so easy and outgoing that I told her of my dilemma. "Don't give it a thought," she said; "Sarah will understand and let you go."

Emboldened by that assurance—after all, it was a *very* small part—I went to Sarah. She looked at me sternly. "YOU have been announced; we have sold tickets on YOUR name."

Forty years of never missing a performance or leaving a show had left their mark on me. I stayed.

But there were times during the week when I wondered if I had made a wise decision. Sarah Caldwell's rehearsals were a mess. To begin with, the auditorium always looked like a gypsy encampment—people cooking on little portable stoves; children playing up and down the aisles; cats and dogs, wandering about, and even a goat on stage. The accompanying bedlam at times made it impossible to hear the person standing next to me.

Sarah herself was always late. The cast would start to direct themselves, and then she would arrive and change everything around—for the better, I must admit, but it was all quite nerve-racking. The Duchess is a singing and speaking part, and Sarah kept giving me new lines. I never saw a writer around; she must have kept some benighted scrivener imprisoned somewhere. My costumes didn't fit; props either weren't there or didn't work. At the dress rehearsal Beverly sat down on a wooden keg and fell through because someone had forgotten to put the top on. I was in despair, filled with the certainty that I had been caught in a production that would bring only humiliation, and that for this hodgepodge I had given up the trip on the *Christina!*

At the theater the next day Beverly came over to me. "I know what you're thinking and how you feel," she said sympathetically, "but I assure you it will all come right tonight. It happens every time."

She was right. The soldiers came down the aisles on cue, the choristers spilled out of the wings with their garlands of flowers, my costumes fit, and someone had nailed the top on the keg. Sarah conducted with panache, and a satisfied audience cheered and yelled bravo and we bowed and bowed until we could bow no more. Which only goes to prove that in the end it didn't matter that there was madness in Sarah Caldwell's method.

I never did cross the ocean on the *Christina,* but I have a lasting friendship with Beverly Sills—a better than fair exchange.

SOME people wondered why I never remarried. Edna Ferber once said of herself: "There were men who wanted to marry me and men whom I wanted to marry, but they were never the same fellow." That was my problem.

I was used to being alone; I had worked and made my own way since I was twenty-one. I never lacked for escorts, and I never felt the need of one to take me to a dinner party. To quote Ferber once more, "Dining is not for mating."

I was without an escort the night I met former governor Thomas E. Dewey at a dinner dance for the Girl Scouts. He told me he'd originally come to New York to study singing. When he discovered he wasn't going to make it as a concert singer, he thought he'd better find a profession where he could earn a

living, so he went to law school. We both liked to dance and he
was a good dancer. He asked questions about me and my children, and appeared genuinely interested in the answers. I confided to him that I was very concerned that night because Chris
had gone on a march to Washington to protest the Vietnam War
and storm the Pentagon. I told Mr. Dewey he had gone on the
famous Martin Luther King march, but that had been peaceful.
"This time I said, 'Chris, are you sure you want to do it? You're
liable to go to jail.' Chris was determined, so I said, 'Well, in that
case, go. Take an extra pair of socks and a toothbrush, and I
won't hold dinner.' " Mr. Dewey thought I was terribly funny.

A year went by, and my hostess of the Girl Scout dance invited
me again to the fund-raiser. I really didn't want to go this time,
but she said, "Tom Dewey is coming, and he has asked especially
for you." I went, and I was quite won when the first thing Tom
said as we sat down was, "How did Christopher fare at the
Pentagon?" (Chris did get home, but not for dinner.)

I saw a lot of Tom that year. We enjoyed each other's company, even though we were worlds apart politically. He knew it,
and teased me about it. He never asked me if I had voted for him
—which I hadn't—but once in a while, when I looked at him, the
thought intrigued me that this man had come within a whisker of
being President of the United States.

Tom was a stickler for punctuality. He'd say, "The sun will set
at five-fourteen. I'll meet you at the entrance to the park at five-
sixteen." It was rather sweet; he'd be standing on the street
wearing his unmistakable square homburg—but because he had
added a pair of dark glasses, he was convinced that nobody
would recognize him.

I met many of Tom's friends, and they all seemed to like me.
They were particularly pleased that I had introduced him into a
whole new world. Tom enjoyed my friends, and they found him
attractive. He was a good listener and enthusiastic about other
people's activities. Arlene Francis said he was quite unlike the
image of the little man on the wedding cake; and Arthur Schles-

inger said that seeing us together gave him an entirely different picture of Tom, and he was glad to have had these glimpses of a very human and agreeable man.

Tom was romantic and stubborn. He kept asking me to elope. I finally said, "Tom darling, I'm very fond of you, but I am never going to marry again." It made me happy that we remained good friends and continued to see each other.

I knew he had a slight heart condition, but it was a dreadful shock some months later when Lowell Thomas, one of Tom's best friends, called and said, "There's no way to soften this. Tom died this afternoon in Florida."

I had lost a friend who would have stood by me no matter what, and it was a bitter loss.

Tom had been offered just about every post a President can offer. At his funeral, watching his coffin being carried shoulder-high out of the church, I remembered his answer when I asked him why he hadn't accepted the Supreme Court. "I'm a gladiator," he said, "not a judge. I like to be down in the arena fighting, not sitting in a tribunal judging." And he was right, I thought: there goes a gladiator.

DURING the college upheavals of the sixties Chris wasn't the only one demonstrating. Cathy was at the University of Wisconsin, one of the most explosive campuses. She went to the demonstrations, but instead of throwing rocks, she set up first-aid stations, a harbinger of her medical career. I thought she should have a change of pace from state troopers, tear gas and riots, so I took her for a weekend to Alfred Lunt and Lynn Fontanne.

The Lunts lived in Genesee Depot, not far from the university. Their house, their lives, and their conversation were pure theater to the exclusion of everything else. They had a new audience in Cathy, and they showed off for her as if she were a whole theaterful of first-nighters. The anecdotes tumbled forth as the Lunts remembered bits of business, which they acted out. At one point Lynn said, "Alfred, do you remember the kiss in *Reunion in Vienna?*" They jumped up and went to the other end of the room, kissed, and holding the kiss, glided across the floor in complete unison. There was not a single jiggle or awkward movement. It was a terribly difficult feat requiring coordination that athletes might envy. They were then both in their seventies, and it was the most romantic thing I ever saw in my life.

Lynn told us about Ellen Terry, one of the greatest actresses of her day. Lynn auditioned for her when she was sixteen years old. She went to her house at eleven in the morning for an interview. The maid who answered the door told her to go upstairs and knock on the first door on the right.

Lynn went up, trembling with nerves and excitement. Miss Terry was having breakfast in bed. "Come here, my dear," she said. "What are you going to recite for me?" " 'The quality of mercy,' " Lynn said. Miss Terry, trapped behind the breakfast tray, muttered, "Oh, my God!"

Miss Terry took Lynn on as a pupil; at one of the first lessons she tied a bed sheet like a bib lengthwise around Lynn's neck. "Walk!" she commanded. Lynn had to kick the sheet out in front of her so as not to become hopelessly entangled, and that was the genesis of her very personal and majestic walk on stage.

The last day of our visit Lynn politely asked Cathy about her college life. I had warned Cathy to lay off politics (Lynn didn't even know who was President). She chose the least controversial subject of student complaints, namely teachers with boring lectures and yellowed notes which badly needed updating. "We're going to demonstrate in front of the president's office," she said. Lynn immediately translated the whole problem into her usual theatrical terms and surprised Cathy by saying, "You're quite right; the professors are the actors, you are the audience, and it's a cardinal sin not to give the audience their money's worth."

Then, struck by another idea, she said, "No! It's the parents who should be demonstrating. They're paying!"

After two years, Cathy, with more than a little push from me, transferred from Wisconsin to Radcliffe. It so happened that the year she graduated, Harold J. Kennedy wrote a play for Cathy and me to take out in summer stock. It was called *Don't Frighten the Horses,* a title taken from Mrs. Patrick Campbell's statement: "I don't mind where people make love so long as they don't do it in the street and frighten the horses." Harold wanted Cathy to play my daughter. He thought it would be good for business for a mother and daughter to play a mother and daughter. Cathy had already had some theatrical experience at a very early age. When she was a year and a half, Moss decided that his "tradition" of presenting children to an audience extended to the second child as well. By the time I did another summer stock show at the Bucks County Playhouse, she was too big to be carried. I made my little speech to the audience, then Moss and I stood on either side of the wings and I launched Cathy onstage, saying, "Go to Daddy!" She toddled across the stage to Moss's waiting arms and received her first taste of thunderous applause.

She was charming in *Don't Frighten the Horses* and got good notices. I thought she might follow her parents and Chris, who was to become a music critic, songwriter, and producer, into the arts. But the week before Labor Day she asked me if we were going on with the play. "No," I said, "we close next week." "That's good," she said. "That's when my job at Massachusetts General Hospital starts." I was astounded. She'd gotten a job as a social worker on a medical team, all on her own!

Cathy's job led not only to medical school and the title of Doctor, but also to another doctor, a marvelous young man named Mark Stoeckle. They invited me to lunch one day and I was quite prepared for the announcement that they were going to be married, but not for the drama of the next announcement that rang through the restaurant: "Is there a doctor in the house?" Cathy and Mark were such very new doctors that it never occurred to them that they should answer the call. It took a second, more urgent call to bring them leaping to their feet to go to the aid of someone who had collapsed. While they rode with the patient to the hospital, I lunched alone and planned Cathy's wedding.

It was going to be everything mine wasn't, and I'm not sure which of us wanted it more—the white dress and train, brides-maids, Chris to give her away, a hotel ballroom, early eigh-teenth-century music, and trumpets for the walk down the aisle. There was dancing and Governor Carey and I sang a duet. I fell in love with Cathy's in-laws, John and Alice Stoeckle, and was not at all displeased at the idea that now I was an in-law myself.

OVER the years lectures have been one of my steadiest sources of income.

They have brought me far more than financial returns. I used to think of performing as facing an audience—rather like a firing squad. It was only through the lectures that I began to change *facing* the audience to being *with* an audience. For the first time, I began to perform without the desperate handicap of stage fright.

On the lecture circuit I am usually met by a delegation. Some-times the ladies expect a movie star's pageantry and there is only me. Seeing me alone at the airport, one of them asked me, "Where is your entourage?" "Right here in my hand," I said. I was carrying my electric curlers.

Once there was no delegation at all, only an extra-large limou-sine. I wondered how such a small town could have such a big car. The driver said he was looking forward to my lecture. The next morning, when the same driver showed up for the return trip to the airport, I asked him how he liked my talk. "Had to miss it," he said regretfully, "had to do an autopsy and a funeral." That, of course, was the answer to the extra-large limo.

Usually the talk takes place at 10:30 in the morning. I don't use a podium, just a standing mike. I don't want anything between me and the audience because I know the ladies like to look me over from head to toe—they take me apart bone by bone. A lunch at twelve follows, and then a question period. I ask for questions to be written out. I read them aloud and answer all of them. I have saved a few:

"Are you as hard on your children as your mother was on you?" "Do you do your own housework?" "What kind of fur is that on your suit?" "What is the stone in your ring?" Sometimes there are comments: "I just spoke to you at the entrance to the cloakroom. Now I know how you must have felt when you met Queen Elizabeth: speechless!!!"

One of the questions most often asked is "How did you keep your figure all these years?" The answer is: "Dieting is a way of life." Along with all the well-known injunctions is one that is seldom mentioned: eat *slowly.* If you tend to wolf your food, put your fork down between bites. It slows up the intake, and it makes you a more interesting table companion. You can't talk with your mouth full.

Some questions are really unexpected. In North Platte, Nebraska, I read, "Would you consider moving to Paxton, Nebraska, and marrying the minister?" Before I had a chance to answer, a voice called out, "That must be from his mother!"

"Who does your hair?" I say there's a little woman named Kitty Carlisle who comes in every day. She also does my makeup, even mixing my face powder, a habit of mine left over from my days on the road.

The ladies try to trap me with ill-disguised curiosity about my age: "How old are your children?" "How old were you when you married?" "How long were you married?" But there is always one person who comes out flat-footedly with the question,

"How old are you?" I save it for last, and I always say, "I've lied so long I can't remember!"

One of the stories that amuse the lecture audience is about the Secretary of Defense and me.

One morning I got a call from the Folger Shakespeare Library in Washington, asking if I would read some Shakespeare at their gala fund-raising dinner. Much as I like to try different things, I know my limitations, and I'm not a Shakespearean actress. I said I wouldn't do it alone. It was agreed that they would ask some other distinguished actor capable of carrying me, and we'd do a scene from *The Taming of the Shrew* together.

One after another was unavailable. I was desperate.

"Don't worry," I was told, "we have the perfect backup." "Who?" I cried eagerly. "Caspar Weinberger!" Caspar Weinberger? But how? And where would we rehearse? Without rehearsal I wouldn't do it.

It was all worked out, I was informed. I was to come to Washington on the morning of the gala; I'd be picked up at the shuttle and driven to the Pentagon, where Mr. Weinberger would give me lunch and we would rehearse.

The idea of rehearsing Shakespeare in the Pentagon with the Secretary of Defense was irresistible.

A nondescript car picked me up at the airport. Though I didn't expect a jeep with flags flying or a tank, it was rather disappointing.

I was driven up to a porte-cochère which had some framed prints of country scenes on the walls. A nice touch, I thought. Then I went up in a private elevator that opened into a wide corridor lined with glass cases filled with military memorabilia, at the end of which was the Secretary's outer office. A Marine was standing at attention, a rifle at his side.

At the inner door, hand outstretched to greet me, stood Mr. Weinberger. He ushered me into his office. "I hope you will give me whatever help you can." "We have to help each other," I said. "I know you've read at the Folger before," I said. "Yes," he answered, "some of Queen Victoria's letters, but it's not the same as Shakespeare."

I had my pages neatly typed, in a black folder, and he produced the same. Very professional. We stood up and began to read our lines until I got to a stage direction in my part. "Mr. Secretary," I said. "Do call me Cap!" "Cap, it says here that Katharina strikes Petruchio. Do you mind if I give you a swat?" All of a sudden my mind jumped to the Kremlin, with the KGB listening to a conversation in the Pentagon and wondering if they had to break a brand-new code: was the United States sending a SWAT team to Padua?

"Go right ahead," Cap answered. So I hauled off and struck a blow for all of us who felt the defense budget was too high.

After lunch we ran through the scene once more, and then I was escorted down to the car, this time a bang-up limousine. I knew right away that it was the Secretary's car; telephones galore, newspapers neatly stacked, and when I tried to open the window the driver said, "They won't go down. They're bulletproof."

At the hotel I was seized with a terrific urge to see the license plate, I don't know why. I intended to scuttle around to the back of the car, but it drove away before I had a chance.

That evening our reading went well. Weinberger did better than I did, and I envied him the sang-froid of the amateur. We were duly applauded—not, I'm afraid, for our sterling performance, but because the idea of our doing it together was so outlandish.

After dinner the Weinbergers offered to take me to my hotel. As we approached his car, Cap turned to me: "Would you like to see my license plate?" Did the Pentagon have a newfangled widget that read people's minds? He led me to the back of the car, and I was stunned. The number was Double-O-Seven!

THE lectures became musical reminiscences when Roger Kennedy of the Smithsonian Institution said, "Let's celebrate something we've invented in this country: the American musical comedy. The people you and Moss knew and worked with span most of its history." I had never thought of it that way, but he was right. Moss wrote the book for two musicals: *Face the Music,* and *As Thousands Cheer,* and he directed *Miss Liberty,* all with Irving Berlin music. He wrote the book for *Jubilee* with Cole Porter; *I'd Rather Be Right* with Rodgers and Hart; and *Lady in the Dark* with Kurt Weill and Ira Gershwin, besides directing *My Fair Lady* and *Camelot* for Lerner and Loewe. And I had worked with George Gershwin, Jerome Kern, Harold Rome, Dietz and Schwartz.

With the help of Roger Kennedy and Lee Adams I strung together an hour of songs and stories about the composers Moss and I had known. I performed it in the great hall of the Museum of History in the Smithsonian, and Rosalynn Carter asked me to repeat it at her annual luncheon for the wives of the senators. Mrs. Carter wanted it to be in the Rose Garden. That worried me. I had been to occasions in the Rose Garden, and I didn't want to compete with birdsong and jets roaring overhead. But it was Rose Garden or nothing, unless it rained. No Hopi Indian ever prayed for rain as hard as I did. It was not till twenty minutes before lunch that the rains came and everything had to be moved inside. There was no time for a technical rehearsal, and I was a nervous wreck.

At lunch I was seated at Mrs. Carter's left, and Lady Bird Johnson was on her right. Mrs. Carter kept getting notes delivered by aides, and my mind was on my upcoming performance, so conversation was exceedingly sticky. Finally, at dessert time, Mrs. Johnson leaned across Mrs. Carter and said to me, "I'm going to New York for a few days; what would you recommend that I see in the theater?" What with my nerves about performing without rehearsal, I had lost track of every play I'd ever seen. But I looked at Mrs. Johnson and I saw *TEXAS,* and I said, "What about *The Best Little Whorehouse in Texas?*" "I don't think I

care to see that," she said coldly, and then, realizing my discom-
fiture and being the kind lady that she is, she kept talking until I
could get my foot out of my mouth.

Foot-in-the-mouth seems to haunt me at the White House. I
had been invited by the Reagans to a showing of *King Lear,* made
for television, starring Laurence Olivier, who was the guest of
honor. He came with Lady Olivier, his son, and his agent. There
were only thirty of us, and it was a wonderful evening. At the end
of the film the President escorted the Oliviers to their car. When
he returned he came over to me and said, "After seeing that
performance I don't think I'll ever call myself an actor again."
And for the first and last time in my life, instead of *esprit d'escalier,*
(thinking of my good line on the staircase after leaving the
party), I said it on the spot: "Well, Mr. President, maybe *you*
never had such good parts!"

If *A Night at the Opera* was my claim to fame with my children's
friends, my last movie, *Radio Days,* almost made me a part of
their generation.

The first time I saw Woody Allen in person I was having
dinner at Elaine's. A young man sort of sidled up to my table and
without any preamble said, "I'm a great admirer of Moss Hart.
When I was a little boy, there was something called 'Library
Period' at school, when we could read any book in the library we
wanted. One day I reached up and took down *Six Plays by Kaufman and Hart,* and it changed my life." He didn't wait for an
answer, but just crept away.

A few weeks later he called to ask if I would sing "They're
Either Too Young or Too Old" and "I'll Be Seeing You" in his
new movie, *Radio Days.*

It was a good thing that I had kept up my singing all these

years, even though doing those scales at times felt as if I were pushing a boulder uphill.

After the filming I asked Woody, "How did you know I could still sing?" "I was told you practiced every day," he answered. I thought to myself, he was taking quite a chance. Florence Foster Jenkins also practiced every day.

In the end he took only half a chance—"I'll Be Seeing You" ended up on the cutting-room floor.

KCH

A soul is a very expensive thing to
keep . . . It eats music and pictures and books
and mountains and lakes and beautiful things
to wear and nice people to be with . . . you
can't have them without lots of money.
George Bernard Shaw
Heartbreak House

In the early sixties I was the moderator and interviewer of a television show called "Women on the Move." It was dedicated to female accomplishment on every level. We had women who were at the top of their professions and fitted into this pattern: Jacqueline Cochran, the first woman pilot to exceed the speed of sound in a jet plane; Mary Roebling, head of the Trenton Trust Company; Dorothy Rodgers, the wife of composer Richard Rodgers, decorator and inventor (the Jonny Mop and non-perishable dress patterns); Dr. Louise Bates Ames, a child psychologist and co-founder of the Gesell Institute; Abigail van Buren ("Dear Abby"); Babe Didrikson, the great athlete; the economist Sylvia Porter; composer-lyricist Sylvia Fine Kaye.

"Women on the Move" didn't have a long life (we lost out to "Leave It to Beaver"), but it created some little stir. Right after it folded, an assistant to New York State Governor Rockefeller, Nina Jones, called me up. She had seen the show and had been impressed. She told me Rockefeller had organized a two-day meeting on Opportunities for Women, and she asked me if I'd like to chair it. Governor Rockefeller had a sharp instinct for ideas whose time had come, and the ability to dramatize them.

I had never chaired anything, but I moved into this new environment as if I knew what I was doing. I introduced the governor and the speakers, and I visited the workshops. The conference created so much interest that the governor asked me to tour the state, gather up the ideas that had been discussed, and write a report ("The Kitty Carlisle Hart Report of 1966"). I was pushed into doing what Moss said was good for me: shake up your life every so often.

It was a pleasure working for Rockefeller. The whole operation resulted in the Women's Unit, a small agency attached to the Executive Chamber, and I was appointed honorary chairman. It was my first volunteer government job. "Governor R. has put me on his committee for Women's Affairs," says my diary, "with an office in his building on 55th Street. Mossie would be pleased and *so* funny about it."

I wrote a monthly newsletter; we set up training courses on how to apply for jobs, for women on welfare who had never been employed, and halfway houses for girls coming out of prison. We also promoted a fairly new idea to accommodate teachers who had children: two women on the same job, with two shifts, mornings and afternoons. I discovered the power that women have to get things done when they band together.

The professional women in the office, Evelyn Cunningham, June Martin, Virginia Cairns, and Nina Jones, guided my small steps into this new world with affection and amused indulgence. Without being aware of it, I was being given a crash course in state government. I learned a little bureaucratese, about agencies and acronyms, one in particular. Going over an agenda one day, there were ten items all headed by initials. I understood them all until the last one. "What on earth is KCH?" I asked, and they laughed. "That's you!"

A door was opening—all I had to do was step forward.

At a fund-raiser for the Democrats, Carol Hausaman and Elinor Guggenheimer asked me if I'd like to think about running for state senator against Roy Goodman.

It never occurred to me to question their authority to make such an offer. I just thought I'd better get some advice. Ever my mother's daughter ("Go to the top!"), I called Governor Rockefeller.

After spending a good deal of time discouraging me from running for the state legislature, he made an about-face, upping the stakes, and said, "You *should* be in public life; you should run for Congress." He was suggesting that I run against my very own congressman, Ed Koch, on the Republican ticket! I was too flabbergasted to say more than "I'll think it over."

Now I really needed advice. After Bennett Cerf's death, Phyllis had married Robert Wagner, who had been mayor of New York for twelve years. He was a most experienced and astute politician, and also one of the kindest men I had ever known. Phyllis suggested that I talk to him. "I think you'd do a fine job," he said, "but Ed Koch is so strong you couldn't possibly beat him. Why make your first try for elective office where you know you can't win?" Next I went to Marietta Tree, by then Ambassador to the U.N.; and to Clayton Fritchey, Adlai Stevenson's closest adviser. They agreed with Bob, but they both said that I should ask for an appointive job.

Before I had a chance to call the governor, he called me. He caught me at the worst possible moment. I was in my dressing room at NBC, getting ready for "To Tell the Truth," surrounded by makeup and wardrobe women and hairdressers. I couldn't say I wasn't there—I had picked up the phone myself. I motioned everyone to leave—it wasn't the kind of call I could concentrate on with all those people fiddling with me. I began to improvise. "Governor darling," (that's what I always called him) "I couldn't win against Ed Koch now, and by the time the party gave me an easier assignment and I won, I'd be too old to walk up the steps of the Capitol unaided. Anyway, I'm a Democrat. What would you think about an appointive job?"

Out of this conversation came one of the most important changes of my life. Three days later the governor called and offered me the vice-chairmanship of the New York State Council on the Arts under Chairman Seymour Knox. "Now you're talking!" I said. "I'd love it!" Then he added, "and someday I want you to be chairman."

The Council on the Arts had been founded in 1960 by Rockefeller, whose interest in the arts was innate and passionate, and
who knew that the arts needed shoring up. Moss had exactly the
same idea at the same time. I just found a 1960 interview in the
Harvard Crimson. He said, "The economics of the theater are
prohibitive. The method for correcting this situation, however,
does not lie in the power of the playwrights, or the producers.
The solution rests only in government subsidy." But he despaired of its
ever happening. Wouldn't he be surprised to know that there *is*
government subsidy, not only for the theater, but for all the arts,
and I have a hand in it!

For five years I served with two chairmen: Seymour Knox,
banker, collector of modern art and the founder of one of the
best small museums in the world, the Albright Knox of Buffalo.
Joan Davidson, who followed him, had innovative ideas and was
very creative. She left after eighteen months to head the J. M.
Kaplan Foundation. Then Governor Hugh Carey offered the
chairmanship to me.

But though I had been on the Council for five years, the
difference between vice-chairman and chairman is like the difference between a bicycle and a rocket ship to the moon. The
chairman is the chief executive officer of a state agency, and is
accountable to the governor, the legislature, and the constitu-
ents for the fair distribution of taxpayers' money. In other
words, so much—and so many—would be depending on me.

I had been helped when I was young by so many people. Now
I would have the chance to do the same for those young artists
coming up behind me. But was the desire to help enough? I
started adding up my qualifications. I knew theater and music;
"To Tell The Truth" had given me nationwide recognition, no
small help; and with the Women's Unit, I had had some experience with state government.

Because I felt the responsibility was overwhelming, I galloped
off again to my friends. I canvassed them all more than once
while I agonized. The advice ranged from "Don't do it, you'll

have a stroke, it will kill you," to "Why not?" I had been calling
Phyllis Wagner more than the others, for I felt she knew more
about it. Late one night I called her once again. Phyllis, finally at
the end of her patience, shouted, "Oh, do it!" That was exactly
what I wanted to hear. I called the governor and accepted.

I never forgot that Nelson Rockefeller had wanted me to be
chairman. I telephoned him at once. "Governor darling," I said
(he was then vice president), "I have something to tell you."
There was a tiny pause on the other end, and he said with real
pleasure, "You're chairman of the Arts Council!"

A few days later I got a letter from him:

Dear Kitty;

Just a note to tell you how thrilled I am with your appointment
as Chairman of the New York State Council on the Arts. I know
you'll do your usual marvelous job. . . .
Again, congratulations and warm personal regards.

Sincerely,
(signed) *Nelson*

Underneath, in his own handwriting, was a P.S.: "I never
thought—or dared hope—it would work out this way! It has
restored everyone's faith! Very best, Nelson."

The friends I had gone to so trustingly to ask advice really
knew little or nothing about the Council. Many of them still
don't. I can't blame them. The Council has become a very com-
plex operation in the sixteen years I've been there, although the
basic structure remains constant.

The Council consists of a twenty-member board appointed by
the governor—all unsalaried, including me—and a paid staff of
about ninety-five. We fund non-profit institutions, large and
small; the rural, the emerging, and the avant-garde. Every request to the Council—this year we received 6,778 requests, of
which we funded 3,634—is examined by the staff for artistic
quality and fiscal responsibility. It then goes to professional peer

panelists, and after that to the board itself. In this way no one's bias can influence final decisions. The Council's budget is recommended by the governor and appropriated by the state legislature, with some small help from the federal government. It is all taxpayers' money—and I think it's the best money the state spends.

The Council's board has always sustained and upheld me, and they have given time and effort to the great demands made upon them. Seymour Knox's faith and trust also eased my way. He came to the first board meeting after my appointment. He stood behind my chair and stretched both his hands over my head in a symbolic gesture of benediction. Governor Carey asked Edward Kresky, a senior board member, to look after me and save me from my own mistakes. As for me, I enlisted everyone's help; once I was on a flight to Albany with Donna Shalala (now president of the University of Wisconsin), an expert on state government, and she later told a friend, "Never get on a plane with KCH, because you'll leave with a long, very detailed list of things you're going to do for the Council!"

I began to travel the state extensively, from Plattsburgh to Staten Island, from Erie to Montauk. In a job like mine the banana peel is always around the corner, but thanks to the staff and their meticulous briefings I knew every detail, from the amount of the grant to the names and political leanings of everyone I was to meet. I went to an awful lot of receptions. Anne Kaufman Schneider said the job was made to order for me. "Kitty is the only person I know who really *likes* receptions!"

THERE was a honeymoon of three months and then I was thrown to the budget lions.

The governor proposes and the legislature disposes.

Neither Seymour Knox nor Joan Davidson had ever taken me with them when they went to Albany to discuss the budget. Now it was up to me to present the Arts Council budget request to the Budget Department and the Ways and Means Committees in Albany. I was terrified. I was about to ask the State of New York for $32 million of the taxpayers' money. It was going to be worse than an opening night—at least then I would have had a chance to rehearse. And that gave me an idea.

I called our budget examiner, Paul Veillette, a scholarly man, and asked if I could have a dress rehearsal for my hearing. He had never heard of such a thing, but he was an unbureaucratic bureaucrat. He said, "Why not?" We sat informally around a table while he and his staff asked me dummy questions.

When it was over I asked Paul for my marks. He said he'd give me a seventy-four. It was the equivalent of a weak notice in the theater. I had three days before the hearing. Fear of failure is the greatest discipline. I came home and learned the budget by heart.

The formal hearing was in the Capitol. I sat at a long table with my staff, facing the Director of the Budget, Dr. Miller, who was to conduct the hearing. It was standing room only. Everyone came to see what this beginner would do. It may not have been quite the spirit in which the Romans came to watch the lions eat the Christians, but I detected slightly amused smiles on all faces, as if the audience was anticipating good sport.

I got off to a shaky start, and limped along till we came to the grants for individual artists. "Why do you feel that artists should be subsidized by the state?" Dr. Miller asked. *"You* weren't subsidized, and *you* did all right." I had a rush of blood to the head. "Of course I was subsidized," I said, "by my mother! I went to drama school and I had lessons in singing, dancing, piano, and languages. Why shouldn't someone without these advantages have the same chance? What better use can the state make of its money than to help artists, who bring in billions of tourist dollars and who have turned New York into the arts capital of the world?"

After my impassioned speech, I looked at Dr. Miller with apprehension. I swear there was a twinkle in his eye. I think he had deliberately given me the opening. "Doll," he said, "that's one up for you!" There was a sound of concerted exhalation around the table as if everyone had been holding his breath.

But we didn't get the added appropriation this time. The notion dies hard that artists will thrive if they starve in garrets, or that like birds they will sing anyway. Artists are always being asked to donate their services to every worthy cause that comes along, and they always do.

In the arts we are always tilting at windmills, but in my heart I knew that if I kept at it, eventually government would be won over.

The budget is a yearly hassle. When it goes up I get most of the credit, but when it goes down I have to take all of the blame. Each time it does, I say to myself, "Our cause is just and we *will* prevail—next year!"

The governor is my first port of call to make a pitch for more money. I don't rely only on myself, I ask everyone I think will see him to carry our message. I even get out-of-staters like Kitty Dukakis of Massachusetts and Governor Tom Kean of New Jersey to speak for us. Governor Cuomo once said to me, "Every time I turn a corner, someone pops up and says, 'Don't forget the Arts Council needs more money!' "

Then I go to the governor's senior staff. They look grave and say there will be no more money. I look graver and say that without more money New York State will become a cultural wasteland. (Every year, however, they look less grave.)

My next call is on the legislature. I'm not allowed to lobby them, but I can educate, exhort and, I hope, persuade them to give us more money. I like politicking. Knocking on doors at the Capitol doesn't faze me.

In the beginning the whole concept of government money for the arts was a foreign notion. The legislature was understandably nervous about giving money to what some of them used to call "those people in New York City who dance around on their toes," or "artists in Greenwich Village who paint themselves blue and run around naked." The legislature has changed radically. When I became chairman the budget was $27 million. It is now over $60 million, a testimonial to their belief in the arts, which now generate upward of five billion dollars. Over the years I have constantly thanked those wise men and women of the legislature who by befriending the arts have increased the economy of the state.

The Arts Council is not a foundation. We buy services for the people of the State of New York, and if these services are not performed, all or part of the funds must be returned.

One of our groups neither fulfilled its contract nor did it return the State funds. We had to go to the Attorney General to investigate some of their financial juggling. They went into bankruptcy, and then *they* took the Arts Council to court to try to force us to restore the funding we had withheld. We appeared before a bankruptcy judge, who seemed to have already made up his mind against us. He had written a report, starting with: "Not since Javert hounded Jean Valjean, not since the Bishop of Beauvais condemned Joan of Arc, has there been such harsh intolerance" (on the part of the Arts Council).

I had never been in a courtroom in my life and I was scared. I was in for a big surprise. As I walked into the chamber, the judge did a double take, jumped up, and came forward with outstretched arms. "Prince Orlovsky!" he cried, *"Fledermaus,* 1967, New Year's Eve at Lincoln Center!"

During the hearing, every time I opened my mouth to rebut something, our lawyer nudged me as if to say, "We've already won, so shut up."

I had only recently become chairman when the legislature asked me to put on an extravaganza for the 1976 Bicentennial celebration. I wanted desperately to make good.

I persuaded George Balanchine, of the New York City Ballet, to give us Suzanne Farrell and Peter Martins for a pas de deux, and Clamma Dale sang "Summertime" and "Amazing Grace." But we needed a grand finale. My oracle, Phyllis Wagner, came up with the perfect idea. Since it was the country's birthday, she suggested I get a big papier-mâché birthday cake and have the leadership of the legislature burst out of it singing a New York song. It was a splendid bit of showmanship, but I wasn't sure I could get them to do it. "They're not all friends, you know." "It matters not," Phyllis replied sternly. "You'll manage."

The night of the benefit, as I stood in the wings waiting for the curtain to go up on that elephantine red, white, and blue cake, I wished there had been a microphone inside; I'd have given anything to hear what Anderson, Steingut, Duryea, Marchi, and Orenstein were saying to each other!

Every once in a while a request turns up that is so unusual that board members feel they must investigate personally. One such came from a "sound sculptor" named Max Neuhaus. I had never heard of sound sculpture, but the Council was there to educate me. Mr. Neuhaus had installed a permanent sound some thirty feet under one of the gratings in Times Square. I asked Dorothy

Rodgers, one of the board members, to go with me to try to hear what was described to us as a lugubrious underwater bell that went BONG, BONG, BONG.

Dorothy, the wife of Richard Rodgers, is one of my closest friends; she is also one of the most elegant women in the city. I dressed up in my best to match her, and the two of us sallied forth to Times Square. We were not told exactly under which grating we would hear the bong, so we went from one to another, leaning down and cupping our ears.

No bong could we find. We were about to give up when along came a bag lady. She stood waiting for the traffic light to change, and we went over to her and asked, "Do you mind telling us if you hear anything down under that grating?" The bag lady, being a New Yorker, was used to crazy people. But she looked at these two rather well-dressed women asking her this ridiculous question, decided we must be barking mad, and fled. And on the spot where she had been standing we heard a sound like a buoy lost in the netherworld.

It is there to this day, and P.S., we didn't fund it.

My job is never routine. We are beset by problems. Each day brings a new crisis. Most pressing is the acute shortage of performance and rehearsal space. Recently the ballet world was faced with the loss of one of New York's best dance spaces. The building was about to be sold to a developer for offices. It had a theater and the best rehearsal studios in town; it housed costumers and wigmakers, and it was home to the Feld Ballet and the American Ballet Theatre. We had ten days to act. This story has a happy ending. I called one of the city's great benefactors, the philanthropist Lawrence Wien, and asked his advice. Mr. Wien's solution was simple and fast. He bought the building and saved the day for the ballet companies. It was a brilliant example of government and private enterprise working together.

There are other areas in the arts where the non-profit and the commercial merge dramatically. The Council's seed money encourages the Off- and Off-Off Broadway; from these plays, many of them Pulitzer Prize winners, the commercial theater selects the best to move to Broadway.

Joe Papp's *A Chorus Line* is perhaps the most dramatic example of the move from non-profit to Broadway. This time the system worked perfectly. When he was sitting under his shower of gold, he put all of it back into the non-profit Shakespeare Festival.

In 1983 Mario Cuomo reappointed me chairman, making it three governors I have served—one Republican and two Democrats.

During Governor Cuomo's tenure the arts environment has expanded to the point where I feel like Johnny Appleseed. There are twenty-four opera companies throughout the state and four major regional theaters in upstate New York alone. There are artists' galleries and alternative spaces where before there were none. We started many new programs, such as capital construction for building purposes and Folk Arts. We are the leader in film and video, and some of the artists we support have been Academy Award winners and nominees. Governor Cuomo is both a practical man and a philosopher. He has set a tone of far-reaching compassion for the state, and he gave us one of our most successful programs, Arts in Education for schoolchildren. It is in keeping with his theme, "The Decade of the Child."

Matilda Cuomo works as hard as the governor. She too is deeply involved in state programs for children. I've been with her when she captivated a whole table of young people at the New York Children's Museum. It's not only children who warm to her. She has a gift for friendship that charms all ages.

It pleased me to read the New York *Times* editorial in March 1984:

. . . The New York State Council on the Arts, for instance, helps fund the hugely famous Metropolitan Opera, but it also gives money to Second Avenue's Ukrainian Museum. The user of the Seneca Nation Library has reason to thank the Arts Council, and so has every child who's ogled the dinosaur eggs at the Museum of Natural History. So have countless theater, dance, and music groups all over the state. . . .

In the more than 20 years of its existence, the New York State Council on the Arts has been the model not only for similar councils in other states, but also for the National Endowment for the Humanities.

What the *Times* doesn't mention is the effort that goes into the balancing act between the large organizations and the small. It doesn't happen by accident. We fund institutions representing every culture and segment of society. I have often gone before the legislature not only to beg for money, but to defend important principles: freedom of speech, freedom of expression, freedom from censorship. There is always the possibility that someone's sensibilities will be offended. We must simply accept the fact that art will be controversial.

Our executive director Mary Hays's commitment to the artists is as important as her ability to manage the three-cornered wire walk: staff, government, and Council members. She has given me so much informed and intelligent help that I bask in reflected glory.

I didn't want to be an honorary figurehead. The Council has been the most important activity in my life for the past ten years. I had no premonition of how many sleepless nights I'd have, how much it would teach me, and how much satisfaction there would be.

Since I've become chairman of the Arts Council, I've begun to see the arts in a new light—a dazzlingly bright light, in fact. I have come to believe the arts provide an occasion in which differences do not matter as much as they seem to in daily life. I see the arts as a kind of cohesive force in which people of all colors and conditions come together. How many times have we been a part of an audience and felt the special power of the arts to touch and bind us all in a common experience.

To paraphrase Robert Frost: The arts begin in delight and end in wisdom.

AT an age when most people's lives are narrowing and diminishing, mine is expanding at a cosmic rate. I don't complain; I'm of the school that thinks if you stop working you go under.

In 1986 I was reappointed by Governor Cuomo for another five years as chairman of the Arts Council. I've received many honorary degrees, which gives me enormous pleasure because I never graduated from anything. I've broken some new ground: I was the first woman commencement speaker at Groton, the alma mater of the Eastern establishment.

The best prescription for keeping healthy and attractive is good genes, a good disposition, and a good diet. The genes are out of your hands; a good disposition is up to you.

There is a trick that often works for me. First thing in the morning I smile at myself in the bathroom mirror. The difference between the face I see at first and the smiling one is so ludicrous that I can't help laughing. I believe that you can make a happy outlook come from the outside in.

You must also forgive yourself for your sins. When I wake up in the morning, I run down the litany of my transgressions of the day before, and if I have been unkind, or made a tactless remark, or done one of the thousand things that cause me to blush at the memory, I say, "Well, Kitty, I forgive you—just try and do better next time."

My children are giving me a fine old age (which will be here in a few years!). I have the best possible relationship with them. They think I'm slightly eccentric, which allows me a lot of leeway. I enjoy them and I admire them with all my heart. I have watched my son the producer produce his father's plays for the stage and for television (he even offered me a part in one episode), while my daughter and son-in-law have produced my first grandchild.

The joy of seeing James Hart Stoeckle at the age of two and a half hours was bittersweet. I walked home from the hospital by myself. I needed time to be alone with Moss—I missed him so. When I sang *Fledermaus* at the Metropolitan Opera, my mother was the one I wanted to share the glory with, but walking back from New York Hospital, it was Moss I wanted, and I talked to him all the way home. I imagined what he might have said about our first grandchild. Witty or sentimental, he would be terribly moved; his feeling for family was so strong. I wept all over again with the ache of my loss.

A book like this has no real ending. The path my mother set my feet on can lead heaven knows where. Mother's pronouncement in the beginning is still true. I wasn't the prettiest girl you ever saw, I wasn't the best actress, and I certainly wasn't the finest singer; but with a bit of courage and a dash of self-discipline, a small talent can go a long, long way.

Index